For Taking Pictures

To Achieve This Result:	Follow These Suggestions:
Avoid shadows in your subject's face	Use the camera's flash as a fill flash or shoot with the sun to your side, preferably not around noon; move the subject if possible
Properly expose subjects that have a bright light behind them	Set the camera's exposure compensation mode to +1 or +2; move the subject if possible
Eliminate red eye	Use the camera's red-eye reduction mode
Take a steady picture	Hold the camera up against your eye, not away from your body; in low-light situations, use a tripod or lean against another solid surface like a fence or table
Take close-up pictures	Use the camera's macro mode
Conserve battery strength	Turn off the flash when you don't need it; disable the LCD display if you can and just use the optical viewfinder; plug into a wall socket to transfer images to your PC; use rechargeable batteries
Squeeze extra pictures into the camera's memory	Reduce image resolution; lower image quality by increasing image compression; delete unneeded images; swap out the camera's memory card for fresh storage space

For File Formats and the Web

To Achieve This Result:	Follow These Suggestions:
Make image files smaller	Save in JPEG format and use image compression
Save an image to use as wallpaper for the Windows desktop	Use the GIF or BMP format
Make an image's background transparent	Save in the GIF 89a file format
Save an image for the Web	Use the JPEG or GIF format
Add a graphic to a Web page	<IMG SRC="image.jpg">
Add a clickable graphic to a Web page	<A HREF="URL"><IMG SRC="image.jpg"></A>

For Image Editing

To Achieve This Result:	Follow These Suggestions:
Apply an effect to just one portion of an image	Use the selection tool; use the magic wand to select an irregular area that is similar in color, like a person's face
Crop an image to improve its composition	Select the part of the image you want to keep with the rectangular selection tool, then copy it and paste it as a new image
Improve the focus of an image after it's taken	Use the sharpen or unsharp mask tool
Eliminate moiré patterns while scanning	Use the descreening tool
Straighten a crooked scan	Use the deskew tool or rotate the image by one or two degrees
Brighten an image	Use the brightness and contrast tool; use gamma if you want to keep shadow regions very dark
Make an image smaller	Use the resize or resample tool
Discover the color used somewhere in an image	Use the eyedropper tool

Instant Digital Photography Answers ...

For Controlling Exposure

To Achieve This Result: **Follow These Suggestions:**

Stop the action

Higher shutter speed (smaller number)

Blur the action

Lower shutter speed (bigger number)

More depth of focus

Smaller aperture (larger f/stop number)

Less depth of focus

Larger aperture (smaller f/stop number)

For Information on Cameras and Products

Agfa: http://www.agfahome.com
Apple: http://www.apple.com
Canon: http://www.usa.canon.com
Casio: http://www.casiousa.com
Epson: http://www.epson.com
Kodak: http://www.kodak.com
Konica: http://www.konica.com
Minolta: http://www.minolta.com
Nikon: http://www.nikonusa.com
Olympus: http://www.olympusamerica.com
Ricoh: http://www.ricohcpg.com
Sony: http://www.sony.com

For Tips, Hints, and Photographic Communities

The Amateur Photography Ring: http://home.earthlink.net/~troise/ring.htm
The Computer Artist's Forum: http://www.geocities.com/SoHo/3103/
The Digital Art Ring: http://pluginhead.i-us.com/digring.htm
i/us: http://i-us.com/
The PC Photography Ring: http://www.mgisoft.com/webring/webring.html
The Ring of Photography: http://www.best.com/~gazissax/paths/ring/index.html
The Sony Mavica Web Ring: http://www.fortunecity.com/skyscraper/data/440/

Digital Photography

Answers!
Certified Tech Support

Dave Johnson

Osborne/**McGraw-Hill**

Berkeley • New York • St. Louis • San Francisco
Auckland • Bogotá • Hamburg • London
Madrid • Mexico City • Milan • Montreal
New Delhi • Panama City • Paris • São Paulo
Singapore • Sydney • Tokyo • Toronto

About the Author

Dave Johnson's writing career started at the age of eight with colorful post-Apocalyptic tales of life with Snoopy in the wake of Godzilla's devastation of New Jersey. More recently, he has focused his writing efforts on computers. His first book, *The Desktop Studio: Multimedia with the Amiga,* was published in 1990. Since then he's written eight books and frequently contributed to magazines like *Computer Shopper, Windows Magazine, Small Business Computing,* and *PC Computing.* He's a columnist for *Digital Camera* magazine and a site editor for CMPnet's Planet IT Web site.

Dave has flown satellites (making him an official "rocket scientist"), instructed college courses, and driven an ice cream truck (making him relatively unemployed). Currently he hopes to finish his science-fiction-rock-&-roll-space-comedy novel-thing that's been collecting dust since college and then travel the country photographing roller coasters and rock bands.

Osborne/**McGraw-Hill**
2600 Tenth Street
Berkeley, California 94710
U.S.A.

For information on translations or book distributors outside the U.S.A., or to arrange bulk purchase discounts for sales promotions, premiums, or fund-raisers, please contact Osborne/**McGraw-Hill** at the above address.

Digital Photography Answers! Certified Tech Support

1234567890 AGM AGM 90198765432109

ISBN 0-07-211884-9

Publisher
Brandon A. Nordin

Editor-in-Chief
Scott Rogers

Acquisitions Editor
Megg Bonar

Project Editor
Madhu Prasher

Editorial Assistant
Stephane Thomas

Technical Editor
Terrie Solomon

Copy Editor
Bill Cassel

Proofreader
Laurie Stewart

Indexer
Valerie Robbins

Computer Designers
Mickey Galicia
Jani Beckwith

Illustrator
Brian Wells

Series Design
Mickey Galicia

*I dedicate this book to the wonderful
models who selflessly posed for me
throughout the production of this book.
That includes my wonderful wife Kris,
my too-cute kids Evan and Marin, and
my nieces Jessica and Rebecca.*

Contents

Acknowledgments

This was probably the most fun I ever had writing a computer book. Not only was the topic as interesting and exciting as they come, but the Osborne team was yet again a great bunch to work with. Specifically, I'd like to thank my editor buddy Megg Bonar, as well as Stephane Thomas, Madhu Prasher, and Terrie Solomon. And whoever it is that keeps coming up with the funky colors for these Answers! books—way to go.

This book was also made possible by the fine folks at various digital imaging companies. Since I can't imagine having written this book without the Kodak DCS 520 and the Epson PhotoPC 700, many, many thanks go to Miller Shandwick's Diana Wong and the folks at Kodak, as well as Walt & Company's Jill Martin and the rest of the Epson team.

I truly appreciate the efforts of Tiffen (and Paul Baldassin in particular) for the array of lenses and filters. Likewise, thanks to Karen Thomas at Thomas PR, Jennifer Chu at Live Picture, Kristy Kozaka at Miller Shadwick for Agfa, Pam Crowley at Radius, and, of course, Dave Sims at Copithorne & Bellows for his assistance with Hewlett-Packard products. Lastly, much thanks to Michael R. Overly, the Special Counsel, Information Technology Group at Foley & Lardner for his assistance with copyright issues.

As always, thanks go to my copyediting wife Kris, who is an indispensable asset for pointing out things like the fact that I fell asleep halfway through Chapter 12 and therefore created six pages filled with the letter "b."

A very special thanks to Kristin Hersh for making *Strange Angels*. As usual, your music was the soundtrack to this book.

Introduction

It's hard to describe how much fun you can have with digital cameras. If you enjoy taking the occasional photo but have never found the "hook" that pulled you into photography, digital imaging might be just the ticket. How would you like to have a camera that never needed film, took pictures that you could publish instantly on the Internet or share with others via e-mail, and was as easy to use as a point-and-shoot camera? Well, based on sales of digital cameras last year, about half a million of your closest friends wanted exactly that. Digital cameras appear to be here to stay, and for good reason.

Today's digital cameras, like any other kind of electronic gadget, are more powerful and less expensive than ever. You can take pictures in a variety of resolutions and download those images directly to your PC. Unlike traditional photography, there's no waiting for the processor to run your images through a printing machine. Want to modify your images? There's no messy chemicals or expensive darkroom. The image editing tools on your PC can help you do anything imaginable to your images, and it's pretty easy to pull off. And your digital images needn't collect dust in a photo album, either. You can post them on a Web page, e-mail them, print them on T-shirts and hats, or hang 'em on the wall.

I've found that digital cameras offer an element of compositional freedom I've never had in traditional photography. In Paris a few weeks ago, I wanted to take a picture of my wife with the Eiffel Tower in the background. Problem: we were on the Arc de Triomphe, and the bars that keep you from falling off ruined the background. Solution? I took the picture anyway, and used the magic of digital editing to "erase" the bars afterwards. Tres cool!

So, I was chomping at the bit to write a book on digital imaging so anyone—35mm experts, novices, and everyone in between—could make the most of this new medium. I compiled about 400 of the most interesting questions and created a comprehensive guide to digital photography. I

doubt you'll find more complete coverage of the topic anywhere—this book has it all, from the basics of choosing a camera to composition to digital image editing. I made it a priority to explain the basics of photography so you can use this book as a single resource, even if you don't yet know a lot about how to take an interesting picture with the point-and-shoot in your closet.

Digital Photography Answers! is divided into 18 chapters. Each chapter tackles a different photo topic, like mastering your camera, taking pictures, storing and processing photos, and getting good printouts. Start with Chapter 1 to read the answers to the Top 10 most commonly asked digital photography questions, and then thumb through Chapters 2 and 3 for some advice on getting started with your digital camera. If you're a photography novice, be sure to read Chapters 5, 6, 7, and 8 to learn about photography basics. If you're already handy with a camera, you might want to buzz over to Chapters 11 and 12 for an introduction to the "digital darkroom," where you can edit images easily inside your PC.

CONVENTIONS USED IN THIS BOOK

Digital Photography Answers! uses several conventions designed to make it easier to find the information you need and follow the instructions outlined in the book. These include:

- **Bold type** is used to indicate text you should enter using the keyboard.
- Small caps like ENTER and SHIFT indicate specific keys on the keyboard.
- Vertical lines separate menu items, as in File | Save or Start | Settings | Control Panel. This helps you make menu selections quickly while following along with instructions in the book.

In addition to those conventions, there are a few symbols specially designed to draw your attention to special information. These are:

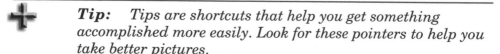

Tip: *Tips are shortcuts that help you get something accomplished more easily. Look for these pointers to help you take better pictures.*

Note: *Notes are, for the most part, interesting facts that won't signal a major change in your life, but might enhance your understanding of the subject. File these items away to impress your friends.*

READY TO GET GOING?

Enough introduction already. Welcome to what I think is the best book on digital photography available at any price. If you have a question or problem that you can't solve with this book or by visiting one of the many Web sites listed within these pages, drop me a line and I'll see what I can do. Be as detailed as you can when you ask your question.

You can also e-mail me with general comments, questions for the next edition of the book, or your own tips, tricks, and techniques. For questions, send an e-mail to questions@radioguys.com. For everything else, reach me at dave@radioguys.com. Also check the Web site—http://www.radioguys.com—for late-breaking information and other digital photography goodies.

Good luck and enjoy the book!

Chapter 1

Top 10 Frequently Asked Questions

Answer Topics!

- What a digital camera is
- How much you should spend on a digital camera
- Digital cameras versus Kodak's Advantix cameras
- What kind of camera to buy
- Peripherals
- Getting photo-quality prints

- Keeping track of digital images on your computer
- Making money from digital photography
- What you can do with your digital pictures
- What file formats to use with your digital camera

Top 10 FAQs @ a Glance

 Digital photography is a new and exciting hobby that can be fun and rewarding, whether or not you already know much about traditional photography. There are a lot of common questions, however, concerning everything from memory to file formats to camera controls. Make this chapter your first stop when you have a burning question about digital cameras—chances are, others have asked the same question before you.

1. What is a digital camera?

First, the dramatic answer: Digital cameras are an exciting new way to take pictures that could very well revolutionize the way people record still images.

Now for the more conservative answer: A digital camera is a new kind of photographic device that works more like a computer scanner than a 35mm camera. Instead of exposing film to light, processing the film into negatives, and then printing the pictures on photographic paper—a process that takes time, money, and the services of a photo-processing shop—digital cameras use light-sensitive chips to store the image in memory, ready to use.

Digital cameras usually look and function very similarly to point-and-shoot 35mm cameras, which means that you probably already know the basics of how they work. The biggest difference with digital cameras is that, armed with a connection cable, you can transfer the images you take with your digital camera to your PC, or you can send them directly to a printer.

If you last saw a digital camera a year or two ago, they're now worth another look. The technology has advanced at such an incredible rate that you can now get an affordable camera that takes images with good quality and resolution, and you don't have to be a computer genius to use it. Instead, all it takes is a computer, some image editing software, and a printer—and this book explains how to get the most out of all of those items.

To learn more about digital cameras, check out the Web sites of some of the most popular camera manufacturers. Here's a fairly comprehensive list to get you started:

- Agfa: www.agfahome.com
- Apple: www.apple.com
- Canon: www.usa.canon.com
- Casio: www.casiousa.com
- Epson: www.epson.com
- Kodak: www.kodak.com
- Konica: www.konica.com
- Minolta: www.minolta.com
- Nikon: www.nikonusa.com
- Olympus: www.olympusamerica.com
- Play: www.play.com
- Ricoh: www.ricohcpg.com
- Sony: www.sony.com

2. How much money should I spend on a digital camera?

Cameras vary quite a bit in price, and as the saying goes, you get what you pay for. Be sure you read Chapter 2 to learn what features are important—and what kinds of cameras you may want to avoid.

That said, there are several excellent cameras available for under $1,000, and a few even cost $500 or less. For about $1,000, you can get a fairly high-resolution camera, though for most applications you may be perfectly happy with a low-resolution, 640×480-pixel camera that may cost as little as $300. These cameras typically work like simple point-and-shoot cameras, since they don't include through-the-lens viewing or advanced "mode" settings like you'll find in an advanced SLR (single lens reflex) camera.

If you're a serious photographer, you may want to set your sights a bit higher and look in the $2,000 or higher category,

where you can get a camera that offers many of the SLR-style features you expect in a camera.

 ## 3. Are digital cameras the same thing as Kodak's Advantix cameras?

No, but they're definitely cousins. A digital camera does not use chemicals or film at all. Advantix (formally known as APS, or Advanced Photo System) is much more like traditional 35mm photography.

APS uses a new kind of film that stores digital information when you snap the picture. It records information like your exposure information, date, time, and most important, the format of the picture you're taking. You can tell your APS to take some panoramas, some "wide screen," and some 35mm format images—all on the same roll of film. Instead of a pile of negatives, APS cameras give you a contact sheet with thumbnail images of all your prints, which you can use to order reprints. With the right hardware, you can even load APS film cartridges into your PC and convert the images into digital pictures.

But while APS and digital cameras share some of the same advantages, remember that they're completely different kinds of cameras that rely on different technologies to make pictures. Each has advantages, but APS systems aren't as easy to use in the computer environment as real digital cameras.

4. What kind of camera should I buy?

Depending upon your skill level, dedication to digital photography, and budget, there's a wide array of choices available. If you're a casual, consumer-level photographer, you should look for a camera that offers features like a built-in flash, a zoom lens, removable memory, and an auto-focus lens. If you have the budget (between $500 and $1,000), I recommend getting a "megapixel" camera. This is a camera that photographs images with at least one million pixels of resolution.

If you're a more serious photographer, you should step up to a camera that includes more SLR-like features. Companies like Canon, Kodak, and Nikon all make candidates, though

the prices are astronomical. Nikon's E3 is about $8,000, and the Kodak DCS 520 is a whopping $15,000.

There is an almost infinite array of cameras and styles to choose from, so shop around and don't buy the first camera that seems to do what you want. The Epson PhotoPC 700, for instance, is an excellent affordable purchase, but it lacks a built-in zoom lens or a red-eye reduction mode on the flash. The Sony Mavica is a popular camera, but it stores images on a floppy disk, limiting its image quality. And the Kodak DCS 210 has a flash, a zoom, and a great interface, but it has a fixed-focus lens. Bottom line? Make a chart of camera features and fill it out for all the cameras you're interested in purchasing. That way you won't get stuck with a camera that doesn't have all the features you wanted. Make sure you see Chapter 2 for more information on buying a digital camera.

5. If I buy a digital camera, will I need to buy lots of other peripherals too?

That depends on how serious you want to get about photography. Many people can do just fine with a plain-vanilla camera for years. Others will want to expand. When I played guitar at home as a teenager, I bought a flanger—an effects pedal that adds a very cool metallic sound to the guitar's voice. I certainly didn't really need one, and years later when I bought my first car, my dad reminded me "not to get a flanger for it."

My dad already knew that I thrive on adding gadgets and accessories to all my major purchases. Likewise, there are a lot of "flangers" you can add to your digital camera.

For most people, I'd suggest the following accessories (if they didn't come with your camera):

- An AC adapter to run the camera off wall power when you're indoors
- Rechargeable batteries and a charging station
- Cleaning supplies to keep your camera in top condition

If you're interested in getting the most out of your camera, the following accessories can add to your enjoyment:

- Additional lenses and filters for photographic flexibility
- Extra memory cards so you can take more pictures in a single session
- A tripod

Of course, there are even more accessories that you can buy, but these are the most important ones. See Chapter 9 for more on all the accessories that can complement your digital camera. And be sure to thumb through the back of the book to find out about some of the vendors who produce digital photography products.

6. How do I get photo-quality prints with a digital camera?

The printout was long the digital camera's weak link. The resolution of digital cameras is much lower than that of chemical film, so pixels were often obvious in the printouts. Plus, older inkjet printers weren't up to the task of reproducing photo-quality colors.

The good news is that today's inkjet printers can create images almost indistinguishable from 35mm prints. You need a fairly recent inkjet printer (one made in the last two years is probably fine) and the right paper. Armed with photo paper (it actually looks like the paper that 35mm prints are made on), your digital camera can print images you can confidently send to friends and family.

In fact, I've used the Hewlett-Packard DeskJet 1120C to print poster-sized 11×17-inch images that are framed and hanging around my house. They look incredible, with bright, vibrant colors, pure black shadows, and sharp details.

7. What's the best way to keep track of digital images on my computer?

Once they're on your PC, digital images have a nasty way of clogging up hard disks and getting lost in the mountains of data already stored on your system. I recommend that you use a document- or image-management program to catalog all your pictures.

Instead of simply relegating images to folders on your hard disk, these programs display small thumbnails of your images for easy searching. Some of my favorites include Visioneer's PaperPort, ThinkStream's Scan-O-Matic, and G&A's PhotoRecall.

8. What do I need to know if I'd like to try making money from my digital photography efforts?

It isn't necessarily any easier to make money selling photographs in the digital medium than in the world of traditional photography. But digital cameras make it much more convenient to develop and hone your skills. If you want to pursue this fun and rewarding hobby as a possible source of income, you'll need to learn how to find and work with photobuyers—I suggest you get a copy of the current *Photographer's Market* and read photography magazines as well. You should also understand the laws that concern photography; these are covered in Chapter 16.

9. What are some things I can do with the pictures from my digital camera?

The best thing about using a digital camera is that the output—your pictures—is already in the world's most versatile format. Directly from the camera, you can print the image on paper or instead use it in any kind of project you can imagine. Here are some of the most common applications:

- Adding images to your Web pages
- Creating a newsletter or report by using images in desktop publishing or word processing documents
- Creating compelling presentations by inserting images in PowerPoint slideshows
- Putting images on T-shirts, calendars, hats, coffee mugs, and other items
- Sending images via Internet e-mail or on America Online
- Publishing your own portfolio of images

● Feeding live images from your camera into your PC to make videos or video teleconference with friends who live thousands of miles away

Be sure to thumb through the back of the book to find out about some of the vendors who produce digital photography products.

10. What do I need to know about stuff like file formats and image size to work with my digital images on my PC?

You certainly don't need to become an expert. If you want to make the most efficient and productive use of your camera, it helps to understand the difference between various file formats—like GIF and JPEG—and know when the best time is to use each one. It also doesn't hurt to know when you need high-resolution images (such as for print applications) and when you need to shrink the size of your files (such as for the Internet). See Chapter 10 for details on this topic.

Chapter 2

Choosing a Camera

Choosing a Camera @ a Glance

Not sure about digital photography? This chapter explains the basics, like how a digital camera works, how it's different from a traditional 35mm camera, and what the relative advantages and disadvantages are. Shopping for a digital camera can be a daunting task. It's bad enough that there are so many models to choose from, but often they have such different features that it's like comparing apples to oranges. And even if you know how to shop for a traditional 35mm camera, that won't necessarily help you much; digital cameras are completely different. Look to this chapter for advice on what features are most important and how much of a good thing—like resolution—you really need in a camera.

Like any other kind of computer product, digital cameras come with their very own set of confusing terms and acronyms. CMOS? CCD? SmartMedia? Compact Flash? What's it all mean? Look here for the answers.

Optic quality is unarguably the most important part of any camera, and it pays to know what you're looking for. What focal length should you buy? Do you need a zoom? Optical or digital zoom? This chapter clears up the confusion and allows you to make a smart, informed decision.

DIGITAL CAMERAS REVEALED

 ## What makes a camera "digital"?

To answer that question, it helps to understand how ordinary, non-digital cameras work. Traditional photography relies on a process invented in the middle of the 19th Century that, while continuously refined for the past 150 years, is fundamentally the same as it was in 1850. In essence, when the shutter of a camera is opened, a film made of silver halide crystals suspended in a thin layer of gelatin, known as an emulsion, is briefly exposed to light. The silver halide is actually light sensitive, and when exposed briefly to light as the shutter opens, it changes chemically. When the film is processed afterwards, particles of silver bond to the chemically altered halide in direct proportion to the amount of light the halide received during exposure. This constitutes a negative. The negative is then exposed to a second development process in which the tonal values are reversed and printed on photographic paper, yielding prints you can file away in a photo album. It's a slightly convoluted process, but actually not a difficult one—many people develop their own negatives to better control the photographic process. The entire process is shown in Figure 2-1.

Digital photography relies on a completely different process. Instead of chemicals, a digital camera has a *charged coupled device* (CCD), which is essentially a hunk of light-sensitive silicon. The CCD is kind of like film, but instead of slivers of silver halide, the CCD is made of *pixels*. Each pixel represents a dot of color in the finished picture.

When exposed to light via a camera shutter, each pixel of the CCD registers a value based on the intensity of the light. Since a CCD is actually an analog device, an *analog-to-digital (A-D) converter* is needed to store that information digitally. For each pixel, the A-D converter stores a value on a scale from 0–255 indicating the intensity of the light to which that pixel was exposed. A single CCD can only capture a grayscale image. But by passing the light through color filters, or using three different CCDs (with each one tuned to red, green, or

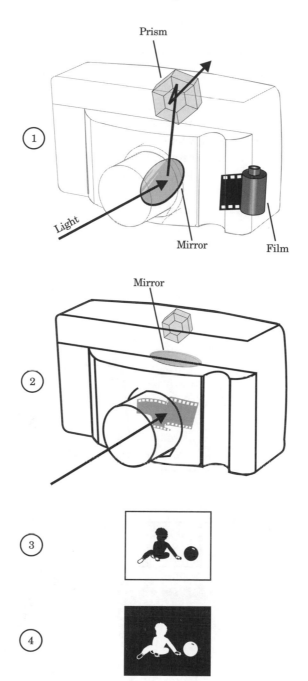

Figure 2-1 From exposure to print, 35mm style

blue), the CCD values can be calibrated for the entire
spectrum and yield color images (see Figure 2-2 for a
depiction of the three-prism system used by most digital
cameras). Afterwards, a computer—such as one in a digital
camera—can process the numerical color values registered by
the CCD into a visual image and store it in memory for later
processing or printing.

In a nutshell, traditional film cameras use a chemical
process to develop images onto paper. Digital cameras use a
photosensitive chip to store the images digitally in memory,
where they can later be manipulated like any other kind of
computer data.

What is a CCD?

CCD stands for charged coupled device. The CCD is the heart
and soul of a digital camera, since it acts in many ways like

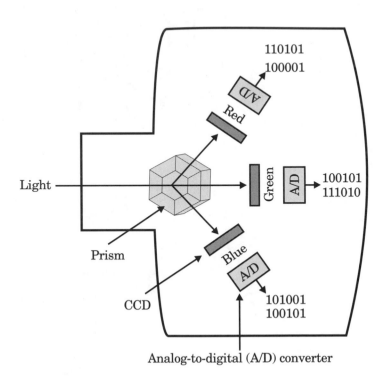

Figure 2-2 A depiction of the insides of a digital camera

the film in a 35mm camera. CCDs are light-sensitive and actually emit an electrical charge when struck by light. By creating a CCD with many pixels, you can essentially paint a picture by monitoring the intensity of the charge on each CCD pixel—this indicates the intensity of the light to which the pixel has been exposed (see Figure 2-3). Oddly, CCDs are analog devices that need an analog-to-digital converter to fill the bit registers in a digital camera. Analog devices like camcorders have CCDs but use the voltages stored in the CCDs directly without converting them into digital values first.

Much of the cost of the camera is embedded in the CCD, since the higher the resolution of the camera, the more pixels the CCD must contain.

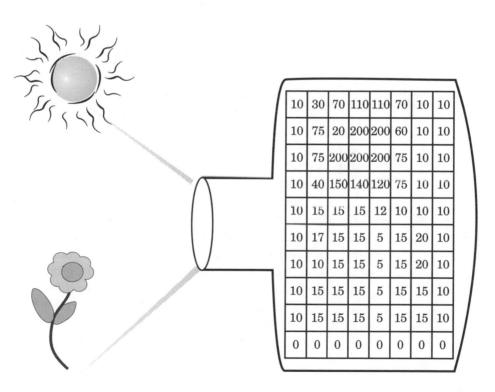

Figure 2-3 Each pixel in a CCD registers a voltage based on the intensity of the light striking it

The Origins of CCDs

CCDs got their start in astronomy. Developed at Bell Labs, these circuits first were used at Lowell Observatory in Flagstaff, Arizona. Today, virtually every observatory in the world uses CCDs to gather light and image the stars.

 ### What is a CMOS?

CMOS stands for complementary metal oxide semiconductor. As far as digital cameras are concerned, CMOS chips can be used in place of CCDs for gathering the exposure information when taking a picture. CMOS chips are cheaper than CCDs, so you find this technology in cheaper cameras. They're less effective than CCDs, however, often introducing noise and errors into the images they photograph, so they've generally fallen into disfavor. I recommend you avoid a CMOS-based digital camera, no matter how good the price may be.

 ### Is the size of the camera's CCD important?

The heart of any digital camera is a light-sensitive imaging array, typically a charged coupled device (CCD). When exposed to light, each of the CCD's pixels registers a value that corresponds to the intensity of light that it observed. Because the most accurate images result when each pixel in the finished image corresponds directly to a pixel in the CCD, you'll generally find that a camera's CCD is measured by the total number of pixels it contains. A camera that takes 640×480-pixel images, for instance, will contain a 300,000-pixel CCD, while a megapixel camera that takes 1,280×960-pixel images probably contains a 1.25 million-pixel CCD.

If you find a camera that offers 800×600-pixel images but only includes a 300,000-pixel CCD, you can be sure that it's a bargain camera that has saved money by providing a less accurate CCD. Since the color and brightness of pixels in the finished image will have to be averaged to get the resolution up to 800×600, the end result will be unsatisfactory. You're better off getting a similarly priced lower-resolution camera, since the results will almost certainly be superior.

What's the difference between CCD and CMOS? Does it matter which one my camera has?

CCD and CMOS are similar technologies, though CMOS is a bit cheaper for camera manufacturers to implement. It's a good idea to stay away from CMOS cameras—CMOS isn't as accurate as CCD in some lighting conditions, resulting in inferior images. And if a camera uses CMOS instead of CCD, it's a good bet the manufacturer cut some corners elsewhere, too. The cost difference between CMOS and CCD isn't great enough to warrant buying a camera with inferior optics, so go with CCD.

How do I get images from my digital camera into a form I can use?

A camera image—no matter how it's created—is of no value if it's forever stuck inside the camera. In most cases, you'll need to periodically transfer the contents of your digital camera's memory to your computer's hard disk. There are several important reasons for doing this:

- To print the images (see Chapter 17)
- To edit the images—crop them, resize them, alter the brightness or colors, or perform other minor adjustments (see Chapter 11)
- To perform special effects—vignetting, turning the image into a Surround Video (or Quicktime VR movie), or making other creative changes (see Chapter 12)
- To send the image to others, such as via the Web or e-mail (see Chapter 14 and 15)

Most cameras transfer images to your PC via the serial port. This is an inexpensive and common method, but it can be slow. Cameras that take very high-resolution images sometimes utilize alternate transfer methods, such as SCSI cables (your PC needs to have a SCSI card installed),

Digital Camera Glossary

- **CCD**   CCD is an abbreviation for charged coupled device. The CCD is a light-sensitive circuit that can be "exposed" to light in much the same way as film.

- **Megapixel**   Some digital cameras are described as "megapixel" cameras. That means that their images contain at least one million pixels, a high resolution.

- **Pixel**   The word "pixel" is short for "picture element." The pixel is the smallest element in a computer image. A computer monitor is made up of pixels, usually arranged in a grid of 640×480 or 1,024×768 individual dots (though other resolutions are also common). In a digital camera, the imaging system uses pixels in much the same way.

- **Resolution**   The amount of information, or overall sharpness, in a computer image is called the *resolution*. It is measured in pixels, and higher numbers are "better," since the higher the resolution, the more pixels (or dots) that are being packed into the same physical dimensions.

- **SCSI port**   The Small Computer Serial Interface (SCSI) port is a high-speed port on some computers that allows your PC to communicate with devices like hard drives, scanners, and even digital cameras. Some digital cameras use this port as a means of transferring pictures from the camera to the PC. Alternatives to SCSI include new standards called FireWire and Universal Serial Bus (USB).

- **Serial port**   Your computer has a serial port—it is sometimes used to connect your modem—and many digital cameras use this port as a means of transferring pictures from the camera to the PC.

Universal Serial Bus (your PC needs a USB port), or FireWire (again, you need to add a FireWire card to your system). For more information on getting images out of your camera and into your PC using these standards, see Chapter 10.

Some new cameras are beginning to appear that have printer ports built right in. Equipped with the right hardware, you can connect the camera directly to your printer and generate prints without ever transferring images to the computer.

Lastly, some cameras have removable memory cards. There are card readers that you can attach to your computer, making it easy to read the card quickly and then return it to the camera. If you have more than one memory card, you can transfer images from one card while you're out with your camera taking more pictures with another.

I've heard that digital images look less "alive" than traditional 35mm images. Is that true?

While some people might think that digital images—devoid of the chemical "soul" that theoretically gives ordinary prints and slides their warmth and personality—look cold and impersonal, that's not the case. It's the same argument that some people use to imply CDs sound more "mechanical" than LPs. The reality, though, is that the CCDs in digital cameras can capture the same depth of color and expression as silver halide, and on a sufficiently high-resolution image, you can't tell the difference in the final product. See Figure 2-4 for an example of an image taken with the Kodak DCS 520.

People who think that digital photos are less expressive may have drawn that conclusion from their experiences with very inexpensive and low-resolution cameras. Just a year ago, state-of-the-art $300 digital cameras would produce images with flat, low-contrast images and severe bluish tints. When used in video-teleconferencing, these same cameras would create jerky, three-frame-per-second movies.

And don't discount the effect of the printer that's used to create the prints. Some new color printers can create essentially photo-quality output; older printers pale in comparison. New printers with great-looking output are actually pretty inexpensive; see Chapter 17 for details.

Remember these facts of life: You get what you pay for and technology is always improving.

Figure 2-4   You'd have a hard time distinguishing this portrait from one taken by a 35mm SLR

 When compared to traditional photography, what are the pros and cons of digital photography?

In many ways, digital and traditional (chemical) photography have little in common. They use different technologies and generally have different applications. But here are some advantages that digital photography has over traditional cameras:

● Did you just cut off the giraffe's head? Most digital cameras give you instant feedback. Thanks to the LCD display on the back of most cameras, you can see the picture you just took and decide whether to keep it or discard it immediately and try again, instead of waiting a day for the prints to come back from the corner store.

● Digital cameras can potentially be cheaper in the long haul, particularly if you take a lot of pictures. Since there's no film to buy or process, all your costs are up front. And you only pay for the printing of the pictures you want to distribute on paper—the others stay in computer memory.

● Because they're stored as digital images on your computer, you can easily edit your pictures with a level of control that's almost impossible in the world of traditional photography. Certainly, it's impossible without your own darkroom and lots of expensive equipment. Cropping and color adjustment are just the beginning; you can add all sorts of special effects and combine parts of different images together in ways that are limited only by your imagination and graphics skills.

● Digital images allow you to cross media formats easily. Armed with a set of pictures of your house, for instance, you can create a Surround Video that lets viewers walk through your home and see it from every conceivable angle. Or you can synchronize images to music and copy them to video. Digital images can also easily be inserted into presentation software like PowerPoint.

● It's easy to take digital images and post them to a Web site, insert them in newsletters and other documents, or e-mail them to friends and family. With digital images, all these applications are one step away. With traditional prints, you need to scan them first to get them into a PC.

● You can transfer digital images to T-shirts, mugs, hats, calendars, and other personalized accessories. There are special transfer papers available for doing this yourself, or you can e-mail your digital images to fulfillment houses that will do it for you.

Bottom line: Digital photography is liberating in that it frees you from film, developing services, and negatives. But digital cameras aren't a panacea for every photography complaint. Here are some disadvantages you need to consider:

● Most digital cameras subject you to delays that are annoying if you're used to a three-frame-per-second SLR with motor drive. There are two delays you need to be prepared for. First, many cameras experience a short (perhaps quarter-second) lag from the moment you press the shutter release to when the image is taken. This can render your digital camera useless for high-speed photography like car races or airshows. And after the image is taken, it can take up to 30 seconds (depending upon the camera) before the camera is ready to record a new image. This is because the image has to be written to memory and the CCDs must be cleared and readied for another image.

- The resolution, or overall sharpness, of digital images is vastly inferior to that of prints from 35mm cameras. Most consumer-oriented digital cameras create 640×480-pixel images, equivalent in size to a standard-resolution Windows display. This will look OK if you print the image as a 4×6-inch picture, but larger prints require larger resolutions, and that's why "megapixel" high-resolution cameras are becoming popular. Megapixel camera have at least a million pixels—that's comparable to a computer display with at least <1,000×1,000 pixels.

- High-resolution images that rival traditional prints have huge file sizes. The Kodak DCS 520, for instance, takes pictures that measure 1,728×1,152 pixels. At this size, the results are perfect for print-quality magazine and newspaper work, or for large posters, banners, and other projects. But each image is about 2MB in size, requiring large amounts of processing power from the computer and big chunks of disk space. And that's the rub—you need lots of pixels to match chemical photography, but that drives the size of the image files up at the same time, making the images difficult to edit and store.

- Digital cameras have considerable lighting requirements. Most digital cameras operate at the equivalent of what would be ISO 100 for a traditional camera. That means they don't function nearly as well in low-light situations as traditional cameras, which can use film rated at ISO 1,000 or beyond as conditions dictate. (ISO is the "speed" of the film. The higher the ISO rating, the better a film

can capture images in low light. For more information, see Chapter 3.)

 I have a film camera, so what would I use a digital camera for?

Digital cameras excel at tasks that require computer processing. Instead of taking a picture, developing the film, and finally scanning the image, with a digital camera, you can transfer an image directly from the camera to your PC. From there, you can:

- Add images to Web pages
- Insert images in presentations, such as PowerPoint slideshows
- Use images in desktop publishing applications
- Send images via Internet e-mail or America Online
- Publish a portfolio via an online service
- Print images onto T-shirts, calendars, and other items
- Feed live images from your camera into your PC and make videos (even though it's a still camera) or video teleconference (see Chapter 18)

 Can a digital camera replace my old SLR or point-and-shoot camera?

Yes and no. It really depends upon how you want to use your camera. Many people can toss their old point-and-shoot aside more or less forever, but you'll need to consider these points:

- Do you want to print every image you take? If so, paper and ink costs for digital photography could start to add up, particularly if you use expensive "photo-quality" paper. And it might simply be more convenient to use an old 35mm camera if you want prints of all your pictures.
- Do you often want to take a lot of pictures at once? If you shoot 100 pictures or more in a given session, you might

need more than one memory card or some way to download the pictures to a computer before you continue. Most consumer-level cameras can only handle a few dozen images at once without a memory upgrade.

● Do you take lots of action pictures? If so, the lag time spent waiting for the camera to recycle might cramp your photo style.

What is a megapixel camera?

The word "megapixel" means one million pixels and refers to the number of pixels in the highest-resolution image a given digital camera is capable of taking. A megapixel camera, therefore, is one that's capable of producing images that contain at least a million total pixels. "Megapixel" is really a marketing buzzword, because it doesn't tell you very much about a camera aside from the resolution—and it doesn't even tell you a lot about that—but it is a useful way to divide the consumer market into low-end and more advanced cameras.

To determine how many pixels are in an image, just multiply the horizontal and vertical pixel counts. For instance, an image that's 480×480 pixels contains about 230,000 pixels (480 × 480 = 230,400). The Epson PhotoPC 700 is an example of a megapixel camera, because it creates images that measure 1,280×960 pixels (1,280 × 960 = 1,228,800, or about 1.2 million, pixels).

Generally speaking, more pixels are better, because they permit the image to show more detail (see Figure 2-5). Remember, though, that the pixel count is not the final word on image quality—just because a camera can render a million pixels, that doesn't mean the optics are any good, and you might be better off with a 640×480-pixel camera that actually takes good pictures.

On my film camera, I can adjust settings like shutter speed and f/stop. Can I also adjust these settings on a digital camera?

In most cases, no. In general, digital cameras operate fully automatically, varying the exposure time based on a fixed

Figure 2-5 The low-resolution image on the left has fewer pixels than the high-resolution image on the right

aperture, or f/stop, setting. In many ways, this is no different from the ordinary point-and-shoot world, but it may offend traditional 35mm photographers.

Most digital cameras work with a very large aperture setting—around f/2.8—and can vary the "shutter speed" down to about 1/16,000th of a second when necessary. There is no actual shutter. Instead, the CCD is electrically active for that period of time, resulting in an equivalent exposure.

A few cameras—particularly more expensive ones—give you more control over exposure settings, enabling you to manipulate depth of field and shutter speed. It isn't until you reach truly professional cameras—like the Kodak DCS 520, priced at $15,000—that you have full control over the aperture and shutter.

SHOPPING FOR A CAMERA

 What kind of equipment will I need to get into digital photography?

It doesn't take much to get started with digital photography. Here's a short shopping list:

- You'll need to get a digital camera, of course, and you should make sure you do some comparison shopping before choosing the camera you'll take home. Establish a budget and figure out what features are most important to you.

- Make sure your PC is powerful enough to manipulate your digital images. You should have enough memory—no less than 32MB of RAM—to display multiple images simultaneously, and a large hard disk or some kind of removable storage medium (like an Iomega Zip drive). Some cameras may have specific and more stringent requirements like 64MB of RAM, or a Pentium processor of a certain speed.

- Stock up on energy. At minimum, you'll need to buy replacement batteries and carry them in your camera bag. A better option is to get rechargeable batteries and a recharger that you can take on trips with you. That way you can reenergize your batteries in the hotel room at night while on vacation, for instance. For transferring images from the camera to your PC, there's no reason to waste battery power—get an AC adapter for the camera. An AC adapter lets your camera use AC power from any electrical plug in your home without using batteries.

- Memory is like film, so if your camera supports removable memory cards, then you should get a spare so you can continue shooting when the first one fills up. You don't need this right away, but it sure comes in handy on a vacation trip when there's no computer around to let you download the first batch of pictures.

- You'll need some kind of image editing software. Most cameras come with an image editing program, but as you explore your camera, you might find that the software that came in the box doesn't light your fire. There's a tremendous array of graphics software on the market right now, much of it aimed specifically at the growing ranks of digital camera owners. See Chapters 11 and 12 for more details.

● Get a good color printer and special photo paper. Eventually you'll want to print your photos, and a quality color printer can make them look virtually as good as a batch of prints from Kodak. There are many special paper stocks available that improve the output when you print photos, so give them a try. Sampler packs are available in most computer stores so you can see how well various papers work without spending a bundle. See Chapter 17 for more details on printing to both color and black-and-white printers.

● Get a camera bag to keep your stuff organized and the dust off your lenses.

● If your camera uses snap-on or interchangeable lenses, you might want to buy a wide-angle or telephoto lens. These extra optics can vastly expand your repertoire of photo opportunities and make your camera more fun.

● A tripod can help you take steady images, particularly if your camera only has an LCD display and you need to hold it away from your eye to see the preview. A tripod also becomes more important as the focal length of the lens increases. A telephoto lens amplifies camera shake significantly.

Should I use a Mac or a PC to process my digital images?

It doesn't matter. The age-old argument is that Macintosh computers are better at graphics and video than Windows-based PCs, but that argument is not nearly as compelling as it used to be. The fact is that Windows can generally do anything a Mac can do these days, and there's probably a better selection of software available for Windows in most cases.

Certain high-end applications may be better served on a Macintosh. If you need to transfer images from the camera to

your computer using SCSI or FireWire, for instance, it's easier to implement those technologies on a Mac than on a PC.

Otherwise, however, either platform should serve you well, and you can use whichever kind of computer you already have for digital photography too. Just be sure when you purchase your camera and any other hardware or software that your choice is, in fact, compatible with whichever kind of system you own. Some camera manufacturers may not make a Mac version of their connection software, for instance, and you should figure that out in the store, not after you get home.

You might worry that the image files will not be compatible with one kind of computer or the other. In reality, most file formats are easily read by both Macs and PCs, and in those few instances where one computer can't read a graphics format, graphics files are easily converted to another format with most paint and graphics software.

How much should I expect to pay for a digital camera?

How much money do you have? Actually, digital cameras are now available in almost every price range. Inexpensive, low-resolution cameras can be had for well under $500, sometimes for as little as $200. Megapixel cameras are often more expensive, usually checking in at between $500 and $1,000. Cameras that cost over $2,000 are usually aimed strictly at the professional photographer, typically coming in a high-end SLR body, accepting interchangeable lenses, and offering tremendous control over exposure.

What features should I look for in a digital camera?

Cameras come in all shapes, sizes, price ranges, and feature sets. You should figure out what you want to use your camera for and buy one based on those requirements. If all you're doing is creating Web pages, for instance, you don't need a 1,700×1,100-pixel camera. A 640×480 will do just fine. Here are the basic features to investigate:

Resolution

Resolution, as you may recall, is the number of pixels in the images a given camera produces. Most consumer-grade cameras generate 640×480-pixel images. They're adequate for many applications, but don't hold up well when printed at high resolution. Some cameras have multiple, user-selectable resolutions, and you can use the resolution you need for each picture.

Optics

Most manufacturers don't talk a lot about the optics in their cameras, but the quality of the lens is just as important as the quality of the electronics. Most cameras come with fairly normal focal lengths, in the neighborhood of 50mm. You might want to consider a more versatile set of optics, though, such as a zoom lens that goes from normal to moderate telephoto range.

Memory

In general, more memory is better. You'll want to be able to hold as many pictures in memory as possible before downloading to a computer. Cameras can include internal, non-removable memory, as well as interchangeable memory cards. If you want to take a lot of pictures, you'll be better off with a camera that uses removable memory cards.

Viewfinder

Some cameras include a parallax viewfinder, as do point-and-shoot cameras, while others feature a true through-the-lens (TTL) optical viewfinder. The advantage to the TTL viewfinder is obvious: It shows you what you're photographing, even up close where parallax viewfinders fail.

LCD display

Most cameras also include an LCD preview display. The LCD is best for showing you a thumbnail image of the picture you just took, though some cameras also let you use the LCD as a viewfinder before the image is taken. Sometimes, the LCD completely replaces an optical viewfinder, such as in Canon's PowerShot 350. Don't assume, though, just because a camera has an LCD display, that the LCD can be used as a viewfinder.

Flash

Most cameras come with a flash built in. Check out the maximum and minimum distances at which the flash is effective. Also note that some flashes are automatically disabled under certain circumstances, such as when the camera is in macro mode or the lens is swiveled off-axis from the main camera body. Professional cameras—like those that are built into a traditional SLR body—rarely come with a flash, since they can use any flash unit from the world of 35mm photography equipment.

Nontraditional photo modes

Some cameras allow you to configure the camera to shoot in a "panorama" mode that is similar to movie letterboxing, or shoot in black and white or with digital zoom. They may enable you to capture a few seconds of audio with each picture or even several seconds of video. These features are often fun but nonessential.

Video out

Many cameras let you display the camera's contents on a television via a video-out jack. This can be handy for quick-and-dirty slideshows, or as a simple business projector.

Transfer scheme

It's worth knowing how well a camera's transfer system for getting images into your PC works. Though most cameras use a serial connection, not all serial connectors are alike—some utilize the maximum transfer speed of the serial port, while others are much slower. Other cameras use SCSI, USB, or FireWire. And if you have a notebook PC, you might want to have a camera that allows you to pop the memory card out of the camera and insert it directly in the PC Card slot of your notebook.

 ## What features do the most popular cameras offer?

No two digital cameras look alike or have the same kinds of features. To better prepare you for that stroll through the

computer store, here's a look at some popular cameras and the features they offer:

● The Kodak DCS 520 is representative of professional-grade cameras that offer all the power of traditional 35mm SLRs while recording their images digitally instead of on film. The Nikon E3s and Canon EOS D2000 are other examples of this genre.

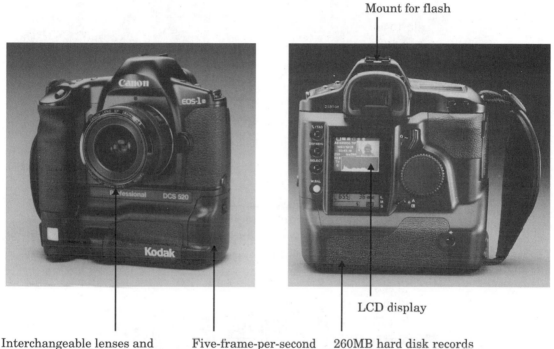

Mount for flash

LCD display

Interchangeable lenses and through-the-lens viewfinder

Five-frame-per-second motor drive

260MB hard disk records over 100 images

● The Canon PowerShot 350 is one of many digital cameras with a fixed-focus lens. Since the lens is always in focus as long as you stay within the camera's useful focusing distance, this is a very easy camera to handle—but it isn't as versatile as an auto-focusing camera.

Built-in flash

Manual macro focusing lever

All controls are easy to access

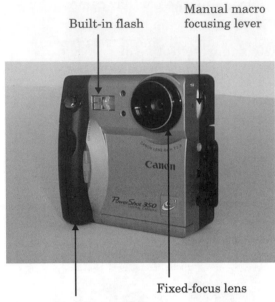

Fixed-focus lens

LCD display

Batteries stored in handgrip

Brightness control for LCD display

● The Epson PhotoPC is an auto-focusing camera that also accepts interchangeable lenses via a Tiffen adapter that snaps on the front of the camera. It's a versatile, fun-to-use camera, but it is missing a few important features like red-eye reduction mode and exposure compensation.

Built-in flash

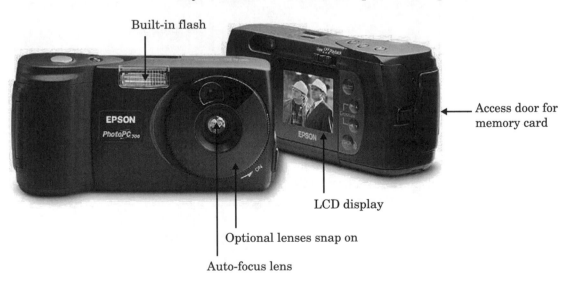

Access door for memory card

LCD display

Optional lenses snap on

Auto-focus lens

● A few manufacturers make cheap CMOS-based cameras like this Umax MDX-8000, a low-end camera that doesn't include an LCD display or any advanced features. Beware of cameras that use a CMOS chip instead of a CCD, don't include an LCD display, or offer very high resolution at a bargain-basement price.

Designed to look and act like a point-and-shoot 35mm

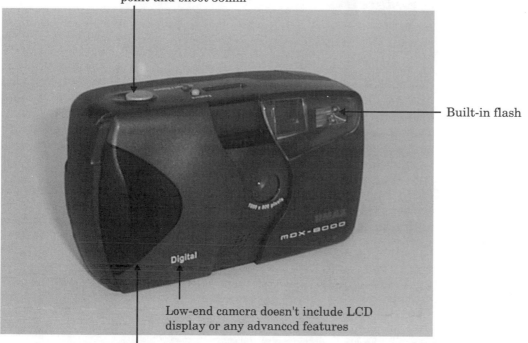

Built-in flash

Low-end camera doesn't include LCD display or any advanced features

Lens cover serves as on/off switch

 Will a camera with a higher resolution mean my digital photos will have better image quality?

Not always. Higher-resolution cameras give you images with more pixels, but be sure that the rest of the camera is up to snuff, too. The only way to do that is to read camera reviews and test it yourself before buying. Beware of cameras that don't have as many pixels in the CCD or CMOS as the image resolution—they need to interpolate to get their resolution and the image may suffer. Cameras can render washed out,

undersaturated, or color-shifted images, so it's important to test-drive any camera before buying it. As you can see in Figure 2-6, not all cameras are alike. These two images were taken with competing cameras; notice how the camera on the right takes obviously inferior images. That's why you need to try before you buy!

How much resolution do I need to get a good image (or picture)?

This is a question that people rarely ask—they just assume they need the best resolution they can get their hands on, or else they take the opposite angle and get an inexpensive camera assuming that's all they'll ever need. In fact, you can key the resolution of your images to specific applications and decide from there what kind of resolution you need. In general terms, you'll want to use low resolution if:

● You'll be displaying your images on a computer screen, such as on a Web page

● You'll be e-mailing images

● Your camera has limited memory

Figure 2-6 Not all cameras produce similar-quality images

● You have little hard-drive space to dedicate to image storage

You should use higher resolutions if:

● You'll be printing the image in high resolution
● You'll be cropping the image, resulting in a final image with fewer pixels
● You have storage space on your camera and hard disk to spare

Specifically, consider these guidelines for camera resolution:

Purpose	Resolution
Onscreen (Web pages)	640×480
Prints up to 4×6	640×480
Prints up to 5×7	1,024×768
Prints over 5×7	1,280×960 or higher

This chart is just a guideline, designed to give you some idea of what resolution is useful for certain applications. By using a somewhat higher resolution than you need, you can edit and crop the image on your PC and still have enough resolution in the final image to get a good-quality print.

 ## I'd like to learn more about specific digital cameras. What Web sites have more information?

Most vendors have their own Web sites where you can learn about the current models and their newest technologies. Check out these:

● **Agfa** www.agfahome.com
● **Apple** www.apple.com
● **Canon** www.usa.canon.com
● **Casio** www.casiousa.com
● **Epson** www.epson.com
● **Kodak** www.kodak.com

- **Konica** www.konica.com
- **Minolta** www.minolta.com
- **Nikon** www.nikonusa.com
- **Olympus** www.olympusamerica.com
- **Play** www.play.com
- **Ricoh** www.ricohcpg.com
- **Sony** www.sony.com

EVALUATING SPECIFIC DIGITAL CAMERA FEATURES

What's the best way to test a digital camera before I buy it?

As with any camera, the proof is in the output. It doesn't matter how good the features are if the images are lousy. If you're in the market for a camera, I recommend that you make a standard color-test sheet that you can use to compare cameras. Go to a paint store and pick out a variety of paint chips, then glue them to an 18% gray card available from most any photo shop. Gray cards are neutral sheets of cardboard that professional photographers use to take exposure readings; you can find out more about them in Chapter 3.

Take this test sheet to the store and photograph it with the camera you're interested in. That way you can immediately and directly evaluate the color accuracy of the camera by displaying the resulting image on a computer screen. Pay particular attention to the way the camera handles flesh tones and primary colors, since these are indications of whether the camera renders colors too hot (red) or too cold (blue).

Since memory is like film, why don't digital cameras have a standard memory format? After all, 35mm cameras all use a standard type of film.

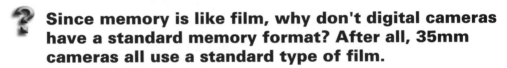

That's a good question. The fact is that there are several major kinds of storage media for digital cameras:

- **Internal only**   These cameras don't allow you to install or swap out memory cards. I recommend you avoid this kind of camera since its storage is so limited.

- **PC Card**   Some cameras use PC Card (also known as PCMCIA) memory. The advantage of PC Cards is that you can usually remove them from a camera and insert them directly into a notebook PC. They're large, however, adding to the size and weight of the camera.

- **Compact Flash**   The Compact Flash is a small memory card that comes in a number of capacities, including 32MB. It's small, light, and semi-indestructible, making it great for portable devices like cameras. Several companies make readers that attach to your PC, allowing you to transfer data directly from the card to a PC while the camera does something else.

- **SmartMedia**   SmartMedia cards compete head-on with Compact Flash—everything you can say about Compact Flash you can also say about SmartMedia. They're incompatible with each other, though.

- **Floppy disk**   Sony uses plain old floppy disks in its Mavica line of digital cameras. By using standard JPEG images with a high level of compression, you can squeeze a whopping 40 or so images on a floppy that can then be inserted directly into your PC's floppy disk drive. It's a convenient medium, but limited forever to low-resolution images.

- **Clik**   New to the digital camera arena, Iomega makes the Clik drive as an inexpensive alternative to flash memory solutions like SmartMedia and Compact Flash. The Clik drive is a tiny 40MB disk that's about the size of a quarter.

The type of storage used in any particular camera is up to the manufacturer—so if you have a preference, consider it while comparison shopping.

Some may think that the memory wars in digital cameras are akin to the old Beta/VHS struggle. In reality, it's a bit different—many of these memory formats have certain advantages, and they'll probably continue side by side for quite some time. Using a PC Card hard disk is essential in a professional camera, for instance, since it allows so many images to be stored. Floppy disk storage is convenient, but it's limited to low-resolution cameras that take pictures with tiny file sizes. Only the SmartMedia and Compact Flash formats are largely redundant, and it's not clear which one will triumph in the end. The future of Clik is very uncertain, and I'm personally going to refrain from choosing any camera that uses it. For more information on storage media, see Chapter 10.

What kind of memory storage should I get for my digital camera?

There's no easy answer to the question of which memory storage is the best, but you can figure out which option is best for you. If you like the idea of using a standard 1.44MB floppy disk to record your images, the Sony Mavica is the clear winner. On the other hand, you can get nearly the same level of portability and convenience from other kinds of memory cards. Both Compact Flash and Smartmedia are small and have large storage capacities, though they're expensive compared to floppy disks or Iomega's Clik drive.

Keep in mind that there are readers available that connect Smartmedia and Compact Flash directly to the PC, so they can be read in much the same way as you might insert a PC Card into a notebook computer. Kodak includes such a handy tool with their DCS 210 digital camera.

Should my digital camera have an LCD display?

Many of the benefits of using a digital camera come from the immediate feedback you can get from seeing the images on the LCD display. Right away, you can see if the image you took was what you were trying to get or if the image needs to be reshot.

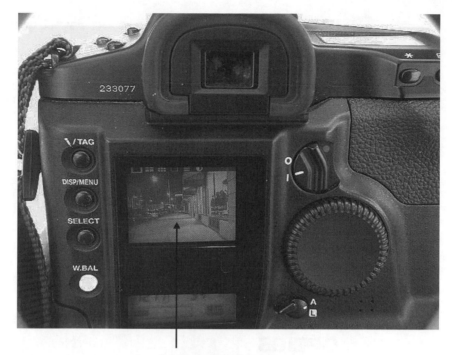

LCD display

The LCD display also lets you delete images from memory, something you can't do with ordinary film. It makes sense, then, that any digital camera you buy meet the minimum requirement of providing a real-time preview via an LCD display. When comparison shopping, though, make sure you consider these aspects:

- Not all LCD displays are also able to show a viewfinder-like preview of the image you're about to photograph.
- Some LCD displays are too small to use comfortably.
- Since many LCD displays get washed out in bright outdoor lighting (and that may be where you're going to take most of your pictures) look for a contrast or brightness control on the LCD display.

 ## What is the video-out port on my digital camera used for?

Many cameras include a video-out port that enables you to look at the images stored in the camera on a television. If you want this feature in your camera, also think about these other features:

● Some cameras include a slideshow mode that plays the images in memory sequentially.

● Some cameras allow you to send images from the PC back to the camera. In this way, you can load graphics, screenshots, and other images into the camera and play it all back on a television display—great for making quick-and-dirty business presentations without the aid of a real video projector or video-out port on your PC.

UNDERSTANDING DIGITAL CAMERA OPTICS

 ## Are the focal lengths of digital cameras equivalent to the focal lengths of 35mm SLRs?

The focal length of a lens is a measure of how much the lens magnifies reality—a short focal length is often called wide-angle, for instance, while long focal lengths are telephoto. For more information on this, see Chapter 5.

But to answer the question, no, they're not. The Canon PowerShot 350, for instance, has a 6mm lens, which on a 35mm camera you might expect to be an extreme fish-eye lens. In fact, it's the equivalent of a 42mm lens on a 35mm camera—a normal focal length. Since a digital camera's architecture is different, focal length specifications aren't the same. When reading camera specifications, therefore, you need to make sure that you read the "35mm equivalence," not just the focal length as marked on the box.

 ## What focal length should I get in a digital camera?

This depends upon how you plan to use your camera. A normal focal length in the 40–50mm (in 35mm equivalence)

All Shapes and Sizes

In contrast to the fairly conservative world of 35mm SLR cameras, digital cameras come in almost every conceivable shape and size. Since the industry is yet in its infancy, manufacturers are trying out all kinds of innovative designs. A look around in a camera store might turn up something that is a perfect match for your needs. Here are some of the most interesting designs:

Minolta Dimage V

This camera's lens swivels around the body, allowing you to take pictures up, down, or even straight behind you. The lens also detaches completely and links up with the body via a tether, allowing you to shoot in cramped and unusual environments.

Nikon CoolPix 300

The CoolPix is a cross between a camera and a pocket organizer—the large LCD on the back is touch-sensitive, allowing you to write notes with the telescoping stylus.

Kodak DCS 520

This flagship Kodak professional camera uses a Canon EOS-1 body. It has a motor drive for three frame-per-second photography, includes complete exposure control, and has a 260MB hard disk for storing over 100 images at once. It costs $15,000.

Sony Mavica

This floppy disk–shaped camera actually uses floppy disks to store up to 40 images at a time.

range is great for general-purpose indoor photography. When shooting portraits and outdoor scenes, however, most photographers prefer to have a lens with a longer focal length, at least 60 or 90mm in 35mm equivalence.

A wide-angle lens (28mm equivalence or less) is handy to have, but not commonly needed, so your money is probably better spent on longer focal lengths. And extreme wide-angle—such as a 14mm-equivalent lens—is only useful when you're explicitly looking for an unusual view of a scene, and it's not useful at all for general-purpose photography. Figure 2-7 shows the effects of different focal lengths on a scene using the Epson PhotoPC and its snap-on lenses.

Figure 2-7 The image on the left was shot with a wide-angle lens; the one on the right was taken with a telephoto lens from the same distance

What's a zoom lens?

A *zoom* is a lens that allows you to change the focal length over a particular range, such as 29–59mm or 35–250mm. The value of a zoom is that it's like carrying a pocketful of lenses on your camera all the time, and you can easily frame a picture by adjusting the zoom.

Many digital cameras include a zoom capability. The Kodak DC210, for instance, has a motorized zoom that spans 4.4–8.8mm, which works out to 29–59mm in 35mm SLR equivalents. That's a good range for general-purpose photography.

One advantage to using a digital camera rather than a traditional SLR is that the camera accepts any interchangeable lens made for that body, including a full array of zoom lenses.

What's the difference between an optical zoom and a digital zoom?

Both optical zooms and digital zooms are found on many consumer cameras. *Optical zooms* use higher-magnification glass optics to enlarge the focal length and consequently enlarge the subject, just as you'd find in a conventional 35mm SLR or an advanced point-and-shoot camera.

A *digital zoom*, on the other hand, works a bit differently. Instead of actually changing the focal length, a digital zoom uses part of the CCD to capture a segment of the total image and enlarge it as if with a magnifying glass. The disadvantage of digital zoom is obvious: It sacrifices the resolution of the image in order to zoom in on part of the scene (see Figure 2-8). Digitally zoomed images are noticeably lower in resolution than ordinary images—even to the naked eye—and thus you should try to avoid them unless the situation demands that level of enlargement. For more information on digital zoom, see Chapter 3.

Figure 2-8   The 2x digital zoom at work in an Epson PhotoPC 700; the image on the left was made using the normal focal length and the one on the right side with the digital zoom

Some cameras include both optical and digital zoom features in the same model. Obviously, the optical zoom should be used whenever possible in lieu of the digital zoom, but for extreme zooming, you can always add the digital zoom on top of the optical zoom.

Chapter 3

Understanding the Features of Your Digital Camera

Answer Topics!

Using a Digital Camera @ a Glance

Digital cameras come with unusual features—unusual, at least, if you're used to point-and-shoot 35mm cameras. Look to this chapter for the scoop on how to use controls like white balance, exposure compensation, and ISO numbers without actual film.

No matter how cool you might think your new digital camera is, the first time you take it to your kid's soccer game, you might be in for a shock: Blurry pictures, delayed exposures that result in nothing but your kid's feet in the picture, and other troubles await you. Unless, that is, you first read how to prevent those pitfalls in this chapter.

Your digital camera's memory is the equivalent of a traditional camera's film. But with a digital camera, how can you tell how much "film" (memory) you have? What can you do to optimize your use of that precious memory for storing your pictures? These are the kinds of questions you may ask as you take your first few batches of pictures. This chapter teaches you how to make the most of your new digital camera's memory.

Batteries, batteries, batteries. Digital cameras go through batteries like ducks go through water, so you should learn whatever you can about how to conserve, extend, and protect your precious power source. This chapter can help you figure out the most practical ways to make your digital camera go longer between battery fill-ups.

UNDERSTANDING THE CONTROLS ON YOUR NEW DIGITAL CAMERA

 What is the ISO number on my digital camera? How is the ISO used in digital photography?

First, it helps to know what ISO actually means. The ISO number—which used to be known as an ASA number, if you're old enough to remember—refers to the speed of the film in the camera. A low ISO rating is good for bright-light photography and produces the most detailed images. A high ISO number is more effective in low-light situations, but the grains in the film are more pronounced. 35mm photographers often use ISO 200 or ISO 400 film for general-purpose photography, since these speeds balance film quality with lighting needs.

That said, digital cameras don't use film, so there's really no true ISO rating at play. On the other hand, the CCD or CMOS chip that collects light when you take a picture clearly needs a specific and measurable amount of light to make an exposure. The electronics of the camera are rated at a particular ISO rating, and information regarding this rating is in your user manual. Most digital cameras need a lot of light compared to the range of lighting that a 35mm can use; you'll find most digital cameras rated somewhere between ISO 100 and ISO 200. Table 3-1 illustrates the issues surrounding ISO numbers.

 My camera lets me change the ISO setting. Why would I do that?

Most digital cameras don't have the capability to change ISO settings. If yours does, consider yourself lucky. Generally found only in professional-grade digital cameras, an ISO setting allows you to specify the "speed" of the virtual film in your camera—in other words, increase or decrease the CCD's sensitivity to light. If you're working in a light-poor environment, go ahead and increase the ISO so that the camera can properly expose your subject. If you're in a very bright situation, you can drop the ISO if your camera is having trouble taking the picture.

ISO Ratings	Light Requirements	Benefits/Drawbacks	Photographic Uses
Low ISO ratings (ISO 64 or 100 film)	Requires more light to create the same exposure as compared to a high-ISO film, so shutter speeds may need to be longer	Creates highly detailed images with barely perceptible film grains	Ideal for outdoor photography
Medium ISO ratings (ISO 200 or 400)	A good compromise for shooting in variable or unpredictable lighting conditions	Grains are not too noticeable	General-purpose photography
High ISO ratings (ISO 1000 or greater)	Requires less light to create the same exposure as compared to a low-ISO film, so shutter speeds can be shorter	Grains are larger, resulting in less-detailed and "noisy" images	Often necessary for low-light photography

Table 3-1   Light Levels and ISO Numbers

For example, let's say that a given scene requires a shutter speed of 1/30th of a second. This is so slow that you're likely to introduce camera shake into the picture. If you can switch the camera from ISO 100 to ISO 200, the shutter speed then doubles to 1/60th of a second, sufficiently fast to capture the image without jitters.

Keep in mind that just as when using real film in a 35mm camera, the lower the ISO setting, the better your final image quality will be.

Many cameras, both film and digital, don't have an ISO dial, but your camera may have a two- or three-position light setting instead. This control allows you to choose between settings for bright, light, and dark environments. While not as precise as getting to actually select your ISO, this serves the same purpose.

 My digital camera has a +/− button that I don't think I've ever used. What is it for and what does it do?

Borrowed from the world of 35mm photography, the +/− button, as it appears on your camera, activates a very important feature called *exposure compensation*. Like your camera, most digital cameras have this capability. Typically,

a camera calculates the exposure of a picture based on the average lighting in the scene. The camera can get confused, however, if you point it at a scene with highly contrasting lighting. Let's say that you're trying to take a picture of someone who is standing with his back to a bright light. The camera will set the exposure for the light behind the person and "stop down" (reduce) the lens opening or raise the shutter speed to send the right amount of light to the CCD. The camera doesn't know that you're really interested in the person in front of the light, and the subject will end up underexposed as a consequence.

Exposure compensation allows you to under- or overexpose a picture in specific increments from what the camera believes is an ideal exposure. To properly expose the person in the example above, for instance, you would set the exposure compensation to +2 or +3. See Figure 3-1 for an example of a backlit image that benefits from exposure compensation.

Exposure compensation on the
Canon PowerShot 350

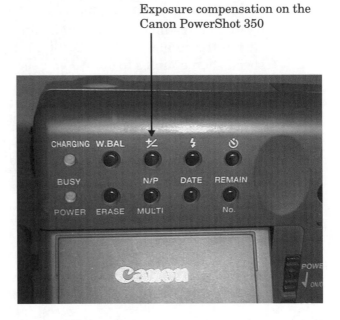

Because setting the correct value of exposure compensation is more of an art than a science, digital photographers have a big advantage over traditional photographers—they can see the effect of exposure

Figure 3-1 The image on the left was shot normally; the one on the right was shot with an exposure compensation of +2 to correct for the bright backlighting

compensation in real time. To see the effect of your compensation, observe the LCD display as you vary the setting—you can choose the correct value before you take the picture. Traditional photographers, on the other hand, typically need to "bracket" the shot by taking several pictures with a variety of compensation settings. Only after developing the image can they see which setting worked best.

Even if your camera's LCD display doesn't show you a preview of the picture you're about to take, you can still see the effect of the exposure compensation right away and decide if you need to reshoot the picture with a stronger or weaker value.

 ## My digital camera's control panel has something called "white balance." What is this option and why would I change it?

Many digital cameras come with a control for white balance. White balance is important because different light sources have different *color temperatures,* meaning that a scene will appear to have a slightly different color tone depending upon how it is illuminated.

Higher temperatures appear warm, or slightly reddish, while cooler light sources add a blue tone to your pictures. It's

not unlike the way a flame has different colors at the outside and center. Why? Because those different parts of the flame are different temperatures.

This chart, for instance, shows the color temperatures of different light sources:

Source	Color Temperature (Degrees Kelvin)
Candlelight	2,000
Sunset	3,000
Tungsten light	3,200
Fluorescent light	5,000
Daylight	5,500
Camera flash	5,600
Blue sky	10,000

If your camera is balanced for one kind of light source (daylight, for instance) and you photograph a scene that is illuminated by a very different temperature of light (such as tungsten), the resulting image won't reflect the true colors. Lower-temperature light sources—like candlelight and sunset—cause a warm, orange glow (see Figure 3-2). Temperatures above 5,500 or so turn out bluish.

The white balance setting on your camera allows you to specify exactly what the color temperature of the scene is. In most cases, your camera can automatically adjust to conditions. If need be, however, you can do it yourself. You'll need to set the color balance using a neutral object.

Traditionally, photographers have used a tried-and-true tool called a *gray card*. An 18% gray card works fine, and you can get one from most any photo-supply store. Place the gray card dead center in the camera's viewfinder. Then photograph the gray card, but make sure that you properly expose the card—don't over- or underexpose it. Once you have photographed the card, you need to then refer to your camera's manual to see how to set the white balance, with your photograph of the gray card serving as a calibration image. You might need to set white balance, for instance, at a birthday party, when the candles from a cake give the camera a false reading about the overall color temperature of the room.

Figure 3-2   Low light is cooler, resulting in warmer pictures (unless you let the camera correct the white balance—in this picture, I forced the Kodak DCS 520 to use daylight balance in low light, resulting in an invitingly orange tone)

One last note: experiment with your white balance. You can get some creative effects by using the "wrong" white balance setting. For example, by mismatching the white balance, you can achieve warm, intimate-looking pictures or get results that look like you're using colored filters. Certainly, you'll want to use the proper white balance setting most of the time, but it can be fun to "step outside the box" and try unusual things.

 My digital camera has aperture priority and shutter priority modes. What are these modes and why would I use them?

A staple of traditional photography, aperture priority and shutter priority options allow you more creative control over

the pictures you take. Here's a quick explanation of what each mode does:

● **Aperture priority**   This option, sometimes called a "mode," allows you to vary the aperture setting—in other words, the size of the opening in the lens—to vary the depth of field of your picture. A small aperture yields the greatest depth of field (in other words, objects both near and far appear to be in focus). A large aperture opening produces a narrow range of sharp focus. Photographers can use this technique to achieve specific effects, like keeping only the subject in focus. This topic is exhaustively discussed in Chapters 5 and 6.

● **Shutter priority**   This mode allows a photographer to directly specify what shutter speed to use (in other words, how long the film will be exposed). A short shutter speed is good for freezing action, while a long exposure can capture motion or an object in very low light.

In both cases, the camera automatically adjusts another element of exposure—either shutter speed or aperture—to take the picture properly.

Some digital cameras, particularly high-end ones, include one or both of these modes. Select the one that is most appropriate to your needs—a car race might benefit from a high shutter speed, for instance, while you may need to select a particular aperture for a portrait to give your photo the focus it needs.

With my digital camera, how do I check to see what my depth of field looks like?

Depending upon the camera, you can't always do this. The view through most digital camera viewfinders is of no value because they're rarely through-the-lens (TTL). Instead, they have parallax viewfinders that always stay wide open, regardless of the aperture setting.

Instead, the best way to get an idea of your depth of field is to actually take a picture and look at the preview in the LCD display. If you don't like the result, you can delete the picture and try again.

Alternately, professional-grade cameras usually have a depth of field preview button located by the lens barrel. When you depress this button, the camera's aperture actually closes down to the position you'll use to take the picture, and you can get a sense of the depth of field. Only high-end cameras have this feature, however.

Depth of field button

 ## How do I use my digital camera's self-timer?

Almost all digital cameras have self-timers that allow the user to press the shutter release and get a short pause before the camera actually takes the picture. The short pause gives you time to get into the picture yourself. In most cases, you merely need to press the self-timer button, compose the picture, then press the shutter release. The camera will go off about five or ten seconds later. In most cases, you'll also see a

flashing indicator on the front of the camera that counts down to the actual exposure.

Self timer on the Kodak DC210

 I keep making the image in the LCD preview brighter; why doesn't it seem to permanently affect the image?

Many LCD displays on digital cameras have brightness and contrast controls. This is particularly useful when photographing outdoors, where the sun can render the screen very difficult to see. You can also adjust the LCD indoors for visibility in particularly dark rooms.

Keep in mind, however, that this control affects only the LCD display, much as the brightness and contrast controls affect a computer monitor or television set. You're not making changes to the actual images stored in the camera, though it's easy enough to do that after they've been transferred to your PC. See Chapter 11 for details.

When should I use—or not use—the built-in flash on my digital camera, and what can I do to get better results?

Thankfully, most digital cameras include a built-in flash. This allows you to extend your picture-taking into low-light

situations that are actually pretty common, but which a 100 ISO–rated digital camera couldn't handle on its own. Most digital cameras have two or three flash modes, and it helps to know when each one works best. Use Table 3-2 to decide how to set your flash.

Flash button on the Kodak DC210

TAKING THE PICTURE

 ### Should I use the LCD or the viewfinder to frame my picture?

In most cases (with the exception of professional-grade cameras mounted in SLR bodies) the viewfinder induces *parallax distortion.*

That's because it isn't showing you exactly what you're photographing. Instead, it's an inch or more away from the actual lens and will induce errors. The closer you get to the subject you're photographing, the less accurate the viewfinder becomes. When performing close-up macro photography, then, you should abandon the viewfinder and rely exclusively on the LCD display.

Flash Setting	Description	Use
Auto-flash	Auto-flash mode decides when the scene is sufficiently dim to warrant a flash and fires—or doesn't fire—as needed.	This is a good mode to leave the flash in when you're concerned about conserving battery life. The flash uses a lot of energy, and you may not want it firing with every single picture.
Fill flash	Sometimes called "forced flash," this mode fires the flash in every image, whether there's enough light or not.	Fill flash is great for illuminating shadowed regions of a picture. If you're taking an outdoor portrait, the flash can evenly illuminate the subject's face even though the sun lights the rest of the scene.
Red-eye reduction	This mode fires the flash several times very rapidly right before the actual exposure, forcing the subject's eyes' pupils to close down. This reduces the red-eye effect commonly seen in pictures taken in dark rooms.	Use the red-eye reduction mode when shooting indoor photos of people. This mode generally works like the fill flash mode (it fires all the time), so remember to switch this mode off when you don't need it.
Off	In this mode, the flash never fires.	This mode comes in handy when battery life is critical. Disabling the flash can extend battery life significantly. Also, disable the flash for close-ups and in macro mode. You don't want to fire the flash when you're focusing on something only a few feet or inches away, since the flash will overexpose the image.

Table 3-2 Flash Setting Guidelines

For more distant photographs, though, even a parallax viewfinder shows you almost exactly what you're photographing through the lens, so it isn't a great concern. Instead, the issue becomes camera shake. To see the LCD display, you generally need to hold the camera away from you, which makes it more difficult to get a jitter-free picture. That's why you should try, whenever possible, to hold the camera directly up to your eye. That allows you to steady the camera against your body and get a more stable photo (see Figure 3-3).

Figure 3-3   It's harder to get a steady picture when the camera isn't resting against your body. Avoid using your camera like the person on the right

What Is Parallax Distortion?

Parallax is a change in the apparent position of an object as a result of your distance from the object. You can observe parallax by driving down a highway and looking at the passing scenery. The closest objects move by very fast, the farthest objects move more slowly. This is similar to the effect of the viewfinder and camera optics being placed apart from one another in your camera—the closer you get to the subject, the less accurate the viewfinder becomes. At a large distance, both viewfinder and optics agree on the position of the object. But as you take the camera closer to the subject, the viewfinder and optics disagree more and more about where the subject is—and that means you can point the viewfinder at something, but the camera may take a slightly different picture.

 ### What is a fixed-focus camera? What is an auto-focus camera? What is the difference between them?

One way camera manufacturers save money on less expensive cameras is by replacing an auto-focus system with a fixed-focus system. *Fixed-focus cameras* are designed so that everything within a given range—such as three feet to infinity—is already in focus. Fixed-focus cameras have one major advantage: Since the camera is already focused, there's no intermediate focusing step that gets between you and the exposure. This can save a precious half-second or more when you're trying to snap a picture.

There's a downside to fixed-focus cameras, though: You can't take close-up pictures unless the camera also includes a macro-focusing mode, and there's no indication that you're too close to focus unless you look at the LCD display. Even then, the LCD display may not be sharp enough to tell you much.

Auto-focus cameras are more common. The camera sends out a short burst of infrared energy and, like radar, gauges the distance to the subject. It then adjusts the lens to the proper focus. All this is done when you slightly depress the shutter release.

 ### How do I focus on a subject when it isn't in the middle of the picture?

If you have a fixed-focus camera, don't worry about it—you're in focus over the camera's total operating range, usually about three feet to infinity.

If you have an auto-focus camera, the system focuses on whatever is in the center of the viewfinder. If your subject isn't in the center of the viewfinder when you focus, the results may be undesirable. In Figure 3-4, the camera locked onto the fence in the foreground, rendering the subject a blur.

However, if you only press the release button halfway, the subject comes into focus but the picture isn't yet taken. You can take advantage of this behavior to focus on a subject that isn't in the middle of the viewfinder.

Do this: Ignore the way you want to compose the picture and instead point the camera at the real subject—the part of

Figure 3-4   An auto-focus camera will lock onto whatever happens to be in the center of the viewfinder, so users must lock focus on the actual subject and then compose the image.

the picture that you want in sharpest focus. Then press the shutter release just far enough to activate the auto-focus mechanism. Continue to hold down the button halfway down while you then compose the picture. The focus should stay locked while you reorient the camera. When you're ready to take the picture, fully depress the shutter release.

You can use this technique for many situations, including scenes where the subject is off-center (a common situation) and where something like slats, posts, poles, or other obstructions might try to steal the camera's auto-focus attention. Just focus between the slats.

Your camera may, in fact, have more than one focusing mode. If your camera continues trying to refocus as you move it with the shutter release partially depressed, it's probably because the camera is in a "continuous" or "servo" focusing

mode. Refer to the manual to see how to switch it to a single-focus setting.

 ## Why do my digital pictures seem to be focused improperly? What can I do to solve this problem?

Out-of-focus pictures are frustrating—but at least with a digital camera, it doesn't cost you any film or developing to experiment and learn how to avoid them. There are several different reasons why it might seem like your pictures have a focus problem. Here's a checklist to review:

- Your auto-focus system may have trouble locking on to the subject because it lacks detail.

- Obstructions in front of the intended subject may steal the focus from it. Make sure you're focused on the actual subject.

- The subject may be off-center, causing the camera to focus on whatever is in the middle of the screen, perhaps at infinity (to solve this problem, see "How do I focus on a subject when it isn't in the middle of the picture?" earlier in this chapter).

- Close-up pictures require extra care. You may need to enable the camera's macro mode, be within a certain focusing range, or perhaps even adjust the focus by hand. Some cameras have a fixed focusing distance for macro mode that is so narrow you'll need to measure the distance from the camera to the object with a ruler.

Or, what looks like a focusing issue may really be a shaky hold on the camera. There are a few things you can do to steady the shot:

- Be sure to hold the camera at eye level if it includes an optical viewfinder.

- Apply light, even pressure to the shutter release. If you jab at it, it can shake the camera right at the moment of exposure.

- If the subject is moving, you might want to pan the camera so it follows the movement of the subject.

 When I press my digital camera's shutter release, there seems to be a slight delay, unlike with my film camera. Why doesn't the digital camera take the picture right away?

This difference between film and digital cameras is a common source of frustration for newcomers. The first time they try to take an action picture they find that the half-second pause causes the subject to move out of the viewfinder before the picture is snapped.

In a traditional 35mm SLR camera, all that happens after you press the shutter release is that the auto-focus system locks in (if it hasn't already), and the film is exposed more or less instantaneously. In a digital camera, however, the computer in the camera has a short list of tasks to perform, including locking in the auto-focus, performing a calibration sequence, and auto-white balancing. This can take several hundred milliseconds, which seems like an eternity when you're trying to take a picture.

There's not much you can do about this delay. You can shave a few hundred milliseconds off the total pre-picture clock by locking in your auto-focus first. To lock the auto-focus feature, all you do is hold down the shutter release partway. If your camera is of the fixed-focus variety, locking the auto-focus feature isn't an issue at all.

Aside from that, most digital cameras have some small lag, and it's something you must learn to work around until technology advances. One notable exception: Professional-grade cameras, like the Kodak DCS 520, can fire off about five frames per second in burst mode, equaling the speed of traditional SLRs.

 Why is there a delay after I take my picture?

Yes, digital cameras typically force you to wait yet again after you take your picture, this time while the image you just captured is written to memory and the CCDs are cleared to make way for the next picture. Probably the biggest source of the delay, in fact, is the image being written to a memory card. While that will take a fixed amount of time for a specific

camera and memory type, keep in mind that some media are faster than others. The Sony Mavica is fairly slow, for instance, because it's writing the image to a floppy disk. A professional-grade camera like the Kodak DCS 520 is extremely fast, offering a burst mode that allows you take about five pictures per second.

Compact Flash and SmartMedia cards come in somewhere in between, usually making you wait between 5 and 20 seconds. This is where you have some control over the delay: Not all memory cards are equal, and some comparison shopping can help you find a card that is significantly faster than the average. For instance, in the debut issue of *Digital Camera Magazine,* a "Compact Flash Shootout" reported on five common brands of memory and showed these times to record a single image in a typical digital camera:

Silicon Storage Technology	5.48 seconds
Nikon	6.00 seconds
Lexar Media	6.03 seconds
Kingston Technology	7.04 seconds
SanDisk Corporation	8.62 seconds

 Sometimes my digital camera turns itself off just as I'm about to take a picture. Can I prevent that?

Most cameras turn themselves off after a short period of inactivity, which conserves battery power. You can miss a shot, however, if the camera goes off at the wrong moment. And since cameras can take ten or more seconds to prepare for their first picture after waking up, that's a photo opportunity that might be gone forever.

One way to stave off the camera's sleep mode is to keep it busy. If you suspect you're going to take a picture soon, make sure that you finger the shutter release frequently, which should activate the auto-focus, or press a control to keep the camera awake.

? How do I clean my camera's lens?

It's important to keep your camera clean. A dirty lens can make your pictures blurry and ruin otherwise good photo opportunities. But be careful how you clean your camera. Follow these guidelines:

● Don't over-clean your lens. It has a special coating that can come off if you wipe it too often or too vigorously.

● Keep the camera under cover—with a lens cap on or in a camera case—when it's not in use. That minimizes the amount of dust that can attack the lens.

● Never use window cleaner or pure water. Get a lens-cleaning solution from a photo-supply store.

● Never pour or squirt liquid cleaner directly onto the lens or LCD display. Always apply it via a tissue, cotton swab, or other clean medium.

With those rules in mind, here's what you should do:

1. Inspect the lens periodically for dust, smudges, and other dirt.

2. Use your breath or compressed air to blow loose dirt and dust off the lens. Otherwise, you'll rub it into the lens, potentially scratching it.

3. Place a drop of cleaning solution on a lens tissue (don't use run-of-the-mill facial tissue—it's too abrasive!) and wipe the lens in a circular motion.

4. Take a dry tissue and gently dry the lens.

Consider equipping your camera with a UV filter from a supplier like Tiffen. The filter can improve your photos, but more important, it protects your camera's lens. It's a lot easier to replace a $20 filter every year than deal with a scratched lens.

UNDERSTANDING MEMORY AND IMAGE FORMATS

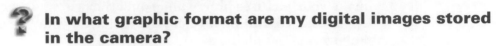 **In what graphic format are my digital images stored in the camera?**

Most cameras store your images in a graphic format that makes the best use of the camera's limited storage space. The format of choice is invariably JPEG, a "lossy" format commonly used by graphics professionals. It's called lossy because in the process of compressing an image in the JPEG format, some data is squeezed out and lost. JPEG is a very flexible and versatile format, however—you can choose how tightly to compress the image, and in the process choose whether to lose only a little information or a lot.

Most commonly used JPEG compression ratios result in very little image degradation—usually too little to see with the human eye. Of course, highly compressed JPEG images can contain artifacts that result from the compression process, but most people stop short of that level of compression.

Some cameras store images in lossless data files, such as 24-bit TIFF files. Only professional-grade cameras with access to a large internal hard disk are likely to use such a scheme, however, since each individual image can consume megabytes of storage space. The Kodak DCS 520, for example, has a 280MB hard disk that can store over 100 two-megabyte images. The advantage of lossless images is obvious—you get 100% of the picture you took—but at the cost of transfer speed and storage space.

My digital camera offers an option of what resolution to shoot pictures at. Which resolutions are best for what purposes?

The quick-and-dirty answer is to always shoot images at a slightly higher resolution than you expect to need in the final application. That way you can crop the image on your PC and still have enough pixels left over to achieve the resolution you wanted to begin with. If your images are destined for the printed page, though, you'll probably want to use a higher resolution than if the images will be e-mailed or inserted in a Web page. Even so, the fact of the matter is that there's no simple gauge to determine what resolution you need, because the printed resolution often depends on the specific printer.

Use a lower resolution, like 640×480, if:

● You're displaying the images on a computer screen or video screen

● Your camera has limited memory

● You have little hard-drive space to dedicate to image storage

You should use higher resolutions if:

● You'll be printing the image at a high resolution

● You'll be cropping the image, resulting in a final image with fewer pixels

● You have storage space on your camera and hard disk to spare

In the digital world, are resolution and image quality the same thing?

No, the resolution is the total number of pixels in an image, such as 640×480 or 1280×960. This is the "size" of the image, both in file size and actual dimensions. Image quality, on the other hand, is a setting that applies to whichever resolution you choose. Digital camera images are compressed to increase the number of images you can store in memory, and the camera's image-quality setting determines how much each image is compressed.

What is file compression and what level of file compression should I use?

Most cameras allow you not only to choose from among two or more resolutions, but also to decide how much the graphics images will be compressed as they're stored in the camera's memory. The lower the compression, the better the image quality (see Figure 3-5). Of course, there's a downside—the

lower the compression, the fewer images you can fit into your camera's memory.

Image-quality selector on the Canon PowerShot 350 determines how much image compression is used.

Figure 3-5 Both dog faces were shot on the Canon PowerShot 350 and were magnified from the original images, but the one on the right—shot in "economy mode"—suffers from a lot more data loss, with obvious pixelation

In general, you should stick to the lowest level of compression available, usually called "fine." This produces images with the greatest detail and the fewest compression artifacts. Of course, some cameras have so little memory that you can only get a few images in memory in this mode before needing more "film." Either upgrade by buying an additional memory card or drop the image quality down one notch.

While "economy" or "low-quality" compression is fine for e-mail and even Web pages, don't use this for print applications, including things like newsletters and T-shirts. In those situations, quality counts.

Does my digital camera offer a panorama mode? What's this all about?

Some cameras include additional modes, including something called *panorama mode*. A panorama mode is very similar to the letterboxing that you can see on some movies on television or video: Bands of black are added to the top and bottom of the image, making it seem more panoramic. Unlike letterboxed movies, however, panorama photos look panoramic because the camera strips away some imaging information. If you're shooting in 1280×960-pixel image mode, for instance, the panorama setting will capture a strip of image through the middle that might measure 1280×480, giving the image a very wide appearance. In reality, the image is still the same 1280 pixels across—no bigger—but the horizontal cropping makes it seem wider.

While panorama mode is fun to experiment with, you can achieve the same effect with any digital camera by cropping

the image at the top and bottom on your PC. This is even better than the preprogrammed panorama mode, in fact, because you can crop it to any dimensions you like. See Chapter 12 for more details.

What is my digital camera's macro mode for?

Most cameras include a macro mode that lets you get extraordinarily close to your subject and still stay in focus. Most fixed-focus and auto-focus lenses can't resolve an image closer than about two or three feet, so macro mode uses a special lens that can focus much closer—sometimes to within an inch or so.

Not all macro modes are alike. Some cameras can auto-focus in macro mode, while others have a manual focusing control that you need to adjust by eye. Still others have a fixed-focus lens that only works within a very narrow range, and for these cameras it's a good idea to have a measuring tape handy to make sure you're "in the zone." See Chapter 8 for details on macro photography.

When should I use the digital zoom on my camera?

The digital zoom is often considered a tool of last resort. A digital zoom works by only using some of the pixels on the CCD, creating a magnified image of the subject but losing resolution in the process (see Chapter 2 for more details). If your camera includes an optical zoom, use it first. If you still need to magnify the subject, try moving closer. If you can't, then enable the digital zoom on top of the magnification offered by the optical zoom.

What do I do when my digital camera runs out of memory?

Get more memory!

Seriously, your camera can only hold so many images. When you run out—or when you're in danger of running out—here are your options:

● Selectively delete images you know you don't need from memory using the camera's built-in controls.

● Drop the resolution and/or image-quality mode to a lower setting for the remaining images. You'll be able to fit more images onto the remaining space. In fact, you may be able to squeeze several images onto the memory card even if there wasn't space for even one image at higher resolution or image quality.

● If you're near a PC, transfer the images from the camera to your computer's hard disk. If you occasionally travel and stay with friends or relatives who have PCs, you might want to build a "mobile transfer kit" into your camera case that includes the installation disks that originally came with your camera and a connection cable. In this way, you can do an emergency transfer of images on the road.

● If you have a spare, swap out the current memory card for a fresh one. If your camera doesn't support memory cards, then you're stuck with the memory built into the camera and you'll have to try one of the other options.

How can I store the maximum number of images in my digital camera?

The way to pack the most images onto your camera is to choose the lowest resolution—usually 640×480—and the highest compression mode. The caveat, of course, is that this creates digital images with the lowest possible image quality. So use this scheme with care.

POWER

Why do the batteries in my digital camera wear out so quickly?

The batteries in a digital camera have a hard life. The same set of four or so AA-style batteries has to not only run the camera electronics, but also to operate the LCD display and fire the flash to boot. It's a lot to ask of any set of batteries, so don't be surprised that they do, in fact, wear out fast. There are things you can do to extend their life, though; see "Can I extend the life of my digital camera's batteries?" later in this chapter.

 ## What kinds of batteries are the best value for my money in my digital camera?

Let's start with the worst value for your money. Considering the frequency with which you change batteries in a digital camera, you shouldn't be putting ordinary alkaline AAs in your camera. They don't last very long to begin with, and ordinary AA batteries simply aren't engineered to work well in an environment like a digital camera, which draws large currents intermittently.

Instead, you should consider rechargeable batteries. Ni-Cad and NiMH (nickel metal hydride) rechargeable batteries may cost more up front, but they can be used over and over several hundred times, making them a very worthwhile investment.

If possible, I suggest you stay away from Ni-Cads as well. They don't recharge as efficiently as the newer NiMH batteries, since they need to be fully depleted before recharging. They don't last as long, either. Look to NiMH batteries as your power source of choice.

Specifically, I recommend that you try QUEST NiMH batteries from Harding Energy. QUEST batteries are inexpensive and, in my experience, last about twice as long as the closest competitor.

 ## Can I extend the life of my digital camera's batteries?

You should be using rechargeable batteries, for starters. Assuming you've gotten that square filled, you should look at the way you use your camera. You can extend the time till the next recharge or battery replacement by following some of these suggestions:

- Disable your flash. The flash is very power-hungry. If you must use it sometimes, put it in its normal auto mode—don't leave it in fill flash or red eye modes, which fire every single time whether they're needed or not.

- If it's an option, disable the LCD display on your camera and only use it when you have to.

- Don't perform power-intensive tasks like formatting a PC Card or floppy disk on battery power.

- Don't play with the auto-focus; making the camera focus constantly, even when you're not preparing to take a picture, can wear down the batteries.

- Don't turn the camera off after every single picture. If you're planning to take a lot of pictures in a short period of time, leave the camera on, since the startup routine is surprisingly power-intensive. If you're shooting pictures very infrequently, however, and the camera would be likely to turn itself off between shots anyway, go ahead and turn it off.

I've heard that rechargeable batteries can develop a "memory." What is that?

The term "memory" refers to Ni-Cad batteries, which are susceptible to this phenomenon. If a Ni-Cad battery is repeatedly charged at the same point in its discharge cycle, it can "forget" about the energy reserve it has below the recharge point and begin to drain only down to there. This memory, then, can effectively reduce the usefulness of a Ni-Cad battery by not allowing it to drain all the way to empty.

This phenomenon was first observed onboard satellites, which used Ni-Cads for power and were subjected to

External Battery Packs

If you want to get a lot of battery life out of your digital camera, consider strapping some batteries onto your belt. Omicron, for instance, sells the NiMH-based DP-1000 Digital Power Pack. This eight-ounce pack plugs into your camera's AC adapter jack and provides as many as 500 pictures on a charge. It clips onto your belt or slips in a pocket.

recharging cycles with military precision. It can affect your digital camera, too, if you consistently recharge it at the halfway point, for instance.

Avoid Ni-Cad memories by using your camera batteries until they are completely drained; then recharge them. Note, too, that newer rechargeable battery technologies—like NiMH batteries—don't develop memories and can be recharged at any time.

My digital camera came with an AC adapter. When should I use it instead of batteries?

An AC adapter lets you plug your camera into the wall and avoid using battery power. It's like using an AC adapter with a camcorder, for instance, instead of relying on its rechargeable batteries.

Your camera's AC adapter can be a lifesaver if you're used to running strictly on battery power. You can use the AC adapter whenever you're shooting indoors, within reach of wall power. But it's most handy for power-intensive situations like:

- Transferring images from the camera to a PC
- Performing image maintenance on the camera, like deleting images
- Formatting the PC Card or floppy disk

Chapter 4

Using a Scanner

Answer Topics!

Using a Scanner @ a Glance

Flatbed scanners are no longer the "mortgage-your-house" kind of purchases they used to be. They're a lot cheaper than most digital cameras, in fact, and make a good camera companion for scanning old photos. Before you shop for a scanner, though, you should understand the technology and terminology behind these devices.

Ready to buy a scanner? There are many kinds and they come in all price ranges. Use this chapter to decide whether you want a scanner that uses an internal expansion card or the computer's printer port. Also consider color depth, resolution, peripherals, and other options.

A scanner can be intimidating, particularly if you need to install an internal expansion card. Look here for step-by-step instructions on installing a scanner, adding peripherals like an automatic document feeder, and troubleshooting problems with your scanner.

Just as taking a good picture is more than just snapping the shutter release, making a good scan is more than just clicking on the "acquire" button. Look here for details on how to make the best use of software tools like sharpening and descreening that accompany your new scanner.

What resolution should you set your scanner to? Look here for a useful formula for setting resolution. You can also determine file size ahead of time with another handy formula, and get lots of other advice on setting color depth and resolution while scanning.

UNDERSTANDING SCANNER-SPEAK

 ### What is a scanner?

A *scanner* is a device that enables you to make a digital copy of a photograph or some other kind of document. The scanner attaches to your computer and "scans" the item you're copying line by line—hence the name—creating a version of the original that you can manipulate on the PC. It's similar to a digital camera, and is handy for getting pictures into a camera when they started out in print form.

 ### How does a scanner work?

A scanner can be thought of as a digital camera that needs a stationary object to work properly. Instead of a digital camera's rectangular CCD that captures the entire image at once (see Chapter 2 for an explanation of digital camera technology), a scanner uses a CCD with a single row of light-sensitive pixels. This linear CCD registers the light value of the image one line or row at a time, and that information is sent to the computer immediately and flushed so that the next line can be read.

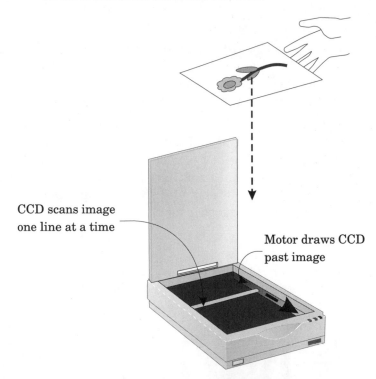

CCD scans image one line at a time

Motor draws CCD past image

The resolution of the scanner is partially dependent on the speed and accuracy of the motor that steps the CCD across the document (or the document past the CCD, depending upon the kind of scanner).

 ## What difference do the varying resolutions in scanners really make?

You can get scanners in a wide variety of resolutions, and the many choices can be confusing. In general, there are two principal reasons to choose a scanner with a higher resolution:

● Higher-resolution scanners typically achieve greater detail, particularly in the lightest and darkest portions of the image, where lower-resolution scanners can't take enough samples to resolve the image properly.

● Higher-resolution scanners let you scan small source documents and print them at a decent resolution. For instance, you can scan a small picture at 600 dpi and then print it larger than its original dimensions, yet still match the printer's resolution of 300 dpi (see "What resolution is right?" later in this chapter).

Why then would you go with a lower resolution? That's easy—they're less expensive. Not everyone needs 1200 dpi, or even a 600 dpi scanner. If your main goal is to scan images for Web pages or send faxes, then a 300 dpi scanner is probably as much as you need.

Table 4-1 offers a brief overview of some common scanners and their prices, resolutions, and interfaces. You can use it as a guide to look for the kind of scanner you want.

Scanner	Manufacturer	Price	Resolution	Interface
ScanJet 5100C	Hewlett Packard	$299	600 dpi	Parallel
ImageReader Ultra Pro	Info Peripherals	$129	1200 dpi	Parallel
ScanMaker X6	Microtek	$179	1200 dpi	Parallel
Plug-N-Scan A3 EP	Mustek	$299	600 dpi	Parallel
ScanJet 6100	Hewlett Packard	$799	2400 dpi	SCSI
Paragon Power Pro	Mustek	$899	4800 dpi	SCSI

Table 4-1 Common Scanners

 What is color depth, like 24-bit or 30-bit color?

As you're probably aware, computers measure colors in terms of bits per pixel. A one-bit display is capable of displaying two colors: The pixel can essentially be turned on or off. The original Macintosh is an example of a one-bit system—rather than displaying true grayscale, each pixel could be either black or white and the impression of gray could only be achieved by "dithering" lots of pixels in a varying black-and-white pattern. 24-bit color is at the threshold of human color perception, with 16.7 million possible colors.

It's an important distinction that a 24-bit computer display can't possibly show all 16 million colors; there aren't enough pixels on the screen to do so. Instead, when we talk about color depth, what we're saying is that each pixel has the *opportunity* to display any one of the 16 million colors visible to humans, and that's what makes the display photorealistic. In reality, a photorealistic scene may only have a few thousand colors actually on the screen at any one time.

Table 4-2 shows the correlation between color depth and the actual color sensitivity of a computer device.

 What's the difference between a scanner with a cold cathode lamp and a scanner with a fluorescent lamp?

Most scanners come with either a fluorescent lamp or a cold cathode lamp. This is the light that illuminates the

Bits per Pixel	Colors	Application
1	2	Original Macs; line art mode for faxes.
4	16	Simple grayscale.
8	256	Photo-accurate grayscale or simple color.
16	65,536	High color mode looks almost as good as true color.
24	16,777,216	True color is generally the threshold of human perception.
32	4,294,967,296	Beyond human perception; good for computer analysis and achieving extra color accuracy.

Table 4-2   Color Depth and Color Sensitivity

document and allows the CCDs to turn it into a digital image. Older—and less expensive—scanners use fluorescent lamps, which have a shorter lifetime, often by a large margin, than cold cathodes.

? I know that different types of scanners hook to PCs in different ways. What's the difference between a parallel scanner and a SCSI scanner?

Most scanners use either a parallel or a SCSI interface. SCSI is the traditional way for scanners to communicate with PCs, and while you need to install an ISA card inside the system (see Figure 4-1) to use SCSI, those scanners tend to be faster. ISA-based cards are the standard way to install peripherals inside your PC. If you've never opened your PC before, don't worry—it's not that hard to do.

Connecting your scanner to the computer with a parallel port results in slower performance, but it's easier to do—you simply plug the scanner into your printer port. Usually, there's a pass-through so you can still attach your printer.

No matter how your computer connects to the scanner, however, they're likely to communicate with each other in the same way: using a TWAIN driver. TWAIN drivers are different for every kind of scanner, but once the driver is installed, your scanner can then be accessed from any software capable of scanning.

What Is OCR?

Optical character recognition, or OCR, is a technology that lets you convert scanned text into digital text—that way you can edit documents like faxes in your word processor. OCR software is often bundled with new scanners, or you might need to buy an OCR program on your own. Some popular OCR packages include Visioneer Pro OCR 100, TextBridge Classic OCR, and Care OmniPage Lite.

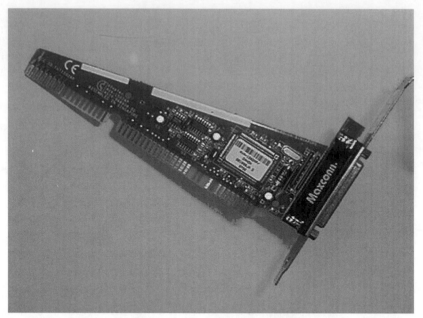

Figure 4-1 Scanner adapters are usually very small ISA-based cards that facilitate SCSI-based communication between the scanner and the PC

What does it mean when a scanner has 600 dpi optical resolution but 9600 dpi maximum resolution?

Many scanners can use sophisticated software routines to interpolate color changes and image information between pixels that were optically observed during the scan. Suppose two adjacent colors in an original document are white and black. If you scan a document beyond the scanner's rated optical resolution, the software then averages the colors and places a gray pixel between the two, smoothing the image.

That means some scanners can render images with a higher apparent resolution—as much as 9600 dpi. In general, this feature is of dubious value. You'll need a lot of memory and hard-disk space to use resolutions beyond the optical resolution, and the final results may not be all that impressive anyway. In fact, they tend to just look a bit blurry.

Don't buy a scanner based on its higher maximum resolution—go by whatever the optical resolution of the scanner actually is.

 ## What's the difference between a one-pass and a three-pass scanner?

In the old days—a few years ago—most scanners made three passes for every document they scanned. Each of these passes captured image information for one of the three color components—red, green, and blue—that would eventually make the final color image. Modern scanners, almost without exception, are single-pass devices. In a single pass of the scan head, the document is sampled for all three colors simultaneously. Obviously, this makes single-pass scanners a lot faster than the old three-pass units. If you have a three-pass scanner, there's no reason to upgrade unless you really want a newer, faster scanner. Just be prepared to wait a long time for documents to get digitized.

What Does TWAIN Mean?

TWAIN flippantly stands for "technology without an interesting name." That doesn't tell you much, though. TWAIN is the standard PC protocol for allowing cameras, scanners, and other imaging devices to communicate with Windows applications in a standardized way. Before TWAIN, every scanner came with its own proprietary drivers for each application. Using TWAIN, once you install the scanner, you can scan from any application that uses scanners.

Don't think it's a big deal? Consider business-card scanners. Even today, these handy little devices rarely come with their own TWAIN drivers, meaning you need to use the software they came with, no matter how awful it turns out to be. With a TWAIN driver, you could buy a business-card scanning program from another company if it worked better than the one that came in the box and live a happier life.

CHOOSING A SCANNER

 I've thought about getting a scanner, but I'm not sure it's worth the money. What can I do with a scanner?

Scanners are valuable if you often find the need to transfer real-world two-dimensional objects—like pictures, faxes, or book pages—into your PC. A year ago, a scanner would have only made sense for someone who needed to do a lot of scanning, but this year you can routinely find scanners for about $100. That means it's cost-effective for someone to get a scanner even for occasional use.

Even if you already have a digital camera, a scanner can be a valuable asset. Your stockpile of old images can be scanned and stored on your PC, ready to get the same kinds of electronic facelifts that we'll discuss in Chapters 11 and 12. Scanners can also be used to convert 35mm slides to the digital world. If you don't yet have a digital camera, your scanner is obviously the only avenue available for getting pictures and documents into your PC.

Scanners can also be used in a number of other, more mundane, ways. You can use a scanner as a copier, for instance. After scanning a document, you can instruct the scanning software to immediately print copies of it on your computer printer. Or you can send documents out as faxes using your PC's modem. Bottom line: A scanner is a general-purpose office appliance.

 I want to get a scanner. What are my options?

Most everyone is familiar with the flatbed scanner. It's good for a lot of different kinds of scanning jobs, but it may be "too much" of a scanner for some people, or just not the right fit for your needs. Here's an overview of the kinds of scanners you have to choose from:

● **Flatbed scanner** A flatbed is typically a long, narrow tray on which you place your document. The scanning head travels the length of the bed to create a digital image of the document. Flatbed scanners traditionally

connect to your PC with an included SCSI card, but now you can find scanners that connect via the parallel port or USB (Universal Serial Bus) port. They generally make high-quality images and accept options like automatic sheet feeders, which enable you to copy lots of pages at once. They can also scan almost any size document, from tiny business cards and 35mm slides all the way up to legal-sized documents. On the downside, they have a big "footprint," so they're hard to integrate into a small office.

● **Sheetfed scanner**   This is a much smaller device that does away with the traditional moving optics and flat scanning bed. Instead, sheetfed scanners typically stand upright and pull documents through the unit—right past the stationary scanning head—to offer a compact scanning solution. Their advantages include a compact footprint and a design that's optimized for scanning sheets of paper and photos. In fact, you can get 25-sheet sheetfed scanners at a small fraction of the cost of a flatbed with a document feeder. Of course, you can't scan thick objects like books or magazines unless you first separate the pages from the source. And some low-grade sheetfed scanners can introduce imperfections in the scan due to the imprecise motor that pulls the page through. While this kind of scanner may be fine for text documents, I highly recommend you avoid it for photographic work.

● **Photo scanner** This relatively new innovation in scanning technology is a class of scanner that is designed to scan just pictures—usually 3×5 pictures, in fact, though some also can handle 5×7s. If all you need is the ability to convert 35mm pictures into digital images, this is a good solution (some photo scanners fit in an empty drive bay of your PC, taking up no room at all). On the other hand, these scanners are completely useless for scanning anything except small pictures.

● **Hand scanner** Handheld scanners have largely disappeared from the PC world—in fact, I was unable to find even a single major manufacturer that claimed to still produce these old relics. In years past, they were a good alternative to flatbeds, but sheetfeds have taken over the role that hand scanners used to serve. Even if you can still find a good hand scanner around, I don't think it's a good investment, particularly if your scanning needs often exceed the width of the scanner (usually just a few inches).

What are the advantages of scanners that have a Scan button right on the scanner?

Simply convenience. Most scanners are fairly dumb; you need to activate them by choosing "Acquire" from the menu of your favorite image editing program. New scanners—like the Hewlett Packard ScanJet 5100C and the Visioneer One Touch—place a button right on the front of the scanner; press it, and the document on the tray is automatically imaged for your convenience. Some scanners even go this one better: The Mustek Plug-n-Scan 1200 III EP, for instance, starts the scanning software as soon as you open the cover to place a new document.

Are these features essential? Not in a million years. But they do make your scanner just a little bit easier to use (see Figure 4-2).

Should I get a scanner that connects through the SCSI port?

A few years ago this question would have been irrelevant, since all scanners used SCSI until recently. Here are some pros and cons of the traditional SCSI port and the new parallel-port scanners:

● SCSI cards are more difficult to install. If you're reluctant to fool around inside your PC, then you may want to avoid SCSI. Additionally, you need to have an expansion slot available to begin with, not always a given in today's peripheral-crazed world. If there isn't an empty slot available in your PC, then you'll either need to remove an existing peripheral from your PC or skip it and get a parallel-based scanner. On the other hand, see "How do I

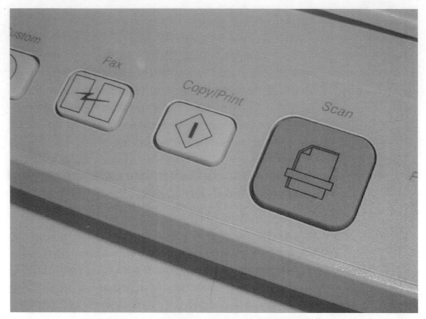

Figure 4-2 A Scan button, like the one on the front of this Visioneer One Touch flatbed, turns the scanner into a push-button appliance instead of a complicated peripheral

install a SCSI-port scanner?" later in this chapter for details on installing your scanner—it's not that hard.

● SCSI scanners aren't as portable as parallel scanners, since they're tied to a specific slot in a particular PC. With a parallel scanner, you can just unplug it and carry it away.

● SCSI cards are faster. In general, you get much better performance from SCSI than from a parallel-port device.

● You may be able to attach other SCSI devices to your SCSI card. This isn't always true. If you use the SCSI card that comes with the scanner, it is probably certified to work with that scanner—and only that scanner. If you want to use other SCSI devices, you'll need to call the scanner vendor and find out what third-party SCSI cards are compatible.

● Parallel-port scanners usually have a pass-through for your printer, but you can experience compatibility problems on occasion.

 If I get a parallel-port scanner, can I still use my printer?

Almost all scanners that use a parallel port also include a "pass-through" port so you can use your printer as well. There are occasionally compatibility problems with certain combinations of PCs, scanners, and printers, but this system generally works without a snag.

 What should I look for when shopping for a scanner?

The most important things to consider when scanner shopping are the scanner's fundamental specifications. In a nutshell, these are resolution and color depth.

● **Resolution**   Scanners are rated by the resolution at which they can convert documents into digital images. Inexpensive scanners are typically rated at 300 dots per inch (dpi). Often, you'll see a rating like 300×600 dpi. The first number is the optical resolution of the imaging system; the second number is the resolution of the motor that moves the scanning head across the document. Since the optical resolution is always lower than the number of discrete steps the motor can perform, the first number— the optics actual resolution—is more important. You should use that number to compare scanners when you shop.

 Note: *Hewlett Packard, while a major scanner manufacturer, doesn't publish the "Y" resolution—that is, the motor's stepping accuracy—of any of its scanners.*

● **Color depth**   Most inexpensive scanners are 24-bit scanners, meaning they can digitize as many as 16.7 million colors, which also happens to be about as many colors as the human eye can see. More sophisticated scanners work at 30 or 36 bits per pixel, meaning they can distinguish billions of colors. Those scanners with more than 24-bit accuracy have more colors to choose from when resolving dark regions and images with lots of rapid color changes. The end result is always a 24-bit (or

less) image, but a higher-quality one. The bottom line is that extremely high-color scanners can produce better images, but that's beyond the needs of most small office and home users.

 ### What are the advantages of a flatbed scanner?

Flatbeds are handy for scanning thick and oversized documents, like books and magazines. You can even scan three-dimensional objects with some success, depending upon what the object actually is. You can scan car keys, for instance.

Because flatbeds are so bulky, however, other scanners have added features to do some of the things that flatbeds are good at. You can find sheetfeds, for instance, that allow you to scan open book pages.

One area where flatbeds will always have an advantage is image quality. Flatbeds offer high resolution and color-depth options that sheetfed models, for instance, can never approach.

USING YOUR SCANNER

 ### What software do I need to use my scanner?

Any graphics editing program, like Adobe Photoshop, Adobe PhotoDeluxe, Jasc Paint Shop Pro, and probably 500 other applications, can scan documents.

Most scanners bundle the necessary software. Unless your scanner came with no bundled software at all, you'll have something right in the box that you can use to scan. If not, then you can buy a program like one of the ones I suggested earlier to use with your scanner.

Should I leave my scanner on all the time or turn it off between scans?

Since most modern scanners are rated for at least 30,000 hours and often more, you can safely leave the scanner on all day when you know you'll be coming back to scan more. Turn it off at the end of the day, however, and leave it off when you don't plan to be scanning for an extended period of time.

Leaving it on has one important advantage: Some scanners need to be powered on with the PC in order to work properly, so leaving the scanner on with the computer prevents you from having to restart the computer just to make a scan.

How do I scan multiple sheets with a scanner without feeding them one page at a time?

Many flatbed scanners accept something called an *automatic document feeder* (ADF), as shown in Figure 4-3. You can determine if your scanner accepts ADF attachments by checking the manual or looking at the back of the scanner. If you see a small port next to the SCSI connector, then that's probably for peripherals like an ADF. Call the manufacturer and see if they sell an ADF for your scanner. Keep in mind

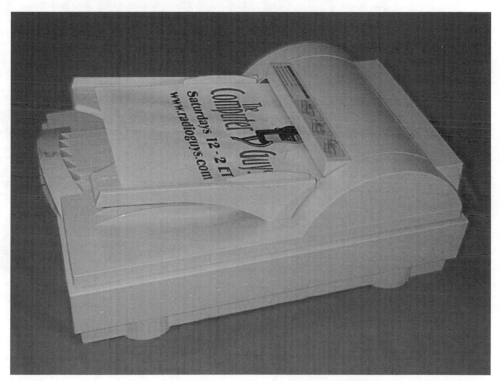

Figure 4-3   A Umax Vista scanner with its optional ADF

that ADFs are often quite expensive—while the scanner might cost $200, the ADF itself could cost another $400.

 ## How do I install a SCSI-port scanner?

Most scanners come with their own ISA-based SCSI cards, so you'll have everything you need to perform the installation in the box. Follow these steps:

1. Shut down your PC and open the cover. Locate an empty expansion slot and remove the screw holding the dust cover in place. Remove the dust cover.

2. Take the SCSI card out of the anti-static bag and insert it in the empty slot. Make sure it is seated perfectly level in the slot and then screw it into place.

3. Set the scanner up on a sturdy, flat, and level surface within a few feet of your PC.

4. Look for the shipping pin that holds the optics in place while the scanner is in transit. It will be on the bottom, the back, or even the top of the scanner. Some shipping restraints come in the form of dials, knobs, or levers— refer to the manual to see how to remove yours and then

do so. It is possible that there is no shipping pin; some scanners are beginning to do away with them.

Warning: *If you turn the scanner on with a shipping pin in place, the scanner will be instantly ruined.*

5. Plug the scanner's SCSI cable into the scanner and then into the back of the PC. Unless the scanner is internally terminated, you'll need to insert the SCSI terminator block (see Figure 4-4) into the other SCSI port on the scanner.

6. Plug the scanner's power cord in and turn it on. You should see the optics turn on and hear the motor initialize.

7. Turn on the PC. When Windows starts, you'll see a New Hardware Found dialog box and you can install the software as directed by the manufacturer.

If the scanner isn't recognized and the scanning software doesn't get installed properly, look ahead in this chapter for answers to troubleshooting questions.

The scanner is now installed. Test the scanner to be sure everything went well. Start an image editing program like Adobe PhotoDeluxe or Microsoft Imaging and choose the Scan menu option. Make sure you select the scanner from the Select Source menu the first time you use the scanner and

Figure 4-4 All SCSI chains need to be terminated at each end

then acquire an image. If you see the scanner control window, that means Windows has recognized the scanner. Go ahead and make a scan.

Tip: *If your shipping pin removes completely from the scanner, save it in case you ever need to ship the scanner in the future. You can usually tape it to the back or bottom of the scanner.*

 ### How do I install a parallel-port scanner?

Many new scanners come not with a SCSI card but with a cable that plugs directly into your parallel port. These scanners are very easy to install—here's how to do it:

1. Shut down your PC and unplug your printer from the parallel port.

2. Set the scanner up on a sturdy, flat, and level surface within a few feet of your PC.

3. Look for the shipping pin that holds the optics in place while the scanner is in transit. It will be on the bottom, the back, or even the top of the scanner. Some shipping restraints come in the form of dials, knobs, or levers—refer to the manual to see how to remove yours and then do so. Check your manual; not all scanners come with shipping restraints these days.

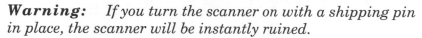

Warning: *If you turn the scanner on with a shipping pin in place, the scanner will be instantly ruined.*

4. Plug the scanner's parallel cable into the scanner and then into the back of the PC. Then plug your printer into the "pass-through" port on the scanner.

5. Plug the scanner's power cord in and turn it on. You should see the optics turn on and hear the motor initialize.

6. Turn on the PC. When Windows starts, you'll see a New Hardware Found dialog box and you can install the software as directed by the manufacturer.

If the scanner isn't recognized and the scanning software doesn't get installed properly, look ahead in this chapter for answers to troubleshooting questions.

The scanner is now installed. Test the scanner to be sure everything worked out all right. Start an image editor like Adobe PhotoDeluxe or Microsoft Imaging and choose the Scan menu option. Make sure you select the scanner from the Select Source menu the first time you use the scanner and then acquire an image. If you see the scanner control window, that means Windows has recognized the scanner. Go ahead and make a scan.

Tip: *You shouldn't have a problem using your printer with a parallel-port scanner, but if you do, unplug the printer from the scanner and reboot everything. Try to get it to work a second time. If it works now (without the printer), contact the scanner vendor to find out if there's an incompatibility with your printer.*

 ## What do I do if my PC can't find the scanner?

If your scanner worked when you first installed it, odds are good that the PC didn't recognize the scanner's presence when you first tried to access it in this scanning session. Some scanners need to be turned on when you boot the PC so they are active when Windows starts; others simply need to be turned on before you first try scanning. The solution to your problem is probably to shut down your PC and restart it with the scanner already turned on.

If your scanner doesn't work at all—you just installed it and there's no response, for instance—it's possible that you need a new TWAIN driver or other software for your scanner. Contact the vendor for updates. Here are some common scanner Web sites to help you look:

- **Acer**   www.acerscan.com
- **Agfa**   www.agfahome.com
- **Canon**   www.ccsi.canon.com
- **Hewlett Packard**   www.hp.com/go/scanjet
- **MicroTek**   www.microtekusa.com
- **Mustek**   www.mustek.com
- **Pacific Image**   www.scanace.com
- **Plustek**   www.plustekusa.com

- **Storm**   www.storm.com
- **Umax**   www.umax.com
- **Visioneer**   www.visioneer.com

I get messages like "Scanner not ready" when I try to scan.

Ah, the wonderful world of scanners. As you can see in the illustration, when the scanner doesn't respond, either you will get an error or the scanner's diagnostic software will automatically start.

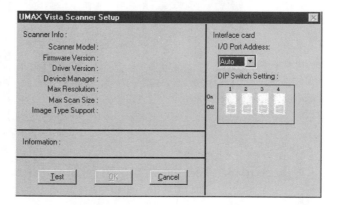

There is a wide range of problems that can cause this. Here are some things you can check, in order from easiest to fix to hardest to fix:

- If you have a cable that is not identical at both ends, check to make sure that the end with the big round lump (this is a magnetic shield called a *choke*—see Figure 4-5) is on the scanner end. This eliminates interference that might prevent the scanner from functioning properly.

- The scanner might not have the SCSI termination block in place (SCSI scanners only).

- The scanner might be using another device's SCSI ID number. Try another number (SCSI scanners only).

- The scanner might have been turned off when the TWAIN driver tried to query the scanner. Reboot your system with the scanner on at the start.

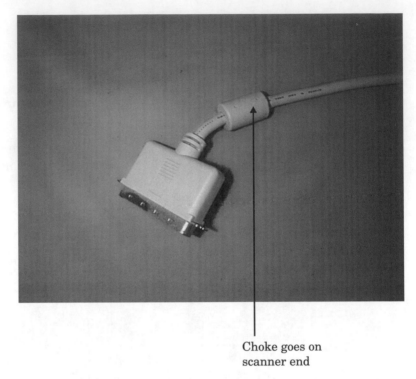

Choke goes on
scanner end

Figure 4-5 The choke should be at the peripheral end, not the PC end, of the connection sequence

- The software might not be installed properly or the drivers may be out of date—check with the manufacturer for an update.
- The SCSI cable might be bad—try replacing it.

I already have a SCSI card in my PC for my hard disk—can I use it for my scanner, too?

You'll have to call the scanner vendor and ask. Scanners are fickle SCSI devices, and they don't all work with just any SCSI card. Even if you can use the card, remember that you may need to replace the SCSI cable, since many newer SCSI cards use a small, high-density connector that won't fit the low-density cable that came with your scanner.

 I'm using a new SCSI card for my scanner, and my images have gotten very "noisy"—they are very poor quality. Is it the card's fault?

Probably not. In the process of switching to a new SCSI card, you probably had to get a new cable, too, unless the new card has the same SCSI connector as the one that came with the scanner to begin with. If you're using a new cable, it may not be properly shielded or it may be too long. A scanner cable should never exceed six feet, and three feet is even better, if your scanner is close enough to the PC.

 How do I add a document feeder to my scanner?

An automatic document feeder (ADF) can make it easy to put a stack of documents in your flatbed and go to lunch while it scans. Here's how to install one:

1. Shut your scanner off. It's quite all right to leave the PC on.

2. Remove the light shield document cover from the top of the scanner. You can usually just pull it off the scanner—generally only two short pegs hold it in place.

3. Take the ADF out of its packaging and insert the ADF's pegs into the same slots that the cover came from. There

may be screws or some other means of securing the ADF in place.

4. Find the accessory connector cable. Plug it into the appropriate port on the back of the scanner (it's usually near the SCSI port).

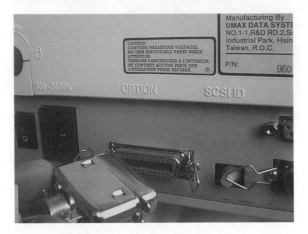

5. Turn the scanner back on.

6. Start your scanning software and look for the media type selector. Reflective is probably already selected. Choose ADF from the list and begin scanning.

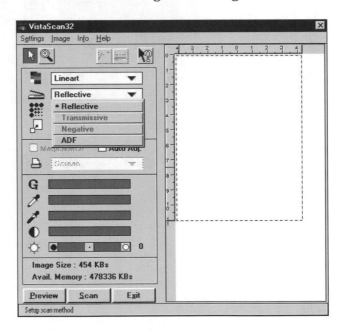

Note that the documents will probably load face up instead of face down. That way the documents will be drawn into the scanner and past the scan head face down.

My document feeder doesn't seem to work.

It is possible that the media type isn't set to use the ADF. There will be an option to change it somewhere on the scanner controller dialog box.

When you select your scanning software, be sure that the media says ADF or Feeder, and not some other setting like Reflective or Transparency.

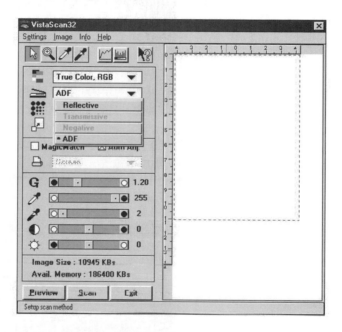

Why does my scanner scan extremely slowly or sometimes crash unexpectedly?

Many scanners come with two versions of their driver software: 16-bit and 32-bit varieties. You might think that you need the 32-bit version, particularly if you're running Windows 95 or Windows 98, but if you experience problems with a particular program, use the 16-bit one instead.

That'll probably fix the problem. You can switch between them when you choose the Scan menu in your graphics

program—select the Source option and choose the driver with a "16" in its name.

Of course, if you are using Windows, you'll generally want to use the 32-bit version of the scanner software since it'll offer better performance, but sometimes it just won't work.

IMPROVING YOUR IMAGES

 Why does my scanner seem to create images with dark edges and a brighter center?

This problem grows more common as inexpensive flatbed scanners become more prevalent. The lamp that illuminates your document may not produce an even level of brightness across the image. Specifically, it may get a little darker at the edges and brighter in the middle, altering the exposure of your document. Usually, this isn't apparent, but it might be obvious with some documents.

There are generally only two ways to avoid this problem: You can upgrade to a higher-quality scanner or arrange your documents in the center of the scanner and avoid the edges. The disadvantage of the latter method is that it can

sometimes be more difficult to ensure that the document is placed squarely on the tray without using the edges.

 ## What is sharpening?

Sharpening is a process that your scanner software can use to increase the apparent sharpness of an image (see Figure 4-6). This is usually done by increasing the contrast along edges in the image, leaving the rest of the scan alone, though some scanners increase the contrast of the entire image instead.

Figure 4-6 You can see how the sharpening filter refined the edges of the trees (most obvious in the sky) of the image on the right. The image on the left was scanned without sharpening

Do you need to use sharpening? Not always. Here's a guide to when to use this feature:

- Images with lots of edges and detail benefit more from sharpening than images that lack detail. Close-up pictures of people, for instance, are less likely to benefit from sharpening than a real estate profile of a house.

- High-resolution images benefit more from sharpening than low-resolution images since there's more detail for the sharpening filter to work with.

- Sharpening is more advantageous in printed images than in screen-based images.

- If in doubt, scan the image both ways and use the one that looks best. Sharpening can ruin an otherwise good image.

What is descreening?

You may encounter a problem scanning certain pictures that have already been scanned, such as newspaper and magazine images. What you see is a moiré pattern caused by the interference of your scanner's screening with the original screening pattern (see Figure 4-7).

To avoid this ugly moiré pattern, you can use the descreening tool found in most scanners' TWAIN driver control panel. Descreening adds time to the overall scan, but it's necessary with these kinds of images.

Figure 4-7 The descreened image on the right is better suited for reprinting than the one scanned normally on the left

Why do my scans seem to have little marks or dots on them?

As with any optical system, you may need to clean the glass scanning bed occasionally. Use a damp cloth and wipe the surface of the bed, but don't spray water or cleaning solutions directly on the glass (it can leak into the mechanism through the edges of the glass).

Surprisingly, dust can accumulate on the underside of the glass (inside the mechanism) after months or years of use. You can remove the glass to clean it, but beware—that can void the manufacturer's warranty, so check first.

How do I retain the sepia tones in an old photograph when I scan it?

To save file space, many people scan images—particularly black-and-white ones—in grayscale. If you do that, however, you'll lose the sepia tones inherent in old black-and-white photos (they aren't really black and white, they're more "brown and white").

The way you keep those old sepia tones is to scan those images in 256 color or true color, not grayscale.

I often get lousy results with my OCR software. Should I upgrade to a new OCR program?

It can often be the software's fault, but don't run out to get new software right away. Consider these factors:

- Newsprint routinely provides about 85–90% accuracy. That's as many as 150 incorrect words out of every thousand.
- Even laser-printed documents only offer 97% accuracy.
- Check the fonts. If you're trying to convert documents with odd or obscure typefaces, you're going to get awful results.
- Scan at 300 dpi or higher and use the line-art mode.
- If your program supports it, choose which parts of the page to convert, so your program doesn't waste time and effort trying to convert pictures or photocopy noise to text.

CONFIGURING YOUR SCANNER

 How many colors are enough?

It depends, of course, on what you're scanning and what the final output is going to be. Table 4-3 provides some general guidelines on what color depth is right for various applications.

 What resolution is right?

Your scanner is capable of capturing images at a wide variety of resolutions—probably from under 100 dpi all the way up to 600 dpi or beyond. Which one do you pick? In general, it's a trade-off between file size and image quality. If you can, I'd suggest you scan everything at 1200 dpi (or whatever the highest resolution of your scanner is), ensuring that you've always got your image at the highest quality for whatever you choose to do with it.

But that's a waste. Often, all you need a scanned image for is a Web page—which requires about 75 dpi—and a 300 dpi or higher scan is just wasted space. The bottom line is that you should attempt to match the scanned resolution to the resolution of the final output. So a newsletter that will be printed on a 300 dpi printer should use images scanned at

Color Depth (bits)	Colors	Application
1	Line-art mode (2 colors)	OCR and faxes
8	Grayscale (256 grays)	Scanning black-and-white images or scanning images destined for black-and-white documents
8	256 color	Web pages, e-mail, and other onscreen applications where size is more important than quality; print applications with a low-quality printer
24	True color (16.7 million colors)	Print applications in which you want the highest-quality output

Table 4-3 Color Depth

300 dpi. Use Table 4-4 as a guideline for choosing the appropriate resolution.

But there's yet another wrinkle. Suppose you scan an image but intend to print it larger than the original. For instance, you have a 3×5-inch picture that you want to print at 4.5×7.5 inches in a newsletter. You need to scan it at a higher resolution in order to keep enough information to make a high-quality print. Otherwise, just enlarging the scanned image results in a low-res, jaggy image. Use this formula to figure out what resolution to scan at:

$$Scanner\ resolution = final\ dpi \times (intended\ image\ width\ /\ original\ image\ width)$$

Thus, let's say you want to print the 3×5-inch picture enlarged to 4.5×7.5 inches at 300 dpi. The resolution would be:

$$300 \times \frac{4.5}{3} = 450\ dpi$$

You would set the scanner's control panel to 450 dpi before scanning the image.

Likewise, suppose you want to crop a scanned image and only include a smaller detail of it in the finished product. If you end up choosing to enlarge the detail, you need to consider the dimensions of the cropped image at the

Document	Scan Resolution
Fax documents	200 dpi line art or grayscale.
Optical character recognition	300 dpi line art.
Pictures for Web pages	75 dpi.
Color or grayscale images for printing	The easy answer is to scan at the resolution of the intended output, so a 300 dpi printer would require scans at 300 dpi as well. A more accurate method of printing to laser printers, however, is to look up the line screen frequency (LSF) and scan at twice that value. If you have a 300 dpi printer, the LSF is probably about 70.
Line art for printing	Scan at the printer's resolution (i.e., 300 dpi).

Table 4-4   Choosing the Right Resolution

outset—not the size of the entire image—and increase the scan resolution accordingly.

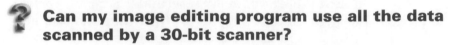

Can my image editing program use all the data scanned by a 30-bit scanner?

No, in general all the image data above 24 bits is discarded when an image leaves the scanner's TWAIN controller and goes to an image editing program. The only exception is Adobe Photoshop, which can handle 30-bit images. Instead, the real value of having a scanner that samples 30 or more bits of color is that the scanner can better distinguish detail in very bright and dark regions of a picture, creating a higher-quality scan.

How big will the files that are created by my scanner be?

The file size of your graphics is an important consideration if you scan a lot, or if you start scanning large documents in full-color mode. You'll be amazed at how quickly your disk space will evaporate.

You can use this equation to determine how big your scanned images will be:

$$\textit{File size} = (\textit{resolution} \times \textit{horizontal size}) \times (\textit{resolution} \times \textit{vertical size}) \times \textit{scan mode}$$

Horizontal and vertical size are measured in inches and scan mode refers to the color depth you used in the scan:

Color Depth	Scan Mode
Line art	1/8
Grayscale	1
Color	3

Using this equation, you can see that scanning a full-color 5×7 image at 300 dpi will result in a file size of about 9MB—but scanning that same image at 600 dpi gives you over 36MB. If you're trying to carry images on a 100MB Zip disk, this formula comes in handy.

Chapter 5

Taking Pictures

Answer Topics!

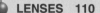

Taking Pictures @ a Glance

Your digital camera has something in common with every other kind of camera in the world, including traditional single lens reflex cameras, or SLRs. That something is optics, and it helps to understand the way your lens or lenses contribute to the photograph. In this chapter you'll find answers to all your questions about some of the basics of optics—focal length, aperture, and how digital camera lenses compare to 35mm lenses.

Depth of field is perhaps the single most important attribute of photography. A master of depth of field can bring a subject to life or manage the focus of a very large scene so everything is in focus. Look in the "Exposure" section for everything you ever wanted to know about depth of field and how to control it. You'll also find information about controlling the exposure of your images so you never again have to be satisfied with the results your camera considers "good enough."

The rules of composition are your ticket to exciting, compelling images that won't just get a few seconds' glance by friends and family. Learn how to arrange your subject, frame the picture, and capture just the right mood by reading the questions and answers on composition in this chapter.

LENSES

What is focal length?

As with most questions, there's a simple answer and a technical answer.

First, the technical approach: The *focal length* of a lens is the distance from the lens to the point at which the rays of light that pass through it focus. The higher the focal length, the greater the distance.

Focal length of lens

That doesn't necessarily tell you much that's actually useful, though. The conventional definition of focal length in photography is simply related to magnification. Larger focal lengths produce greater magnification; hence long-focal-length lenses are great for capturing far-away action or enlarging objects that are moderately far away (see Figure 5-1).

 Note: *Focal length is not the same as f/stop, which is a measure of how large the opening in the lens is. In a nutshell, f/stop measures the amount of light the lens can admit, while focal length is the magnification of the lens.*

Figure 5-1 Three views of a cyclist, all taken from the same position using different-length lenses on an Epson PhotoPC 700

The focal length of a given lens also affects the camera's angle of view (see Figure 5-2). Because a telephoto lens magnified distant objects, it has a very narrow angle of view. As you move toward smaller focal lengths, the magnification goes down and hence the angle of view increases. At the extreme end of the scale—wide-angle lenses—the image is actually shrunk (with respect to what a human eye could see) and the angle of view becomes extreme, sometimes greater

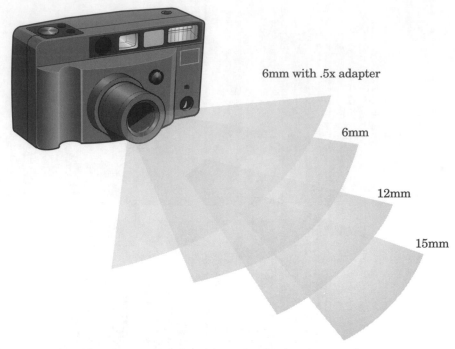

6mm with .5x adapter

6mm

12mm

15mm

Figure 5-2 The longer the focal length, the less area a lens can see

than 180 degrees. This kind of wide-angle lens is known as a *fish-eye lens* due to the peculiar effect of the angle of view.

What is the lens aperture and what is its effect on my pictures?

The *aperture* of your lens is the size of the opening that determines how much light reaches your camera's CCD or CMOS chip. In a traditional camera, the aperture settings are indicated by a series of numbers, called f/stops. F/stops generally vary from about f/1.2 to f/22, and each increment is exactly half as large as the preceding number—so f/16 admits twice as much light as f/22. The smaller the number, the larger the opening. Incidentally, the numbers aren't consecutive (like 2,3, and 4) because they're derived from the relationship between the lens diameter and the focal length.

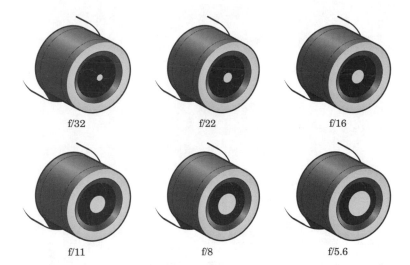

f/32   f/22   f/16

f/11   f/8   f/5.6

A small aperture (like f/22) admits relatively little light. As a consequence, you'll need a longer exposure to capture the image. In addition, a smaller opening also produces more depth of field, so a deeper ranger of foreground and background will be in focus.

Only professional-grade digital cameras actually allow you to dial in a specific aperture setting. Other cameras choose this automatically, or sometimes provide a two- or three-position switch for bright and dark lighting situations. Most digital cameras offer a fairly large-aperture lens, typically between f/2 and f/4.

What is the relationship between shutter speed and aperture?

There is a direct relationship between the aperture and shutter speed of a camera. Together, these two factors determine the proper exposure of a picture, and if they are not synchronized correctly, your images will likely be under- or overexposed.

Aperture determines how much light is allowed. Shutter speed is a measure of how long the camera's imaging circuits are exposed to the light. Both settings can change in doubles and halves, such as 1/1,000, 1/500, and 1/250 of a second. In any given lighting condition, your digital camera typically

Optics Definitions

Depth of field   The region in a photograph that is in sharp focus.

Fixed-focus lens   A lens that is sufficiently wide-angle to ensure good focus over a large range of distances without requiring an auto-focus mechanism.

Focal length   The distance from the lens to the point behind the lens where the light rays focus (when set at infinity). The longer the focal length, the longer the lens, and the greater the magnification the lens provides.

F/stop   A number that indicates how many times the diameter of the lens's aperture can be divided into its focal length.

Full stop   A change in aperture setting such that the lens admits exactly twice or exactly half as much light as it did at its previous setting.

Gray card   Also called an 18% gray card, this is commonly used to determine the correct exposure in a scene; you can use it to set the white balance with a digital camera.

finds the fastest shutter speed that will capture the scene and then assigns the proper aperture setting to take the picture.

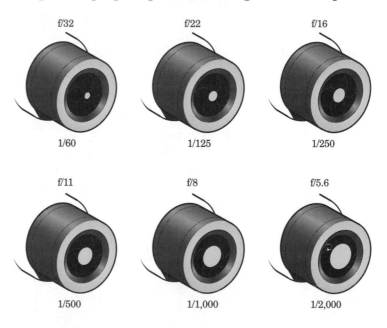

If the aperture is very large, the shutter will be open only a short time. But if the aperture is closed to a smaller diameter, less light can get through and thus the shutter must be left open longer. It's this tradeoff between shutter speed and aperture size that determines how well action can be frozen and how much depth of field is available around the focal point.

Since I understand 35mm lenses pretty well, is there an easy way to figure out the "equivalency" of digital camera lenses to 35mm lenses?

Yes, there is. This is important if you want to buy a telephoto or wide-angle lens for your digital camera from a third party. You can often snap or screw on these lenses for more photographic options, and sometimes the focal length in 35mm equivalents isn't immediately obvious. Most people understand that a 50mm lens is "normal" magnification and a 200mm lens is a moderate telephoto; but what is a 6mm focal length lens on a digital camera? Who knows?

Simply use this equation to figure out the 35mm equivalent of a lens that you know the actual focal length of:

$$35mm\text{-}equivalent\ focal\ length = \frac{(NLE \times RL)}{NL}$$

where:

- NLE is the 35mm-equivalent rating of the lens that comes with your digital camera.

- RL is the actual focal length of the new lens you're thinking of buying for your digital camera.

- NL is the actual focal length of the lens that comes with your digital camera.

You can almost always find the NLE value right on the lens itself, on the box, or in the user's guide. Let's say you have a digital camera with a focal length of 4.4mm, which according to the box equates to a 29mm lens. You are trying to decide whether to buy a 6mm, 9mm, or 12mm replacement

lens. Here's what each one would work out to in 35mm equivalents:

$$\frac{(29 \times 6)}{4.4} = 40\text{mm}$$

$$\frac{(29 \times 9)}{4.4} = 59\text{mm}$$

$$\frac{(29 \times 12)}{4.4} = 79\text{mm}$$

What do I use a wide-angle lens on my digital camera for?

Wide-angle lenses are great for capturing large, expansive scenes or moving in close and getting a unique perspective on smaller environments (see Figure 5-3).

The key thing to remember about wide-angle lenses is that since they can see more than a human eye can, they distort perspective:

● Objects in the scene tend to appear farther apart than they would in real life or with a longer lens.

Figure 5-3 A wide-angle lens can help you include more information in a picture compared to a normal lens

- Objects in the periphery of the scene can appear distorted—the shorter the lens, the more distorted they appear.

- These lenses favor objects near the center of the scene, making them handy for emphasizing the subject in a crowded setting.

- Wide-angle lenses typically offer a lot of depth of field, meaning that you can often get everything from the subject to infinity in sharp focus. Many digital and point-and-shoot cameras come with wide-angle lenses for exactly this reason.

What do I use a telephoto lens on my digital camera for?

A *telephoto lens* is typically considered to be any lens with a focal length beyond that of the normal focal length lens. Telephoto lenses act like binoculars for your camera, pulling distant objects in and magnifying the scene (see Figure 5-4).

Many photographers love telephoto lenses—particularly zoom telephotos—because they expand your range of options significantly. Here are some telephoto factors to keep in mind:

- Objects in a telephoto lens get compressed, making everything seem somewhat closer together.

Figure 5-4 The telephoto attachment for the Epson PhotoPC allows you to get a closer view of the same scene

● In contrast to the distorted perspective offered by wide-angle lenses, a telephoto image looks very flat.

● Telephoto lenses reduce the depth of field of an image. Typically, only the subject of a telephoto shot is in perfectly sharp focus (and this effect is more pronounced with greater focal lengths).

What are the pros and cons of using a telephoto lens?

Virtually every photographer should own a telephoto lens. Since there are many subjects you simply can't approach safely—like lions at the zoo, airplanes flying at an airshow, and spouses who don't enjoy being photographed—a telephoto allows you to stand off some distance and still fill the frame with the subject you're trying to capture. Because of the flat, compressed perspective of a telephoto shot, these lenses also bring a level of intimacy to a scene that a wide-angle lens can't match; the stretched feel of wide-angle images makes you feel like you're looking in from a distance, instead of being right there in the scene.

Telephotos have a downside, though. You may need a tripod or some other kind of support to ensure there's no camera shake, particularly with very long telephoto lenses. Telephoto lenses also have smaller apertures, meaning that the shutter speed must be slower—and that only aggravates the jitter problem. For the same reason, telephotos can't easily be used in low-light situations.

How do you take a "zoomed" picture?

Zoomed images are a popular "effect" shot, taken with a zoom lens and a somewhat long exposure. This isn't the sort of picture you'll want to take all the time, but it can add an artistic flair to your portfolio. These pictures suggest action where there may otherwise just be a static scene, and they can gets "wows" from the people you show it to.

Unfortunately, most digital cameras can't manage the traditional zoomed shot, either because you can't directly control the shutter speed or because the zoom lens is motorized and doesn't go quickly enough. You can simulate the look of a zoomed photo after the fact in an image editor; for details, see Chapter 12. If your camera is up to the task, however, you can try to capture the effect "in the lens" instead of on the computer:

1. Choose a scene to zoom through. You'll get the best results with a brightly colored subject and a simple scene that won't be too "busy."

2. Mount the camera on a tripod to minimize camera shake. Or you can try to hand-hold it if you have a steady grip.

3. Set the shutter for 1/4 or 1/8 of a second. You'll need that much time to slide the zoom lens. Obviously, you may need to take this picture early or late in the day to be able to properly expose the image. If you can't set the exposure because your camera is an automatic, it's always an option to apply a neutral-density filter over the lens to effectively slow the camera down—or shoot in the shade or late in the day.

4. Just as you press the shutter release, start zooming with a firm, steady, and consistent motion. Just as in baseball or golf, ensure that you follow through the zoom motion even after the shutter releases—that way, you won't stop moving the zoom in the middle of the exposure. You may need to practice this a few times to get the shot right, but electronic film is free.

EXPOSURE

 ### What is depth of field?

Depth of field refers to the region of proper focus available in any given photographic scene. When your camera focuses on a subject, some distance in front of and behind the subject will also be in focus—this entire area is the depth of field. See "What is the lens aperture and what is its effect on my pictures?" earlier in this chapter for more information.

 ### How can I control depth of field?

Depth of field depends on three factors:

● Large apertures always have less depth of field than smaller apertures for any particular lens. Thus, an f/22—

which has a very small opening—will generally yield a huge depth of solid focus in a scene as compared to an opening of f/1.2, which typically has a very narrow depth of field.

● Your distance from the subject determines how much depth of field you get in your scene. If you photograph a subject that is far away, the depth of field will be much greater than it is for a subject that is close to the camera. In practical terms, that means the region of sharp focus for a macro shot—where the subject is only a few inches from the camera—is extremely narrow and you need to focus very, very precisely. If you're photographing something very far away—like a distant horizon—then a vast region in front and behind the image will be in sharp focus. Note that this affects all kinds of exposures, so while an f/22 lens might still have a greater depth of field as compared to an f/4 lens, their relative depths of field will change depending upon how far they are focusing.

● The focal length of the lens has a significant effect on the depth of field you can capture. The longer the focal length, the smaller the depth of field becomes for any given f/stop. A wide-angle lens—like a 4mm digital camera lens—has much more depth of field at the same f/stop and distance from the subject than does a 9mm telephoto lens.

How do I get the most—or least—depth of field?

There are three ways to maximize the depth of field in your images:

● Use a short lens, one with a normal or wide-angle focal length.

● Focus on a more distant subject. If you're trying to get a nearby tree and a more distant house in focus simultaneously, for instance, focusing on the house is more likely to deliver both objects in focus than focusing on the tree.

● Use a small aperture, like f/11 or higher (if you can control this aspect of your camera).

To minimize the focal length, the opposites apply. For more information, see "How can I control depth of field?" earlier in this chapter.

Using Depth of Field

Depth of field is a powerful artistic tool that, while more difficult to tap in a digital camera than in a traditional SLR, is still worth employing. Remember the three rules for controlling depth of field (see "How can I control depth of field?" and "How do I get the most—or least—depth of field?" earlier in this chapter) and experiment.

Shallow depth of field is a powerful tool, and one that I try to use often. You can use it to isolate the subject and make the scene more dramatic by showing the viewer exactly where to look.

Large depth of field has the advantage that you can get lots of the image in sharp focus, but if it's not composed well, the picture lacks impact—there's no focal point to interest the eye.

Remember, of course, that any photographic trick, if overused, gets boring. Experiment with taking the same picture with both deep and shallow depths of field, and see which works better in various situations.

 When do I use the various exposure modes on my camera?

Most digital cameras come with just one exposure mode: fully automatic, similar to what you'll find in ordinary

point-and-shoot cameras. Go over about the $1,000 price point, however, and you begin to encounter cameras like the Fujix DS-300, Nikon E3, and the Kodak DCS 520. These cameras all provide exposure modes that mimic traditional 35mm cameras. Here's what each mode does:

- **Automatic**   In this mode, both shutter speed and aperture settings are selected by the camera to match the lighting. Usually, automatic modes try to select the fastest shutter speed possible in order to minimize camera shake when you take the picture. There's nothing you can do to change the settings the camera chooses, but you can externally influence the settings. By putting a neutral filter over the lens, for instance, you can darken the scene and force the camera to use a larger aperture. This will decrease the depth of field.

- **Aperture priority**   This setting is usually indicated by an "A" on the mode dial. Using this mode, you dial in the aperture setting you like and the camera accommodates by setting the appropriate shutter speed to match. Use this mode if you're trying to achieve a particular depth of field and you don't care about the shutter speed.

- **Shutter priority**   This is the opposite of aperture priority—choose a shutter speed and the camera sets the complementary aperture opening. This mode is ideal for locking in a speed fast enough for action scenes. It usually is identified by an "S" on the mode control.

- **Manual**   The manual mode ("M") is like old-style, pre-computerized cameras. In manual mode, you select the aperture and shutter speed on your own, sometimes with the help of the camera's recommendation. Use this for long exposures and other special situations.

 Tip: *Aperture and shutter priority modes are different sides of the same coin. If your camera only comes with one or the other, get the exposure you want by thinking backwards. To capture action in aperture priority, for instance, open the aperture up as much as possible, forcing the shutter speed to increase.*

What can I do to take pictures in low lighting?

If there's not enough light to take a picture, you generally have three options available: add light, open the aperture, or use a long exposure. You can add light using the camera's flash or with external lights (see Chapter 7). Alternately, you can get interesting effects by using a long exposure. Most digital cameras are fully automatic, and they'll extend the shutter speed for several seconds if necessary to capture enough light to shoot the scene. If you choose to use a long exposure, remember these points:

- You'll absolutely need a tripod or some other support to stabilize a camera during long exposures.

- Don't try to photograph moving subjects during a long exposure unless you're explicitly attempting to get a special effect (see Figure 5-5).

- Certain subjects—like city lights and the night sky—can make particularly effective subjects via long exposures.

Your last option is to increase the aperture size. Many cameras have a night or low-light setting that allows you to do this.

Figure 5-5 This carnival ride was exposed for about 1/30 of a second to show a sense of movement

 ## How do I correct for an unavoidable, bright background?

In general, you should avoid taking pictures directly into a bright light, since it gives your camera a false reading and underexposes the subject. Remember that your camera tries to average the light in the scene and the background tends to have a greater overall effect on the exposure than the smaller subject (see Figure 5-6).

Of course, there are always situations where you can't avoid taking these kinds of pictures. When that happens, use the exposure compensation control on your camera to overexpose the scene. The exposure compensation can be used to over- or underexpose your picture in increments of

Figure 5-6 The first picture is OK, but a +1 overexposure on the right corrects nicely for the bright background (the sun is behind the subject)

half or entire f/stops. For more information on your camera's exposure compensation control, see Chapter 3.

In general, try setting the control to +1 and see if that solves your exposure problem. You may need more or less, depending upon the actual scene you're shooting. Here are some common situations that require exposure compensation:

- Photographing a person against a bright background, such as a bright sky, white wall, water, or snow
- Photographing a landscape, city scene, or some other situation in which you are including the sun or a large portion of bright sky
- Photographing a bright subject, such as a metallic aircraft, a white car, or a snow scene

 ## How do I correct for dark subjects that overexpose my images?

This is exactly the opposite of the situations described in "How do I correct for an unavoidable, bright background?" Again, you need to make use of the exposure compensation control on your camera to ensure that the scene is corrected from what the camera's meter would like to do to your picture (see Figure 5-7).

In this situation, I suggest you set your exposure compensation to –1 and see if that solves your problem; if not, vary it as appropriate. Here are some situations that warrant exposure compensation:

● Photographing a person against a dark background, such as a dense crop of trees, a dark wall, or a shady scene.

Figure 5-7 The ghost on the left is badly overexposed, since the dark grass determined the exposure. Underexposing improved the ghost significantly

Keep in mind that exposure compensation will only be needed if the subject is in the light and the background is in shade. If they're both in uniform shade, the camera can probably resolve the exposure issue on its own.

- Photographing a dark subject, such as a black car or people in tuxedos or dark dress.

Bracketing

The term "bracketing" comes from the world of 35mm photography, and it refers to taking a series of pictures of the same scene with slightly different exposures to capture the best image. Typically, photographers use the exposure compensation control on their cameras and take a sequence of exposures, from +0 to +3, for instance. The reason is obvious: Film is cheap and you don't know exactly what you're getting until the pictures come back from the developer.

Digital cameras are a bit different—thanks to the LCD display built into most cameras, you can instantly get a pretty good idea of what you just photographed, without waiting for the development process. In addition, the fact that the images are digital means you can process the images to your heart's content afterwards on your PC. See Chapter 11 for a discussion of how to change the apparent exposure of images.

On the other hand, there's something to be said for getting the picture right the first time. LCD displays can rarely show you all the detail in an image, particularly outside in bright light, where LCDs become relatively ineffective. To add insult to injury, post-processing can't add information back into a photograph that wasn't there to begin with. For example, post-processing can't brighten a shadow to show what's hiding there if the pixels are just plain black. So I recommend what might seem like an anachronistic technique for photographing tricky images with a digital camera: Bracket your exposure to ensure that you got it right. When you can evaluate the

sequence in detail, you can then delete the images that don't cut the mustard and just keep the good one.

COMPOSITION

 What is the focal point of a picture?

The focal point is the main subject of a picture, such as a building or a person. In other words, the focal point is the main point of interest that the eye is drawn to when looking at the picture. You should always strive to consider what the focal point of your picture actually is and plan your photos accordingly.

When your subject is too expansive to really be considered a focal point in and of itself (like a mountainous landscape, for instance), try to contrive a focal point that adds some relief for the viewer (see Figure 5-8). In the case of the mountains, for instance, you could frame the shot so it includes a tractor, cabin, or hikers to allow the viewer's eye to rest on something familiar.

Figure 5-8 Secondary focal points add interest to landscapes

Can I have more than one focal point in a picture?

Be careful with this technique because it's easy to include too many things in an image that all seem to have roughly the same importance. One way to avoid this problem is to position your shot so the various subjects are arranged in an interesting way that leads the eye through the picture. A family portrait, for instance, is usually framed in tiers of people that form an interesting, leading shape. In Figure 5-9, my son forms the point of a triangle that branches up and down to lead your eyes to the left.

What are the "rules" of composition?

The rules of composition in photography are not so much rules as general guidelines—ones that are made to be broken,

Figure 5-9   Create lines or shapes (triangles are common) in group
photos so they don't just show a gaggle of people

experimented with, modified, or outright ignored as the
occasion warrants. If you're a beginning photographer,
however, it pays to practice taking pictures by obeying the
rules and seeing what kinds of results they give you. After
you feel comfortable as a photographer, then you can break
out and try things that are really novel. Also, remember that
the rules of composition—at least the ones in this book—are
just common-sense suggestions that contribute to
well-composed pictures. They're not magical, and you'd
probably figure them out on your own anyway.

● **Follow the rule of thirds.**   Many novice photographers
don't think a lot about the organization of what they see
through the viewfinder, so the rule of thirds helps restore

some balance to their photos. Draw lines through a picture dividing it into thirds and you'll find that the image is broken into nine "zones" with four interior corners. It is these corners that constitute "sweet spots" in your picture. If you place something—typically the subject—along any of the "third lines" or right on one of the sweet spots, you'll typically end up with an interesting composition.

Center of attention

● **Fill the frame.** Novices sometimes obsess about the principal subject in the viewfinder and forget that a good picture is about composition and balance. A lot of that is embodied in the rule of thirds, but also don't forget to get the most mileage you can out of the frame. There's nothing wrong with backing up to get other elements in the picture, but also try getting close and entirely filling the frame with your subject. By filling the frame, you

eliminate distracting elements from the picture and add impact to the shot. Whatever you do, don't use the viewfinder like a gun's crosshairs. Move the subject around in the viewfinder or get a different angle on it to improve the shot.

Tip: *When shooting portraits—both formal and informal—try to leave some head room at the top of the image. A photo with ample head room looks more professional than one that's too tight. But remember, there are exceptions to every rule.*

● **Frame the photograph.**   Many kinds of pictures look good if they've been framed with something resident in the scene you're photographing. This can be something natural, like a tree, or something man-made, like a doorway. Usually you'll want the frame to be in focus along with the subject, so focus on the more distant object and use a smaller aperture. Sometimes it's appropriate to allow the frame to be out of focus, though—experiment.

● **Don't put the horizon in the center of the image.**
This is a corollary to the rule of thirds, and it bears
explicit mention. Since the horizon is such a strong
element in many pictures, you'll usually want it to fall at
the top or bottom horizontal line in your picture. If your
image is of landscape and sky, logic implies that the
horizon should go along the bottom horizontal line.
"Sea-centric" images often benefit from a horizon along
the top horizontal line.

● **Use lines to lead the viewer's eyes through the
photo.** Lines can also create a sense of depth and
perspective that is often lost in the two-dimensional

photograph. Lines can be formed in almost any situation—a row of trees, the shape of a skyscraper from the ground, the route of a backyard fence. The effect of these lines is usually best seen through a normal or wide-angle lens, since telephoto lenses compress the scene and make it harder to see long, sweeping lines.

● **Look for repetition and patterns in your images.** Patterns like those you can see in nature or man-made objects can create interesting effects that, like lines, can add a sense of depth and motion to your images.

● **Use foreground to balance background.** If you are trying to photograph a distant subject—like a landscape or cityscape—a common trick is to place something of interest in the foreground to provide a sense of balance. The viewer's eyes are drawn immediately to the foreground object and then they wander to the background—a very effective technique for adding depth, perspective, and scale to a photo (see Figure 5-10).

Some pictures really seem to pull your eyes through the scene. What tricks do they use to do that?

As mentioned in "What are the 'rules' of composition?" earlier in this chapter, the use of lines can help lead you through a picture. Lines can be obvious and tangible—like a line of trees, the line of a seashore, or the line of cars on a bridge—or

Figure 5-10 The anchor is the fence post in the foreground, followed by the pier midway through the picture; finally, your eyes reach the top of Pike's Peak

Keep the Horizon Straight

This may seem obvious, but how many times have you seen a friend's photo in which the horizon was cockeyed? Vertically oriented pictures can get by with a slightly off-kilter horizon, but if you take a horizontally oriented image and the horizon is not straight, it affects the feel of the photo. Try to be as careful as possible while photographing expansive horizons, but if you goof, remember that it's a digital photo. You can always correct for an angled horizon on the computer (see Chapter 11).

less tangible, formed by the motion of your eyes as they move from focal point to focal point in a photograph. Cleverly arranging people in a picture or lining up the various natural subjects in a composition can create compelling lines that bring a photograph to life.

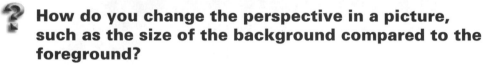 **How do you change the perspective in a picture, such as the size of the background compared to the foreground?**

This is where a selection of lenses—or a good zoom—can come in handy. When we say that a telephoto lens "compresses" the image, one of the things we mean is that the foreground loses its status as distinct and far away from the background. In fact, a telephoto lens seems to enlarge the background more obviously than the foreground, making them more similar in size. This can be used to great effect, for instance making an individual in front of a building seem closer to the structure. In Figure 5-11, notice the relationship between the background and the foreground and the way it changes in the normal and telephoto images.

What makes the best pictures—horizontal or vertical shots?

Don't get lulled into taking just horizontal pictures because the camera is shaped that way. Don't be afraid to turn the

Figure 5-11 The stuffed animals haven't moved, though the telephoto lens makes it seem like they're much closer together in the image on the right

Zoom with Your Feet

Don't have a zoom lens? That's okay—you can always move in closer with a normal lens. In fact, people sometimes get over-reliant on zoom lenses, using zoom for all their photographs. The reality is that the first place you try to frame a picture is probably not the best—walk around and try composing your picture from several vantage points. Try to the right and left, from behind, and even from higher and lower elevations, if possible. Standing on a chair is a great way to get a unique and unexpected perspective on a scene. Sure, use the zoom, but use your feet, too.

camera on its side and try it vertically. In fact, I recommend that beginning photographers try to compose *every* picture both vertically and horizontally. Why? First, it gets you thinking along those lines, and you'll remember that there's more than one way to see a scene. But second, unless you try lots of compositions vertically, you won't be able to recognize a scene that's begging for the vertical treatment.

Of course, you have a digital camera, which means you can crop images in the computer any way you want afterwards. See Chapter 11 for coverage of this kind of image editing. The downside of cropping, though, is that you'll throw away a lot of pixels in the process, and lose enough resolution that the picture may not print well (depending upon the resolution you started with).

There are obvious applications for both camera orientations. Horizontal shots are good for landscapes and other wide, sweeping panoramas. Vertical pictures are good for photographing man-made vistas like buildings and bridges. There's a sense of motion conferred to the photo by the direction of the shot; also, vertical images often seem to be bolder and convey more energy (see Figure 5-12). As always, experiment.

? Why are the corners of my pictures dark?

It's one of two things: Your fingers are in front of the lens (and I doubt that's the case—you wouldn't do that, right?) or you're using a wide-angle lens attachment that darkens the edges of the image. This effect is called *vignetting,* and it commonly happens when you use optional lenses with certain cameras. The Epson PhotoPC, for instance, allows you to attach a wide-angle and super-wide-angle lens to the camera. The vignetting can be edited out on your computer afterwards (see Chapter 11).

Figure 5-12 Two views of Colorado

Vignetting

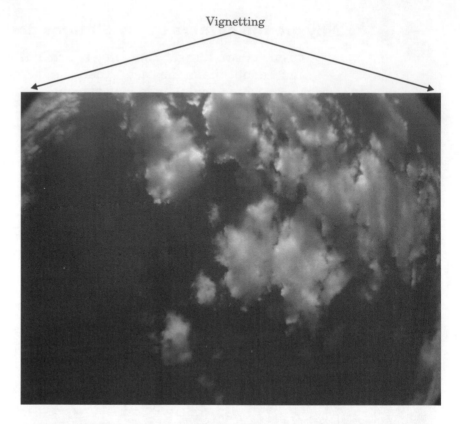

Why doesn't my auto-focus focus on the subjects?

There are a few possible reasons why you're having focusing problems:

- You haven't perfected the auto-focus maneuver. It helps to "pre-focus" your scene by slightly depressing the shutter release as you compose the image. This way, you can check to make sure you're locked onto the appropriate subject before the picture is taken. If you wait until you actually take the picture to focus, you really don't know what the camera did till you review the image later.

- It may not be a focus problem, it may be a steadiness problem. Don't jab the shutter release suddenly or the force can make the camera shake. You may also want to use a tripod, or use the self-timer so you can hold the camera steady while it takes the picture for you.

- The camera might have trouble locking on to the subject due to lighting or contrast problems. Try another position.

- Your subject might not be in the middle of the picture, where the camera is trying to focus. You need to pre-focus on the subject, then compose the picture while holding the shutter release partially down. For more details on this procedure, see Chapter 3.

Chapter 6

Subjects

Answer Topics!

Subjects @ a Glance

In all likelihood, people will be the most common subject that you photograph. Friends, family, children…people are the single most commonly photographed topic on earth. But unless you want your digital images to collect digital dust or be deleted shortly after you capture them, it helps to understand something about how to best capture people on "film." This chapter has tips on what kind of equipment to use, where and how to compose people pictures, and how to put your subjects at ease and make them look their best.

Action is arguably the most exciting kind of photography subject. Fast cars, fast planes, athletic events—it's all in there. To take compelling action shots, you'll need to become familiar with fast shutter speeds, telephoto lenses, and panning. Look for help in this chapter.

At the other end of the photography spectrum is landscape and nature photography. This category is more ponderous, sometimes more poetic, and it takes a different mindset to approach it. You'll need a somewhat different set of equipment and an eye for landscapes, patterns, and natural beauty. This chapter gives you tips on taking all sorts of outdoor photography, from backyard nature scenes to mountainous landscapes to the lion cage at the zoo.

Digital cameras are a great choice for taking on a trip because they are typically pretty small, and if you take a shot you don't like, you can delete it instantly, conserving memory for other shots. This chapter addresses all kinds of travel questions, including topics like how to photograph buildings and cityscapes, what equipment you should pack, how to protect your camera, and more.

PEOPLE

 ### What focal length lens should I use to take portraits?

Most portrait photographers like to use a moderate telephoto lens. This allows you to photograph the subject from a less intimidating distance so they can relax a bit. Also, a telephoto offers two great advantages over a normal lens:

● Telephoto lenses compress the features of the subject, usually resulting in a more pleasing appearance. If your subject has a pronounced nose, for instance, it won't be quite so large using a telephoto.

● Telephotos reduce the available depth of field, making it easier to blur the background and emphasize the subject.

For a 35mm SLR, you'd expect to use a lens in the neighborhood of 100mm. This usually translates to about a 9mm lens in digital photography. For a handy way to convert digital camera focal lengths into the 35mm equivalents you may be more familiar with, refer to Chapter 5.

You can use a camera that comes equipped with a zoom lens or search out a telephoto adapter for your camera, such as one made by Tiffen. While I would never, ever attempt to take portraits with a normal or wide-angle lens (the distortion would render the subject unattractive), don't feel constrained by my advice. Photography is an art, and you should experiment to find your own voice through the lens.

 ### What's different about photographing kids?

Just as with adult portraits, you should choose a moderate telephoto—but while you can usually get by just fine with a fixed-focal-length lens when taking portraits, I suggest you use a camera with a zoom lens for kids. They're unpredictable and spontaneous, and that means you won't always be the right distance from your subject when the picture you want to capture happens. I'd suggest using a camera like the Agfa ePhoto 1280—it offers a range from 38 to 114mm in 35mm camera equivalents. The Kodak DCS 210, while an all-around good camera, has an anemic zoom range from 29 to 58mm. It's not quite there for taking portraits and stalking kids.

Don't forget to back off the zoom button sometimes. Remember that kid pictures are often best when they include some of the surroundings, and you may want a normal focal length for those kinds of pictures.

What settings work best for portraits?

Portraits come in all shapes and sizes, so it's hard to say that any one variety of camera settings is best. In general, though, formal portraits work best when the background is out of focus, dictating a larger aperture. Since digital cameras rarely let you control the aperture setting precisely, you should try to take portraits in settings that aren't awash in midday sun; a slightly less well-lit situation will cause the aperture to open all the way up and blur the background. Early morning and late afternoon sun, in fact, produce warmer pictures that go well with portraiture.

Avoid bright, head-on light, such as you'll get from a camera-mounted flash. Whenever possible, try to take your pictures outside. Flash is harsh light that doesn't flatter your subject.

If you're adventurous, you might want to try your hand at soft focus (see Figure 6-1). You can use a soft-focus attachment for your camera to "de-sharpen" the features of your subject's face. This is a great effect if not overused (see Chapter 9 for details). For a peek at what soft focus can do to your pictures, keep a sharp eye out on television for the appearance of female protagonists. They'll often benefit from a soft-focus lens while their male counterparts—often just a cut scene away—are filmed with rugged, harsh lighting and razor-sharp focus.

Note: *You can always add effects (like soft focus) to your pictures afterwards. That's the beauty of working digitally—you can make almost any kind of change imaginable once the image is stored on your computer. See Chapters 11 and 12 for details.*

Figure 6-1   Soft focus is a great way to flatter your subject's features or introduce a new alien female for Captain Kirk

How should I pose my subjects for a portrait?

There are lots of ways to pose your portrait subject, but remember that one of your goals is to make them feel at ease. No one looks good if they're rigidly posed or nervous, so establish a rapport with them and don't be overly concerned about eliciting a militarily precise pose.

There are a few popular poses that work particularly well. You can choose to have your subject sit or stand, and you can compose the image fairly tightly around the head and shoulders or go all the way down to the waist. If there are multiple people in your picture, you'll need to back off, of course, and include more area in the shot. If the picture involves more than one person, think about the discussion of lines and shapes from Chapter 5—specifically, try to compose the picture so your subjects form a triangle or are divided into tiers.

Give some thought to how your subjects are using their hands. They can rest their hands in their laps or place one or both hands on their heads. Hands in laps tend to make a "formula" portrait that looks serious and perhaps a bit contrived. Instead, try having the subjects put their hands up under their chins or on their cheeks; if done well, this adds a sense of drama to your portrait (see Figure 6-2).

What kind of lighting works best for portraits?

Since most digital cameras are forced to use the flash that's built into the camera, using the flash as your primary source of lighting is a last resort. Instead, take your portraits outside and shoot before noon or in the late afternoon, when the light is a bit warmer and less harsh.

Figure 6-2 Two typical portrait poses. Note the hands

While you may have heard that you want your subject to face into the light, that's only because backlight causes underexposure. Direct, frontal sunlight is just as bad—the light blasts into your subject's face and makes them squint. Instead, I believe the best light for outdoor portraits is that which comes from an overcast sky. If you shoot on a cloudy day, you'll be impressed with the results that come from the even, shadowless lighting.

You can't always wait for bad weather, though, so another alternative is to arrange your shoot so that sunlight comes in from the side. If you can, use a reflector to bounce some of this light into your subject's face. As an alternative, set your camera to fill-flash mode. This makes the flash work even though there's already enough ambient light, and the result is a little extra light filling in your subject's face.

My subjects hate cameras. What do I do?

You can simply give up now, or you can try to work with your subjects so they are a little more at ease. If you're trying to catch spontaneous, candid moments, then back off and try to blend in with the background. You want your prey to be unaware, as much as possible, that you're stalking them, and let them behave naturally. It is that natural activity that you're trying to capture on film, and it won't happen if you're constantly thrusting an intimidating camera in their face.

Luckily, most digital cameras look pretty innocuous, so you're already at an advantage as compared to the guy with a huge 35mm SLR hung around his neck. But be sure you're using a telephoto lens—at least the equivalent of 85mm—so you can hang back far enough that you're not noticed.

If you're trying to capture a fairly formal-looking portrait, you have a little more work cut out for you. It's up to you, the photographer, to put your subject at ease. Talk to your subject and get him or her to respond—if you can get them to loosen up, they'll exhibit more natural responses and look better on film. Take pictures periodically as you pose your subject to get them used to the shutter going off, even if it isn't a picture you intend to keep—remember, digital film is free.

Using Window Light

Another common technique is lighting portraits via window light. Window light is particularly effective at making moody, dramatic portraits, but you can try putting lots of things in front of a window and experiment for yourself. Remember these tips:

- Don't use windows on the east or west side of your house, since light pours in those windows directly. Stick to the north- or south-facing windows.

- Shoot the picture with your back to the window and turn your subject so they face almost head-on into the window, with some light spilling over to their side.

- If necessary, fill in the side of the subject's face with a reflector to eliminate harsh shadows.

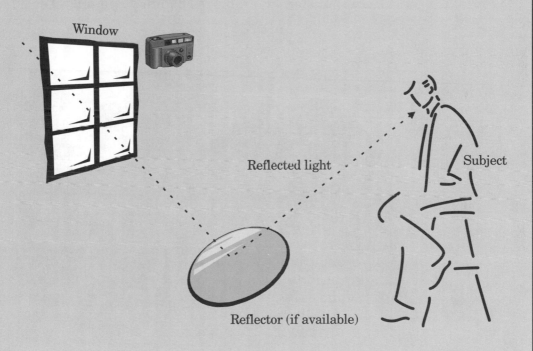

Window

Reflected light

Subject

Reflector (if available)

If your subject is a bit of a ham, let him or her take some control over the pose; if they feel in charge, they'll be more relaxed and look more natural on film (see Figure 6-3). If they are reticent, offer suggestions for how they should pose for you.

Is there a way to get a lot of images quickly— like with a motor drive—so I can catch that perfect expression?

Well, sure—a motor drive will work. But most digital cameras can only take two or three pictures per minute, not per second, which can severely affect your ability to catch fleeting expressions on people's faces. You can step up to a professional-grade digital camera with a multi-frame-per-second motor drive, but that will cost a small fortune.

Or, you can get one of the new digital camcorders, like the Canon Optura. These devices work like traditional video cameras but store their images digitally at a full 30 or 60

Figure 6-3 An informal portrait sometimes brings out personality better than a formal one

frames per second. You can film your subject with a digital camcorder and then extract each frame as a separate high-resolution still image and choose the one that works best. Some photojournalists, for instance, have abandoned their normal cameras in favor of these camcorders, and they use a product like Radius' MotoDV to retrieve each frame from the camera and store it on a PC. For more about digital video, see Chapter 18.

My camera is never ready when I want to take a candid, spontaneous shot. How can I prevent that?

Digital cameras are very frustrating—after a few minutes of inactivity, they shut themselves off to conserve battery power. That may be great for the battery, but it's a pain in the neck if you are ready to capture a shot only to discover the camera is off.

If you're planning to take a picture but you're waiting for the right moment, finger the shutter release (if it's an auto-focus camera) or another control on the camera frequently to keep the camera awake. That way, when you're ready to take a picture, the camera is, too.

Avoid the Tree in the Head

Many beginning photographers pay so much attention to their subject that they forget the picture has a background. That's how we get pictures of little Evan with a tree growing out of his head (see Figure 6-4). While you may not notice the background a whole lot when you're framing the picture in the viewfinder, it'll be an integral part of the finished picture. Remember that the foreground and background are compressed in a two-dimensional picture, and the effect is more pronounced with longer-focal-length lenses. And because most digital cameras offer little control over depth of field, you need to be keenly aware of your composition. In most cases, you'll have lots of depth of field behind the subject, perhaps more than you really want.

Figure 6-4 Moving a little to the right or left would have prevented the reindeer effect

---

 Note: *If you have a fixed-focus camera, you'll need to play with a button other than the shutter release, since there's no partially depressed mode. With a fixed-focus camera, as soon as you press the shutter release, you've taken the picture.*

What's the best way to photograph children?

The attention span of kids varies dramatically over a span of just a few years. A three-year-old simply won't hold a pose, for instance, in the same way that a six-year-old can.

But photographing children is rarely about holding a specific pose anyway; the real heart and soul of shooting kids is in capturing their honest and spontaneous activities. Give them something to do—either ask them to play a game and take their picture unaware or let them play with their toys and wait for the right moment.

My children are now six and eight years old, and they've been in front of the camera enough that they're little hams—they can always seem to conjure up an adorable smile and look quite natural (see Figure 6-5).

If your subjects aren't quite that accommodating, shoot pictures anyway—you can catch pouts, grump faces, and other less-than-adorable poses that are actually quite endearing nonetheless. Here are a few pointers for those kid pictures:

- You can hold younger kids' attention with a favorite toy or by making goofy faces.

- If you're trying to capture a specific kind of image that needs some level of cooperation from your little subjects, don't forget bribery. Taking pictures at the park, you can

Figure 6-5 My daughter Marin is so used to the camera that she has no problem being uninhibited in front of the lens

promise a trip to the ice cream cart when the photo shoot is over.

- Instead of relying on the old "say cheese" ploy, one trick that works well is to let kids do their own thing and photograph them when you see the right moment.

- You can get good candids by having kids look right at the camera and by making it seem like they're unaware of your presence (even if it isn't really true). If you want the kids to look at the camera, try calling their names and snapping a shot as soon as they look toward you. That doesn't give them time to strike a pose.

- Don't point the camera down at them—kneel or sit down so you're at their level. Some pictures benefit from unusual perspectives (like pointing a camera down at them from the top of a set of monkeybars), but most kid pictures should be at their level.

 Tip: *Take a trip to the portrait photographer in the local mall to see how they deal with young children and apply some of the lessons at home when you take your own pictures.*

 Do I need permission to publish pictures of people?

Nope. See Chapter 16 for more details, but in a nutshell you can publish someone's likeness without their explicit permission. If you publish their picture for commercial applications, however, you'll need their permission, and in most situations you'll probably want their consent in writing anyway. For one thing, it's a simple matter of courtesy. For another, if you ever use their picture in a context that they consider inappropriate, you'll have their written consent to protect you.

ACTION PHOTOGRAPHY

 What focal length lens should I use to take action photos?

Action photography is often considered the most exciting kind of photography, but it's also the most demanding from a technique and equipment point of view. As in all kinds of photography, you can no doubt take some compelling images with anything from a super-wide-angle lens all the way up to the photographic equivalent of the Hubble telescope. And wide-angle lenses do, certainly, have a role in action photography. But the essence of many action shots is a kind of "in your face" immediacy, something you can only get with a telephoto lens (see Figure 6-6).

If you want to photograph sports and action, I highly recommend that you get your hands on a long telephoto lens—like 200mm. In digital camera lingo, that focal length translates into focal lengths on the order of 25mm or more. Typically, the only way you can pull off that level of magnification with a consumer-level digital camera is to use the built-in 2x or 3x digital zoom and attach a 2x telephoto lens to the camera in addition to that.

 What shutter speed and depth of field work best for action pics?

If you have any control over the shutter speed and aperture on your digital camera, you should take advantage of those

Figure 6-6 This barnstormer was cropped from a larger mega pixel photo

controls when shooting action scenes. To freeze action, you'll need to use a fairly fast shutter speed, which often works to your advantage by opening up the aperture and diminishing the depth of field.

In general, I recommend that you use the fastest shutter speed available to capture action—that way there's no second-guessing about whether a particular setting is quite fast enough and you know you've nailed it. If you're looking for a rule of thumb on whether your camera can handle the kind of action you want to photograph, use Table 6-1.

Keep in mind that this is just a rule of thumb and you should always try to use a higher shutter speed, if possible, to capture motion. If you can't freeze the scene using a fast shutter speed, try panning, as described in "How do I convey a sense of motion and action in my images?" later in this chapter.

 ## What equipment do I need to take action photos?

You can get your feet wet in action photography with any kind of camera, but I recommend that you have a fairly long telephoto lens, preferably in a zoom. Few consumer-level

Speed	Possible Subjects	Distance from Subject	Minimum Shutter Speed	
			Action Moving Across Viewfinder	Action Moving Toward or Away from Camera
Slow (<10 mph)	Runners	25 feet 50 feet	1/500 1/250	1/125 1/60
Medium (<50 mph)	Cyclists or horseback riders	25 feet 50 feet	1/1,000 1/250	1/250 1/60
Fast (>50 mph)	Cars, boats, or planes	25 feet 100 feet	1/2,000 1/1,000	1/250 1/125

Table 6-1   Action Photography Shutter Speeds

digital cameras currently offer a beefy zoom, so you'll need to either get a digital camera that uses interchangeable lenses or get a telephoto attachment for your camera.

A tripod or monopod (a one-legged support used to steady the camera in the place of a full-blown tripod) can also come in handy for keeping the camera still when shooting fast-moving action.

 ### How do I keep a fast-moving subject in focus?

It can be difficult to keep a fast-moving subject in focus. If the subject is far enough away—like an airplane at an airshow—then you can generally leave the camera set to infinity and take pictures as they occur (though this is only effective if you can turn off auto-focus).

If you have an auto-focus lens without any sort of manual override—and that covers most of the digital cameras out there—then you need to learn the technique of constantly adjusting the focus as you track the subject in the viewfinder. As the subject nears, passes, and departs, keep applying a little pressure to the shutter release so the camera focuses; then lift your finger and do it again so the subject is in focus whenever you need to actually take the picture. Remember that if you don't pre-focus in this way, there will be a painful lag between the moment when you press the shutter release and the moment when the picture is actually taken.

 ## How do I convey a sense of motion and action in my images?

You can use a technique called *panning* to capture the subject in good, sharp focus and the background as a motion blur. This is convenient both when you want to make a somewhat artistic statement about the subject's motion and when you know the camera can't muster up a fast enough shutter speed to freeze the motion the ordinary way.

Panning involves some effort on your part: To create a good pan, you need to twist your body in sync with the motion of the subject as you press the shutter release. Here's how:

1. Position yourself where you can twist your body to follow the motion of the moving subject without having the camera's line of sight blocked by something else.

2. If you have control over the shutter, set it for about 1/60. Feel free to experiment with this, but if you set the shutter speed too slow, you can't capture the subject effectively—it blurs—and if the shutter is too fast, you won't get the pretty blur in the background. If you can't slow the shutter with a camera control, try applying a

neutral-density filter over the lens to slow the camera down or shoot the picture in the shade or late in the day.

3. Twist your body with the motion of the subject and track it through the camera's viewfinder or on the LCD display. Press the shutter release and continue tracking the subject until after you hear the shutter close again. Just as in baseball or golf, ensure that you follow through the motion even after the shutter releases—that way, you don't stop panning in the middle of the exposure. You may need to practice this a few times to get the shot right, but electronic film is free.

 Tip: *The farther away the background is, the less motion-blur effect you'll get. For best results, get close to the object and its background; if the background is too far away, the blur will be minimal and it'll just look out of focus.*

Panning with a digital camera is often easier than it is with a traditional camera. Because most digital cameras don't have through-the-lens optical systems, you can still see and track the subject during the exposure. That's a luxury SLR users don't have!

Want to add a very neat effect to your panned action shots? If you're close enough to the subject for the flash unit to work, enable it in fill-flash mode and take the picture while panning. It will add a unique ghost-like effect that can look good in some situations.

What can I do to improve the odds of freezing the action?

With most digital cameras, you get whatever shutter speed the camera feels like giving you. Since you have little creative control over the camera's settings, use these tips to ensure better action photos:

● Compose the picture with the subject moving directly toward you. As you can see in Table 6-1, if the subject is moving toward or away from you it takes less shutter speed to capture the action. So while it may not be exactly

what you want, head-on motion is easier to capture with a slow shutter speed.

● Take the picture from farther away. The closer a moving object is to your lens, the more shutter speed it takes to freeze the action. Find a compromise between getting in the action's face and being so far away that the picture isn't interesting. If you shoot the picture in a high-resolution mode, then you have the opportunity to later crop and edit the image in your PC to bring the subject to the forefront (see Chapter 11).

● Even if you're not trying to get a dramatic motion blur in the background, you can improve the sharpness of the image by panning as you take the picture (see "How do I convey a sense of motion and action in my images?"earlier in this chapter).

LANDSCAPES AND NATURE

 ### What focal length lens should I use to take landscape pictures?

Unlike action photography and portraiture that relies on telephoto lenses to compress the action into an intimate experience, landscapes typically work best with wide-angle lenses that allow you to include huge, expansive swaths of land, air, and sea in a single frame.

Most digital cameras come with normal or wide-angle lenses, so you're all set for landscape photography with what came in the box. If you want to expand the range of options available, then you should look into a wide-angle or super-wide-angle lens adapter from a company like Tiffen. Many digital cameras have threads on the lens to accommodate other lenses or allow you to snap a lens adapter over the built-in optics.

Be careful when using extremely wide-angle lenses—not only do they produce "fish-eye" effects by warping the perspective of your image (sometimes a good thing), they may also vignette the image by darkening the corners of the picture.

How do I find landscape photography opportunities if I don't happen to live in Colorado or some other scenic location?

I grew up in New Jersey, which arguably has some of the least scenic spots in the nation. Even there, however, I was able to find locations to produce interesting nature photos (see Figure 6-7). Now that I live on the Front Range of Colorado, I don't have to look nearly as hard to find gorgeous scenery—but if I take a bad picture, it's still a bad picture. The fact that it has a mountain lion lapping up water from a creek in the Maroon Bells can't make up for terrible composition.

Explore your local area and look for interesting places that may be nestled in local parks or even between housing complexes. And experiment with those locations to find the best way to photograph them. By making use of close-ups, unusual angles, or different times of day, you can capture a scene in a way that no one else ever has before. For example, the Maroon Bells in Aspen are sometimes called the

Figure 6-7 These ducks lived at a park near my home in New Jersey. Really

most-photographed mountains in America. How was I to compete with that? I found an unusual perspective from which to shoot them and I'm happy with the final result (see Figure 6-8).

For those unique opportunities at home, scout out all the landscape or nature photo opportunities you can and walk every inch of them. Look at the locations from the ground, from a second-story window, and even from the top of a tree. Keep an eye out for natural objects like trees that you can use to frame your scene. And experiment with modifying the images afterwards in an image editor (see Chapters 11 and 12), where you can turn a mountain scene into a mountain with a lake, or crop the image for a unique perspective.

Figure 6-8 Landscape photography is all about finding unusual vistas

 ## How can I capture a very wide panorama that doesn't fit in the viewfinder?

Panoramas are great, and more and more photographers are discovering the beauty of a very long photo that captures the entire horizon. That's due in part to the emergence of film cameras that take panoramic scenes.

You can do it yourself, though, with a little digital trickery. Take two, three, or even more pictures of a scene that, when strung together edge-to-edge, depict the entire panorama. Then, after you get them into your PC, you can manually "stitch" them together or let special software do it for you. The advantages to stitching are several:

- The overall image is higher in resolution than it would be if you took a panorama "in the lens." Each portion is, say, 640×480, so it'll print with higher quality than a single image would.

- A panorama filmed in sections and stitched can be composed with less unwanted detail in the sky and ground because you can zoom in or shoot closer. To take a panorama in a single shot, you need to back up or zoom out and reduce the quality of the composition.

So how do you do it? First get some stitching software (I like Enroute Software's QuickStitch, though several different packages will do the job). Then follow these steps:

1. Figure out how you're going to frame the picture. It may take just two or as many as ten pictures to capture the entire scene; map it out in your head first before you take the series of photos.

2. Start on the left and take the series of pictures, turning to the right for the next image and making sure that about 40% of each photo overlaps into the next photo.

3. As you take each picture, pivot your feet so that you turn, but don't move your feet away from the position of the first picture.

4. When you're done, transfer the images to your PC and use the stitching software to combine them into a single image (see Chapter 12).

Tip: *You can get better results creating panoramas by using a tripod, though you'll usually get passable results with handheld shots.*

Can I photograph landscapes in bad weather?

Absolutely. You can experiment with a variety of weather conditions, from bright and sunny to overcast to rain. Clouds make exciting props in landscape shots, and the effect of the sun breaking through a storm and lighting the landscape can be beautiful. If you have the capability to set your camera to a long "bulb" exposure, you can even capture lightning during an electrical storm.

In other words, weather that you may not want to barbecue in can be great for landscape and nature photography.

How do I photograph a waterfall or a running stream?

There are two ways to capture running water in a photograph: with a fast freeze-frame shot or with a longer exposure that blurs the water into a continuous stream effect. Both effects can look good, but I have a fondness for the latter. The effect looks great, and it's very easy to do; you simply need to take a long exposure of the water. Here's how to do it:

1. You need to ensure that your camera will give you a long exposure, on the order of a half-second. You can get this by shooting in the early morning or late afternoon, using a neutral-density filter, or setting the exposure manually if your camera allows it.

2. Set your camera on a tripod (the long exposure requires a steady support).

3. Compose the image and take the shot.

What focal length lens should I use to take nature and wildlife photos?

If you're photographing big game—be it a lion, wolf, elephant, or squirrel—you want the same basic equipment that you'd need for action photography. In a nutshell, that's the biggest zoom lens you can lay your hands on. This is particularly true for digital cameras, which often lack access to the really big lenses that 35mm photographers take for granted. If you can make use of standard interchangeable lenses, then focal lengths equivalent to the range of 200–400mm will do just fine. This allows you to zero in on animals from a comfortable distance (comfortable for both you and the animal, that is). In most cases, though, you'll need to enable your camera's digital zoom and then add a 2x or 3x telephoto converter to the camera.

For less carnivorous (or skittish) subjects, you can use your camera's macro mode to take pictures of the details in the wild. Leaves, water, plants, insects, and more are great subjects, but you need to be able to magnify them properly. While the macro mode in many cameras is adequate, I recommend that you pick up a few close-up lenses from a company like Tiffen. They come in a variety of classes, measured in diopters, typically from about +1 to +10 (the larger the number, the greater the magnification). If you can afford it, I recommend getting

several, so you can use the magnification appropriate to the scene you're trying to capture.

 ## Where can I find wildlife to photograph?

If you're asking this question, I can only assume you don't live where deer roam right through the streets. If you're in a city, there are a few good places to look for wildlife: your own yard, the local park, and most notably, the zoo.

There are a surprising number of photo opportunities right around your house if you look. Squirrels and birds make great subjects, particularly in the spring when they're most active or might even have babies.

The zoo is a favorite photo opportunity of mine (see Figure 6-9). You'll find all sorts of animals there that you'd rarely, if ever, have the opportunity to shoot otherwise, and if you visit frequently you'll get an idea of when is the best time to shoot various species. Feeding times are great, for instance, to shoot animals that are hand-fed. Afternoons are rarely good times to photograph predators like big cats, because they're sleeping to conserve energy.

Figure 6-9 Baby tigers and their mom at Colorado's Cheyenne Mountain Zoo

How do I eliminate the cage from my pictures when taking wildlife pictures at the zoo?

The problem with the zoo is that the animals are, for the most part, stuck behind a glass window or iron bars. As much as you might want to take pictures that look like they were taken on the savannah, these animal restraints reveal the ruse.

You can minimize or eliminate the appearance of metal bars in your pictures, however, by a combination of position and exposure. If you can get close enough, put the lens of the camera right up next to the bars. Since you're focusing on a far-away subject—like a lion 50 feet away—the bars will be drastically out of focus and they won't appear in the picture.

An alternative is to make use of depth of field to eliminate the bars. Shoot in early morning or late afternoon light, where the aperture will open all the way up and again eliminate the bars through a narrow depth of field.

As for glass, it can surprisingly be even more tricky than metal bars. You'll need to get the camera right up to the glass—and even then, the camera's flash may reflect back into the lens. If you get the lens right up to the glass and there's still flashback showing up in the image (as seen in your LCD preview window), then turn the flash off and shoot the picture with whatever natural light there may be.

Tip: *There's one other way to eliminate bars from a photo—by using your image editor. See Chapter 12 for details on how to use the clone tool to erase the bars from a photograph.*

Photograph Your Pets

You may have some animals living with you already, and they can give you some good practice. On the plus side, your pets are already pretty comfortable with you, so you can get real close, compose your images carefully, and capture special scenes that would be impossible with their wild cousins.

 Why do my wildlife pictures lack the impact I see in calendars and postcards?

Often, the problem with wildlife pictures—as well as pictures of other living things—is the focal point. You should concentrate on focusing explicitly on the animal's eyes. Forget about the rest of the body and make sure the eyes themselves are in sharp focus. If you don't have direct control over the camera's focus, try to take pictures in early morning or late afternoon, when your depth of field is greatest.

 How do I photograph animals discreetly in the wild?

By "in the wild," we generally mean animals that aren't in a zoo, so that includes local deer, squirrels, birds, and other animals you might encounter in a park, the woods, or other areas. If you're on an actual safari in the wilds of Africa, you might be better off with Osborne McGraw-Hill's *African Safari Answers*.

The key is to remember that animals spook easily, so you need to keep a low profile by staying fairly still, dressing in dark, natural colors, and keeping your distance. Use the longest focal length you can get your hands on, ensuring that you won't have to get too close. And don't even try to use the flash—turn it off via the camera's controls before you start shooting.

If you know of an area with wildlife to which you have automobile access, you can "hide" in your car and wait for photo opportunities there. Animals can get used to seeing cars and come out into view if the area remains quiet for a short time.

Lastly, most cameras come in all black, which shouldn't alarm any wild animals, but if you use a tripod or other equipment that has shiny metallic parts, be sure to wrap them in black electrical tape.

TRAVELOGUE

 Can X-ray machines affect my digital "film"?

Believe it or not, X-ray machines are a problem again. For a long time, the conventional wisdom was that film was safe from the effects of X-ray machines in airports, because the dosage was very low. Well, now the new machines entering service are designed to identify a new class of weapons, and therefore generate substantially stronger X-ray fields. 35mm film exposed to these machines can get clouded and ruined.

Digital cameras, on the other hand, are impervious to X-ray machines and can therefore be safely inspected by X-ray. If you're looking for one less distraction and annoyance on a long plane trip, this is a point in digital technology's favor.

What kind of digital photography equipment is best for a long trip?

Any long trip involves a compromise between what you'd like to have and what you need to have. If you're vacationing, for instance, you may want to take pictures, but unless you're a die-hard photographer, you may not want to lug around a big case full of equipment. Even if you are a photographer by trade, the concept of carrying lots of stuff in the summer heat may still not appeal to you.

So you'll need to decide for yourself what you want to bring. I suggest the following minimums:

- A digital camera
- Several sets of replacement batteries
- Extra memory cards (decide how many pictures you expect to take and bring twice as much memory as you think you'll need to accommodate them all)
- Telephoto and wide-angle lens attachments (if they'll fit your camera)
- A camera case that you can wear like a backpack to leave your hands free

Since a digital camera is pretty light, that won't weigh much. If you're game, I'd also suggest taking a lightweight tripod or monopod. If you're traveling to a very wet climate, throw a desiccant into the camera bag to keep everything moisture-free. You can get bags of desiccant from most local camera stores. Don't forget cleaning supplies so you can deal with dirt accidents (you never know when you'll drop the

camera into the mud). Cleaning the lens is discussed in Chapter 3.

If you are so inclined, you can always bring an image transfer kit with you. This includes the camera's connection cable, installation software, and preferably an AC adapter. If your camera's memory fills up, you can use the portable transfer kit to download images from the camera to a notebook PC or a relative's computer. Remember that if you're traveling internationally, you'll need the appropriate conversion kit so you can plug your stuff into the wall at your destination.

Choosing a Camera Bag

Do you need a camera bag for your trip? It's certainly not essential, but it can make your life much easier. On the plus side, digital cameras and their accessories take up much less space than traditional 35mm SLRs, so that means you can get a smaller bag and still have room for extras like medicine, sunglasses, maps, and other daily essentials. When you look for a camera bag, keep these pointers in mind:

● Get a bag that doesn't look like a camera bag. You have enough to worry about without having your camera equipment stolen, so choose one that could pass for an ordinary gym bag or backpack. If it has a popular camera company logo on it, pass.

● Get a bag that's big enough for your camera and accessories, but not a lot bigger. Bring your camera to the store to check.

● I recommend you get one that you can sling over your shoulders—you don't want to lug a camera bag in your hand all day. Alternately, digital cameras fit well in fanny packs, which have the added advantage of being very compact and light.

● Get lots of pockets, zippers, and compartments. That way you'll have lots of places to store things. Some bags even have clips that let you store your car keys.

How do I protect my stuff from getting stolen?

Digital cameras may look like inexpensive point-and-shoot cameras, but we all know that they can cost a not insignificant sum of money. Here are some tips for making sure your camera remains your personal property:

● Record the camera's serial number and keep it in a secure place. It may not prevent the camera from being stolen in the first place, but it might help the police recover it sometime.

● Store the camera in an unobtrusive bag that doesn't look like it's designed to hold an expensive piece of electronic gear (see the sidebar "Choosing a Camera Bag" earlier).

● Keep it on your body as much as possible. That means not putting it in the trunk of a taxi, not trusting it to a hotel's lobby storage, and taking it with you when sightseeing— don't leave it in a hotel room when you're not in.

● Don't leave the camera alone in airports. You may have heard stories about how thieves arrange for delays at the X-ray machine and walk off with your expensive equipment, like a laptop computer, when you can't get through the line to retrieve your bags that were placed on the conveyor belt. The stories are just urban legend— they're not true—but they have a good moral nonetheless. Hang on to your stuff.

● If you travel internationally, bring the original receipts for your hardware. When you go through customs in some countries, officials will try to assess duties or keep the hardware if you have no proof that you did not buy it on your trip—particularly if your camera is not made in the United States.

 ## Where do I find additional memory cards for my camera when I'm on vacation?

You don't. There are very few digital camera-savvy camera stores or computer shops in Paris, at the Grand Canyon, or at Niagara Falls. Unlike with 35mm film, you can't replenish

your supply if you understocked before leaving home. Your only choices are:

- Selectively erase images on your memory cards to make room for new ones.
- Transfer images from the camera to a PC. But that means you'll need to visit a relative or lug a notebook around on your trip.
- Drop the resolution and/or image quality of your pictures to fit more.

So plan ahead and plan carefully.

 What temperature limitations affect a digital camera?

This certainly varies from camera to camera, so check your manual or ask the manufacturer if you think you might be operating near the camera's design limits. In general, though, keep in mind that digital cameras are essentially tiny computers. They are affected by extreme heat and extreme cold, so don't leave a camera locked up in a car for extended periods of time. Likewise, you shouldn't expect a digital camera to function in the arctic. On the other hand, at least one camera manufacturer told me about an Antarctic explorer who took their standard consumer-grade camera to the South Pole, and it worked flawlessly even when the mechanical parts of SLRs failed.

 Are there circumstances where a digital camera isn't as good as a 35mm SLR?

Certainly, if you're an experienced 35mm photographer, there may be times when the compromises necessary with a consumer-grade digital camera—such as not being able to control shutter speed or aperture size—are unacceptable. If you're already used to the point-and-shoot camera environment, though, using a digital camera isn't much different, so you may be quite happy with the digital camera.

Should I count on a digital camera to record a one-of-a-kind vacation, or should I bring a 35mm SLR?

If I were traveling to Europe, for instance, I'd probably bring both a digital camera and a traditional SLR. That way, I'd still have the ability to take pictures even if all my memory were completely used up—but I like redundancy to begin with, and you might not want to dedicate that kind of space to photographic equipment.

Also consider the end use of your pictures. If you want to be able to send prints of the Tower of London to your friends when you get home, perhaps a 35mm camera is in order. But the digital camera allows you to post the images on a Web page or send them via e-mail without first scanning them into a PC.

Are there locations that I can't photograph?

In many locales, you may find that there are things you're not allowed to photograph. Be careful to obey the rules or you may have your camera confiscated (or the memory erased, if the local authorities understand a digital camera well enough to do that). In some extreme places, you may find yourself in trouble with the law. Look out for these potential problem situations:

- Some government and military buildings may not be photographed. In Figure 6-10, we see two foolish people photographing a military sign that essentially says "No photography allowed." Yes, I was one of the foolish ones.

- Sometimes you cannot photograph transportation routes like roads and bridges, or street signs and border locations.

- Some social situations may be illegal to photograph. In the former Soviet Union, you couldn't take pictures of food lines.

- The inside of some religious structures and museums may be off-limits to photography in general or perhaps just flash photography.

Figure 6-10 Obey "no photography" warnings—the danger is real

Whatever country you're visiting, read warning signs and be aware of the restrictions.

What tips do you have for shooting a wedding or other special family occasion?

Going to a wedding? Take your camera! Weddings and other special family occasions are great times to take pictures. When you arrive, stay out of the "real" photographer's way, though. It's OK to stand to the side and take some of the same pictures that the photographer is staging, but remember that they're a paid professional and getting in front of them or delaying the next shot is a nuisance to the entire wedding party.

When looking for shots, go for candids more than staged shots since the wedding party is already in a tizzy—they don't need you asking them to pose for yet more pictures (see Figure 6-11). Capture people's reactions to the event in close-ups as well as wider-angled group and activity photos.

How do I photograph architecture?

Architecture is the soul of a city, and can help convey the experience of a visit to that city better than most other kinds of pictures. Taking pictures of buildings isn't particularly difficult, and you'll be off to a good start with these tips:

● Tall buildings can look like they're falling down on you if you shoot up from street level. This effect can be just what

Figure 6-11 The wedding photographer may not catch the groom making a fool of himself with a guitar, but you can get that magic moment with your digital camera

you're looking for, but in other cases you'll get better results by taking the picture from farther away or from a higher elevation, like an upper floor of a nearby building.

 Photograph older stone or marble buildings in early morning or late afternoon light. Modern steel-and-glass structures look better with bright, even harsh light to create dramatic reflections.

 Give a sense of scale by including people or other objects of known size in the image.

 You can get some great perspectives on a building or entire city from a plane—either from the window while flying in or out, or on a chartered tour plane.

How can I capitalize on the digital format to make a foreign cityscape or landscape look truly exciting?

You can capture 360-degree panoramas of famous—or not-so-famous—locales and turn them into Surround Videos or QuickTime VR movies. They're not really movies; they're still images that you can pan around inside to see a scene from any angle.

To make such an image, just photograph a location as a series of still images that can be glued together like a panorama. See Chapter 15 for details on this exciting use of digital imagery.

Look for the Angle

Don't take the same picture that everyone else already has. Go up to higher ground, get down on the floor, and generally look for unique perspectives on famous landmarks and universally recognized scenes. Take the standard touristy shot of the Eiffel Tower too, just in case your family doesn't like the more artistic ones.

Chapter 7

Lighting and Flash

Answer Topics!

Lighting and Flash @ a Glance

An electronic flash is an essential tool for taking pictures. It represents a way to bring extra light with you and brighten up many kinds of pictures. But most people don't really know how to take advantage of the flash on their cameras, so this chapter discusses techniques like fill flash, red-eye reduction, and bounce flash.

Many people spend a lot of time taking pictures outdoors at events like picnics and carnivals, or just taking snapshots of kids and portraits by a tree in the park. Whatever your subject, though, you need to understand how to control outdoor light to bring out the best in your subject.

Indoor photographs present their own lighting challenges. Usually, you can solve these problems with an electronic flash, but don't forget to try the house lamps you already have. You can also create a low-cost studio in your home—look here for pointers on getting started.

Getting the lighting right in a scene is half art, half science. Before you can exercise your artistic judgment, though, make sure you know the basics. How do you compensate for exposure problems? How do you eliminate glare and hot spots in an image? Look here for the answers.

Night photography is a lot of fun, but challenging for digital camera owners. In some cases, you can use manual exposure features to capture good images in the dark, but in most cases you'll have to use exposure compensation controls to get the effect you're looking for. This chapter includes information on photographing cityscapes, light trails, stars, and the moon.

FLASH BASICS

 My camera doesn't have a flash. Can I add one?

Most digital cameras have electronic flash units built right into the camera body these days. But if your camera doesn't have a flash, there may yet be hope. Your camera needs either a hot shoe or a jack for a synch cable in order to accommodate an optional flash. Check your user's manual to be sure, or call the manufacturer.

In most cases, digital cameras that are built into 35mm SLR bodies will use a hot shoe and an optional flash—all you need to do is add a flash that's compatible with the camera and start taking pictures.

Hot shoe

 What is the range of my flash?

Flash units vary dramatically in strength. Many digital cameras have a maximum range of about ten feet, though the

electronic flashes that are compatible with SLR-type bodies typically are much more powerful, with a range of 50 feet or more. Keep this limitation in mind when you're taking pictures in low-light conditions—a digital camera's electronic flash will usually have no effect whatsoever on a picture in which the subject is 25 feet away (see Figure 7-1).

Another important thing to remember is that your flash has a minimum range as well. You'll find that most flash units don't work when you're closer than about two or three feet from your subject (see Figure 7-2). Look in Chapter 8 for ways to avoid overexposing a close-up photo.

If you try to shoot a picture and the flash fires from less than the minimum distance, your picture is guaranteed to be

Figure 7-1 These two shots show the falloff in flash intensity as you back away from the subject

Figure 7-2 Most flash units overexpose close-up photos

badly overexposed. In these situations, you need to turn the flash off and use natural light instead. Or, bounce the flash if you have that capability—see the following section for details.

 ## The flash on my camera pivots and tilts. What's that for?

Some electronic flash units—mainly those that attach to SLR bodies—have pivot heads that allow you to turn, twist, and tilt the flash. This capability, called *bounce flash*, can be quite useful when you're trying to photograph certain subjects.

Typically, you want to bounce your flash to create a softer, more diffuse light in a picture. Bounce flash is particularly good in portraits, for instance, so you don't have the light of the flash creating harsh highlights on the person's face.

Another use of bounce flash is to diffuse the flash in close-up situations. If you know you're too close to properly expose the picture with the flash, bounce it to reduce the intensity.

To use the bounce flash capability of your pivot head, determine at what angle you need to position the flash in order to get the light to strike your subject. Often, just tilting the flash up about 45 degrees will cause the light to bounce off the ceiling and onto the face of your subject. But that's not always the case—sometimes you'll need to spin the flash head so that the light fires more or less straight up. You can also bounce off a wall or reflector by twisting the head to the right or left.

When using bounce, keep in mind two important factors:

● You're increasing the total distance the light must travel, and it's possible you may exceed the range of the flash unit. Make sure you can still properly expose the picture when bouncing.

● Your picture will take on the color cast of whatever surface
you bounce off of—so if you bounce off a bluish wall, you'll
add blue tones to the picture. In general, this doesn't look
very good, so try to only bounce off white surfaces.

Unfortunately, some camera manufacturers design their
cameras in such a way that it is difficult (or impossible) to
bounce the flash. The chief design limitation you'll see is
when the flash is mounted next to the lens, even on a
swiveling, two-part camera. On a camera like this, such as
the Agfa ePhoto, the flash can only be fired directly in line
with the lens axis (see Figure 7-3).

The flash is mounted with the
lens on some digital cameras

Figure 7-3 Not all cameras have bounce-flash capability

 When I take pictures with my flash, the pictures seem bleached out; is there a way to soften this effect?

There are a few ways to change the effect of your flash on pictures, and you should experiment to see which works best for you:

- Shoot from farther away, and use the zoom (if you have one) to bring the subject closer in the viewfinder. The fact of the matter is that many flash units overexpose an image if used from less than about three feet.

- Bounce the flash if you have this capability (see the preceding section).

- Set the exposure compensation on your camera to underexpose the image. You may want to bracket the exposure and try taking the picture at two or even three stops.

- Diffuse the flash by placing a thin material over it. You can sometimes get a nice diffuse light effect by hanging a very thin white cloth or tissue over the flash unit. Here you can see a thin layer of tissue over the camera's flash.

 Should I only use the flash at night or in the dark?

No, that's one of the biggest misconceptions about the use of flash in photography, whether you're talking about digital or traditional.

The flash is a valuable asset even in broad daylight. Have you ever taken a picture of someone outdoors that resulted in harsh shadows on the person's face? Perhaps the subject's face wasn't exposed badly, it just seemed a bit too dark, hiding features and making the image unsatisfactory. You can solve that problem by using a *fill flash*. Turn your flash on and take the picture—sunlight provides most of the light for exposure, and the flash fills in extra light in the subject's face, which might ordinarily be a bit underexposed since it's in shadow (see Figure 7-4).

Figure 7-4 Firing the flash eliminated the shadows in this outdoor portrait

Almost all digital cameras have a fill-flash mode, even if it's not called that. Look for the mode that's called "fill flash," "force flash," "manual flash," or "always on." This is different from the auto-flash mode, which only activates the flash if the light level is too low to properly expose the picture.

Why shouldn't I just use the electronic flash all the time?

If you're familiar with the benefits of fill flash, you might be inclined to simply leave the flash on all the time. That way, you'll get the benefits of the flash unit without consciously thinking about it.

You may not want to simply leave the flash on all the time, however. The biggest reason to use fill flash selectively is battery life. You probably already know that digital cameras eat batteries at a phenomenal rate, and indiscriminately using the flash accelerates battery discharge—significantly. If you take a lot of outdoor photographs, I recommend that you leave the flash off most of the time and only turn it on when you're close enough to the subject—within about a dozen feet—to make the use of the flash worthwhile.

Also remember that in some indoor situations—like museums and churches—it's inappropriate to use a flash. If you get used to switching the flash on when you need it, you won't be embarrassed by having it go off unexpectedly.

I've seen photographers use more than one flash on a camera. Why would I want to do that?

In some situations—usually portrait photography—photographers like to set up more than one light source. This lets you illuminate a subject from more than one direction, giving more uniform light, eliminating shadows, or creating other exciting special effects. Some photographers use a light to illuminate the subject from behind, for instance, to add highlights to a person's hair.

Whatever your motivation, in order to illuminate a subject from more than one direction you'll need the appropriate hardware, like a slave unit that can trigger extra

flash units at the appropriate moment. Alternately, you can get "hot lights," that is, studio lighting that's always on and doesn't need to fire at the moment of exposure. You can get either of these solutions at your local camera shop.

When I use my flash, the edges of my pictures aren't as well exposed as the center. What's wrong?

What you're experiencing is *flash vignetting*, an effect that occurs because the electronic flash on your camera hasn't the range to properly expose your picture. You'll most commonly see this when taking pictures with a wide-angle attachment over the built-in lens; the flash is probably calibrated to work well with a normal focal length lens and can't reach the edges of a wide-angle scene (see Figure 7-5).

Flash is concentrated here

Figure 7-5   The flash can't reach the edges of this wide-angle shot

Unfortunately, there's nothing you can do about this in most cameras. You'll simply need to be aware of the potential problem and avoid overtaxing the flash. Some flash units have a mode selector that adjusts for telephoto and wide-angle images, but you probably won't see that control in a consumer-level digital camera.

Finally, a little flash vignetting may not even be particularly noticeable. If it doesn't "ruin" the picture for you, then it may not be a big deal.

My flash makes people's eyes red. How do I avoid that?

The effect is called *red eye*, and is caused by light from the flash reflecting off the person's retinas, making them look red in the final image. And it's not just people, either—perhaps the worst offenders are animals, since a red-eyed dog can look downright creepy.

Most digital cameras give you a way to keep red eye from happening: a red-eye reduction mode that pulses the flash several times very quickly right before the picture is taken. This makes the pupils in the subject's eyes close down and

prevents light from bouncing off a huge exposed retina. You can see the fairly universal symbol for red-eye reduction mode in Figure 7-6.

If your camera doesn't have a red-eye reduction mode (surprisingly, some new digital cameras don't), then you can use software on the PC to reduce or eliminate the red-eye effect afterwards. See Chapter 11 for details.

Should I leave the red-eye reduction mode on all the time?

If you're worried about red eye in your photographs, you might be inclined to leave the camera in red-eye reduction

Red-eye reduction mode indicator

Figure 7-6 The Canon PowerShot's LCD display indicates that red-eye reduction mode is enabled

mode any time you shoot. There are a few disadvantages to this method, though:

- Using the red-eye reduction mode drains the battery even more than leaving the flash in fill-flash mode all the time, so you'll reduce battery life significantly.

- The flash isn't appropriate in some indoor settings, like churches and museums.

- The red-eye reduction system delays the actual exposure slightly from when you press the shutter release—which means you may miss the picture you're trying to take. This is particularly important when dealing with action photography.

OUTDOOR LIGHTING

 My outdoor pictures always seem to have regions that are over- or underexposed. Why do outdoor photos never look as good on the computer as they did in the viewfinder?

That's because a digital camera works very differently than your eyes do. As you look at a scene and frame it in a viewfinder, your pupils—the apertures of your eyes—change diameter constantly to adjust for varying light conditions in a scene. Look to the sky, and you pupils close so you see a deep blue sky. Let your eyes drift to a person under a tree, and your pupils immediately open to take best advantage of the limited light that's there. Thus, your eyes are constantly adjusting the "exposure" of the scene as you look around, and the result is that the entire view seems to be evenly lit and properly exposed.

Now compare that with what your camera does. The camera can only use a single exposure setting for the entire image, no matter how different the lighting conditions are from one part of the picture to another. So the camera averages the light in the scene and sets a single aperture and shutter speed, and the end result may have shadows that are poorly lit or highlights that are overexposed.

If you encounter this problem often, it means you're trying to photograph scenes with too much contrast. Practice composing scenes that have a more narrow range of lighting conditions. If you want to photograph the person under the tree, for instance, move in so there's less bright sky to cause an underexposure. But there's good news—you can repair a lot of the damage caused to these poorly exposed pictures afterwards on your PC. Look in Chapter 11 for details on how to do this.

Can I force my camera to set the exposure based on the lighting in a specific part of the picture?

If you rely on your camera to decide how to expose a picture, it'll average the lighting in the middle of the viewfinder and expose for that. So if you have a bright subject in the middle of the picture but shadows on the side, the shadows will be underexposed and turn out black, without any detail. This might be what you want—or it might not be. Luckily, many cameras have a way around this quandary.

Most auto-focus digital cameras lock the exposure when you pre-focus (press the shutter release down halfway). So if you want to make sure that a particular part of the scene is properly exposed, point the camera at it and then pre-focus. Holding down the shutter release, compose the image you want to capture and then finish taking the picture. You'll get a picture in which the key subject is properly exposed.

Tip: *I recommend that you expose for the shadows in a picture with high-contrast lighting conditions. If you expose for the highlights, the shadows will underexpose as pure black. That means brightening the scene on a computer afterwards will have no effect, because the camera recorded no information about what was in the shadows.*

Should I always shoot pictures with my back to the sun?

That's one of the biggest fallacies of "old school" photography advice, and it's no more valid with digital cameras than it was with old 35mm SLRs. The problem with shooting pictures with the sun at your back is that people pictures turn out less than satisfactory. First, your subjects end up squinting and making odd faces—they're looking right into the sun! Second, midday sun is harsh and unflattering, so there will probably be unattractive shadows in people's faces. Instead, try putting people in the shade or using side light for better outdoor portraits (see Figure 7-7).

What is the best kind of outdoor lighting to photograph with?

There are two kinds of outdoor lighting that are particularly popular with photographers: the even lighting that comes from a slightly overcast day, and the less intense, warm light that comes in the late afternoon. You can also shoot in the morning hours for a similar effect. Keep in mind that the reason many people like to use these lighting conditions is that midday, clear-sky sunlight is harsh and unflattering for many applications. The very bright sun also makes it difficult to achieve shallow depth of field (see Chapter 5 for a discussion of the relationship between depth of field and shutter speed).

Figure 7-7   Avoid shooting pictures with the sun at your back; it makes people squint and produces harsh facial features

If you do photograph in those conditions, I recommend trying to take pictures in shade or angling the light so it is over one of your shoulders, not at your back.

Of course, use these guidelines as just that. You can get good photos in many kinds of lighting conditions, though as a beginner you need to recognize that it's hard to get good results without a lot of practice and experimentation (and, quite often, some fiddling around in an image editing program).

 The sun is too harsh for me to take pictures now. How can I make the sun seem less bright and the scene dimmer without coming back later?

You have a few options available for softening the light in a scene. Here are some things you can try:

● If direct sunlight is an issue, try to move the shot under some shade, like behind a building or under a tree.

● If you can't move the scene, sometimes you can block the sun. Ask someone to hold a large piece of poster board overhead to create some artificial shade.

● Underexpose the image by a half- or full-stop using the exposure compensation control on your camera. This can create impressive results—skies can be much bluer when underexposed, for instance.

INDOOR LIGHTING

 Can I use lamps in my house to add light when I'm taking photos indoors?

Absolutely! There's no need to spend money on expensive photography lights when you probably already have adequate desk and floor lamps available. Try them out—lamps can be particularly effective for brightening up a dark room or giving mood to a people-scene.

On the other hand, keep in mind that house lamps have a different color temperature than your digital camera is used

to photographing. If your camera has a white balance control, use it to ensure that your images come out properly.

Sometimes you might like the yellowish or orange glow that comes from these lamps, however. Think of photographing a birthday cake in natural light without a flash—the candles will cast an orange glow, and that's probably an effect you'd like to keep in the picture.

My indoor pictures have colored tints. What's wrong?

This might be the result of your camera picking up the color of light bouncing off walls or coming from house lights. You can adjust the color of your pictures using the white balance control on your camera (see Chapter 3 for details), turning off floor lamps or fluorescent lights, or using the electronic flash on your camera.

My subjects have "hot spots" from the flash. How do I avoid that?

It's all too easy to get hot spots, those bright spots of light that show up on people's faces or other delicate subjects when you use a harsh electronic flash, particularly at close range. There are three solutions for this:

- Use the flash as a fill in concert with ambient light. Position your subject in front of a window or some other source of natural light and use the flash to help fill in the shadows.
- Bounce the flash, if your flash supports this feature, off a ceiling or wall.
- Drape a thin piece of fabric or tissue in front of the flash to diffuse the harsh light it generates.

I'd like to create a desktop studio for photographing plastic models or other small items. How do I do that?

Creating a home studio setup for photographing small subjects is fun and easy. You can do it, in fact, for under a dollar!

At the simplest level, you can get good results by purchasing a piece of white poster board and using it as a backdrop. Get the largest one you can find—I use a piece that is about three feet on each side. Arrange the board so that it sits on a tabletop and then curls up in back to form a wall behind. Curl it gently to keep the transition from horizontal to vertical smooth. You can prop it up in back or have someone hold it for you.

Place the object you want to photograph on the board and arrange the camera (preferably on a tripod) so that the frame is filled by white. The advantage of this system is that you can photograph your object against a sea of white, so there's no distracting background at all. If you need extra help making the background disappear, you can illuminate the scene with a flash or hot lamp.

Tip: *Don't use a colored light like a floor lamp to illuminate your mini-studio, since the lamp will color the background and it will no longer be white.*

I'd like to create a portrait studio to take pictures in my home. How do I do that?

It doesn't take a lot to start taking nice portraits in your home, particularly if it's just a hobby. You'll need a few items:

- **A stool or some other seat for the subject to sit on** I recommend a bar stool since it has no back, making it very versatile for reorienting your subject.

- **A backdrop** I recommend getting an old 35mm slide projector screen and using it behind the subject. You can use the plain white background it comes with, or hang other materials from it that will contrast with the subject.

- **A light source** You can keep things cheap and easy by using the flash on your camera, though later you might want to experiment with positioning multiple light

sources via hot lamps or electronic flashes that are "slaved" to the one on your camera.

- **Reflectors**   It's not a bad idea to invest in a reflector, available at most photo shops. The reflector can be used to get more flattering light—like that from a nearby window—into your subject's face.

- **Soft focus**   You may want to experiment with soft focus tools. See Chapter 9 for details.

- **Props**   I like flowers, candles, wine glasses, and other small props that you can use as secondary subjects in your composition.

GETTING THE RIGHT LIGHTING

 The subject in my picture is underexposed (but the background looks great!). What can I do to fix it?

If your subject is underexposed, it will appear dark and lack detail. This probably means that the camera used a faster shutter speed or smaller aperture because of the average lighting in the scene. If you're close enough to the subject, you can overcome this problem by using your flash in fill-flash (or forced flash, depending upon your camera) mode to better illuminate the underexposed portion. Just set the flash to the appropriate mode (see "Should I only use the flash at night or in the dark?" earlier in this chapter) and take the picture normally.

As an alternative (particularly if a flash isn't available), you can try overexposing the picture by setting the exposure compensation to +1. I recommend taking several pictures and bracketing the exposure to be sure you get the right effect.

 How do I take pictures so the subject is shown in silhouette?

When beginning photographers get a silhouette, that is, with the subject completely dark and utterly lacking in detail, it's generally due to a mistake. In reality, though, silhouettes are powerful and can look great if done properly.

The essence of a silhouette is simply underexposure. The easiest way to take a silhouette is to shoot into a bright sky (so the subject is underexposed) and then adjust the exposure compensation on your camera to underexpose a little more, perhaps one or two stops.

I need extra light when taking close-ups, but the flash is too much. Is there another solution?

Yes, there are ways around this problem. Unfortunately, the close-ups that beginners take are often badly overexposed since the built-in electronic flash is only effective when you get at least two or three feet away from the subject—if you're only a few inches away, the flash will make the image hopelessly overexposed.

Instead, try some of these alternatives:

- Get an inexpensive hot lamp from a photo shop and place it nearby. It can offer enough light to illuminate the subject without overwhelming it.

- Use the exposure compensation control to overexpose your picture by a few stops.

- Take the subject outdoors and use natural sunlight to take your photograph. Remember that the sun is hundreds of times brighter than indoor light, so even in the late afternoon you can get great results from outdoor light.

- Use the flash, but bounce it or shield it from directly shining on the subject.

How do I reduce glare from glass or shiny objects in the picture?

One problem with very bright objects in photographs is that they can introduce lots of glare into your images. That can make a background object—like a car or windows in a distant building—overwhelm the real subject and ruin the picture. One solution is to use a polarizing filter (see Chapter 9). The polarizer will dramatically cut down on the glare created by objects like these. Figure 7-8 shows two views of a car, one taken with a polarizing filter and one without. As you can see in the image on the right, the polarizer eliminates the glare from the windshield, and also helps deepen the color of the sky.

Is there any way to make a multiple exposure with a digital camera?

Multiple exposures are a lot of fun—by putting different images on the same section of film, you can get very creative and interesting results with a traditional 35mm camera.

Figure 7-8 A polarizer can eliminate glare in bright sunlight

That capability doesn't appear to be available in digital cameras, though.

Well, fear not. In Chapter 12, you can see how to create multiple exposures with digital camera images after the fact, in post-production. It can be done, and in some ways it's even easier than doing it with chemical photography.

 Tip: In traditional 35mm photography, you need to underexpose each picture in a multiple exposure fairly accurately so it comes out fully exposed in the end. In digital photography, don't worry about that. We'll modify the images afterwards on the computer and it'll come out just fine.

TAKING PICTURES AT NIGHT

 Can my digital camera take interesting night pictures, or will they be completely underexposed?

That depends, to some degree, on your camera, so some experimentation is certainly in order. Most cameras, though, have the ability to take very long exposures to capture night scenes.

If you have a manual exposure mode, that's great—you can set the camera to "bulb" and let it sit with the shutter open for minutes or even hours as necessary. If your camera is fully automatic (as most digital cameras are), then your options are more limited. You can set the camera up on a tripod, compose your scene, and press the shutter release. Your results may be less than great, but there's no harm in trying and seeing what your camera is capable of doing.

When you set up your night shot, be sure to pre-focus (if your camera is of the auto-focus variety) on the darkest part of the scene. That way your exposure won't lock onto lights, which would underexpose the image. Figure 7-9 was taken just after sunset.

 My camera gives me manual control over exposure. Can I trust the light meter at night?

No, you can't. Night photography is a very special situation, and the radically different lighting in any night scene will

Figure 7-9 To get a glow from the store windows, I pointed the camera at the darkest part of the scene and pressed the auto-focus lock

cause your camera to get false readings and miscalculate the exposure time. This is a textbook time to use exposure bracketing (see Chapter 5) with the exposure compensation control on your camera. If the scene is mostly dark, be sure to overexpose the image; if the scene is mostly bright (like the moon), then underexpose. In Figure 7-10, the image on the top was taken at the camera's suggested exposure setting. The image on the bottom was overexposed using the exposure compensation control and came out much better.

Is there a rule of thumb for how long to expose pictures at night?

Yes, this is a fairly well-documented question for 35mm photography. Traditional photography books usually have elaborate tables that suggest exposures for different film types, aperture settings, and subjects. For most digital

Figure 7-10 Overexposing by one or two stops creates much more satisfying night shots

cameras, you're stuck with the biggest aperture setting the camera has and a fixed equivalent film speed of about ISO 100 or ISO 200. With that in mind, and assuming you have control over the shutter speed of your digital camera, you might want to try some of the values in Table 7-1 as a starting point. Note that I've provided a range of times since each exposure is so subjective, depending upon lighting conditions, time of evening or night, distance from the subject, and the particular way your camera works. In fact, there's such latitude with night photography that you can get good (but different) effects from any exposure from one to ten seconds. Figure 7-11 was shot with a wide variety of exposures, and this four-second shot was the best.

 Tip: *If your camera doesn't include a manual "bulb" control for leaving the shutter open, then don't forget that you can use the exposure compensation control to under- and overexpose your pictures. Since each stop on this control doubles or halves exposure, you can actually get a fairly wide range of exposures out of an automatic camera at night.*

 ### How can you photograph the moon?

The moon can be a challenging subject for digital camera owners. Make sure that you underexpose the scene; you may need to set your exposure compensation control to the lowest value it allows. Remember to use a tripod and the longest

Subject	Exposure Time
Cityscape just after sundown	1/30 to 1/2 second
Illuminated cityscape	4–10 seconds
Street scene	1/30 to 1/2 second
Neon signs	1/125 to 1/60 second
Moving traffic	5 seconds–1 minute
Moon	1/60 second
Home interior	1/30 to 1/8 second
Candles	1/30 to 1/4 second

Table 7-1 Suggested Exposure Times for Night Photography

Figure 7-11 Experimentation is the key to getting interesting night photos

focal length you have available—you'll generally need the equivalent of a 200mm lens to get an interesting picture.

If you don't have a very long lens but you do have a megapixel camera, remember that you can always crop the

image down somewhat and still have enough resolution left over to make a good picture.

 ## How do you photograph the stars?

If you can leave your shutter open for an extended period of time, then you can take some really cool photos of the night sky.

In general, taking a short exposure of the night sky won't yield any interesting results; the stars can't deliver enough light to give you more than a black image. Instead, you can take star photos in two ways:

- Mount the camera on a tripod, point it toward the sky, and expose it for several hours. The result will be a fascinating star trace, showing the path the stars seem to take as the earth spins underneath them. Be sure to shield your camera from stray ground light, or the image will fog.

- Mount the camera to a clock drive mechanism like those on telescopes. Make a multi-hour exposure and you can photograph constellations without any motion effects, since the clock drive will keep the camera in synchronization with the stars. You can learn more about such drives at telescope supply stores.

Don't get overanxious—it can take hours to get a good, solid star photo, so you can only take one or perhaps two in a single evening. It's a good activity to do when camping, far away from ambient lighting. Keep in mind that while it's worth a shot, most digital cameras won't return decent results for star shots. For more details, read the following section.

 ## Why do my pictures have speckles all over them?

Digital cameras aren't the ideal medium for taking low-light pictures, and you won't always get great results. I personally don't mind stretching the envelope of what has been done with digital imaging, and you might want to try as well. But remember, you're venturing into territory that few other people have tried because of the medium's limitations.

That limitation, in a nutshell, is that CCDs aren't tuned to image very dark situations very well, and as a consequence, they tend to litter your picture with lots of phantom pixels of white. This snow can make your picture look grainy and hazy, as if you shot it with very high-speed film and ran it through an X-ray machine three or four times before getting the film developed.

The speckling problem becomes more pronounced as you set the exposure longer—so the scene of downtown Colorado Springs in Figure 7-12, exposed for about ten seconds, is particularly bad.

All is not lost, however. You can reduce the effect of these stray white pixels by running a despeckle filter on the image in a graphics editor. The despeckle filter is fairly common and we'll see how to use it in Chapter 11.

How do I get those cool pictures of light trails from cars?

One of my favorite nighttime photo opportunities is to capture the light trails of moving automobiles. It's easy to do,

Figure 7-12   A despeckle filter can improve this very long exposure

too—just set up a camera on a tripod in a position that sees auto traffic. Make sure that the surrounding area is fairly dark, or ambient light will ruin the picture. Set the camera to a manual "bulb" exposure and let it go for as little as a few seconds or as much as a minute, depending on how much traffic comes by and how much stray light you're dealing with. The longer you expose the image, the more trails you can capture (see Figure 7-13).

 Tip: *Don't have a bulb setting on your camera? Pre-focus on a very dark part of the scene and set the camera to underexpose by the maximum number of stops the camera allows.*

Figure 7-13 Light trails are easy to get as long as your digital camera can keep the shutter open for more than a few seconds

Chapter 8

Taking Close-Ups

Answer Topics!

Taking Close-Ups @ a Glance

Taking close-ups, or macro photography, is an exciting area to experiment with. For someone used to only seeing the world through human eyes and from about five feet off the ground, the world of close-ups is like visiting an alien vista. To take close-ups you'll need some special equipment, like a macro mode on your camera or a set of add-on close-up lenses.

When you get very close to your subject, such as within a few inches, the basic rules of exposure become very important. Depth of field, for instance, is a key ingredient in good close-ups. Read this chapter to master the basics and bring home great close-ups every time.

Lighting is the most important variable in any picture, and it was discussed in detail in Chapter 7. But close-up photography is a unique case in which special tricks can help improve your pictures dramatically. Check out this chapter to learn how to use artificial lights, homemade reflectors, and filters to improve your close-ups.

CLOSE-UP EQUIPMENT

 What is a "close-up"?

When we talk about close-up photography, we usually mean macro photography of all sorts of subjects, not just getting a close-up portrait of a person's face. Thus, we're talking about any photo that is within a few inches of a subject and attempts to magnify it, showing the subject from a closer perspective than humans ordinarily see. Using 35mm SLR equipment, you can get incredibly magnified views of small subjects. In digital photography, we typically can't get quite as close as that, but we can take impressive close-ups nonetheless. All the close-ups in this chapter, for instance, were taken with the Epson PhotoPC 700 by itself in macro mode, or in conjunction with Tiffen close-up lenses.

 Can I take close-up pictures with the lens on my digital camera?

That depends upon your particular camera. Many digital cameras have macro-focusing lenses, and they're perfectly adequate for taking close-ups (though they're often not nearly as powerful as serious close-up photographers would like).

Nor does it matter if your camera is a fixed-focus or an auto-focus model; both can and do have macro modes. They do all tend to work a bit differently, though. The Epson PhotoPC is an auto-focus camera, for instance, and it will auto-focus in its macro mode as well. The Canon PowerShot 350 is a fixed-focus camera that makes use of a manual-focusing lever when in macro mode. The Kodak DCS 210, otherwise a great camera, has a single fixed-focusing distance in macro mode—about eight inches—which makes it difficult to use this camera for close-ups.

Another issue is whether you want to use the built-in lens for close-ups, even if a close-up mode is provided. While some

people may be perfectly happy with the magnification provided by the camera, others will want more. If that's the case, see if your camera accepts optional close-up lenses for greater close-up flexibility.

Which button on my camera turns on the macro mode?

Of course, this varies from camera to camera, but typically the macro mode is indicated by a tulip. To enable this close-focusing mode, you might need to press a button (see Figure 8-1), or in the case of cameras that rely on you to perform the focus manually, move a lever or dial.

As soon as you move the macro-focusing control out of its normal position, the camera only focuses at close distance—so be sure to return it to normal-focus mode when you're done.

Macro buttons are usually marked with a tulip

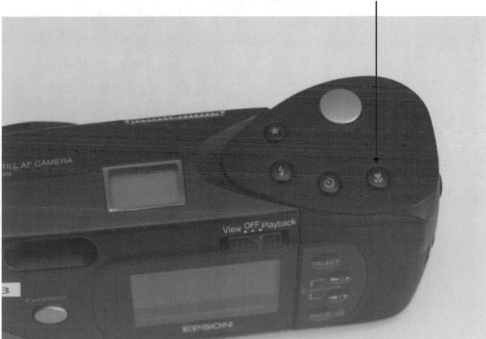

Figure 8-1 The macro mode button on the Epson PhotoPC enables close focusing

What kind of specialty lens can I get to take close-ups?

Close-up lenses magnify the subject and let you get much closer (to within a few inches of the subject) than you could with a normal lens.

If you're in the market for close-up lenses, there's good news and bad news. The good news is that in many cases, you can, in fact, add more powerful lenses to your camera. The bad news is that they're not necessarily easy to find.

Can your camera accept a close-up lens? There are four different ways of getting optional lenses onto a digital camera:

● **Interchangeable lenses**   This option is typically only available on high-end cameras that use 35mm SLR bodies. If you have such a camera, you're in luck—you can put any macro lens you like onto your camera.

● **Snap-on lenses**   Some cameras—most notably the Epson PhotoPC series—use a snap-on adapter that allows you to add lenses and filters to the camera as long as they have 37mm threads. Tiffen makes a series of close-up lenses that you can use with this camera.

● **Special camera adapters**   Tiffen's name comes up a lot in this book, but they've really embraced the digital camera market by making lenses, filters, and other peripherals for these cameras, including custom adapters that slip over the lens to provide access to the optional lenses. Contact Tiffen or your camera manufacturer to see if your camera can benefit from them.

● **Screw-on lenses**   Check your lens. If it has threads on the inside front surface, then you can probably buy close-up lenses and simply screw them on. You'll have to measure the diameter of the threads (a common diameter is 37mm) or call your manufacturer to find out what size lens to use.

In most cases, your camera will fall into one of these four categories. If not, then sorry—you need a better digital camera to take close-ups.

 I see lenses described with "diopters." What does that mean?

Close-up lenses aren't described in terms of focal length, since they're essentially just magnifying glasses that go in front of the camera's normal lens. Instead, they're described using the

term "diopter," which is an indirect measure of focal length. It tells you both how close you can get to the subject and what relative magnification the lens provides. Close-up lenses typically come in a variety of powers, from +1 to +10, though far and away the most common are +1, +2, and +4. Tiffen sells a set of these three close-up lenses for some digital cameras (see Figure 8-2).

Can I combine close-up lenses to increase magnification?

Surprisingly, yes. Close-up lenses typically are threaded (since they're designed to screw onto a normal lens in the same way you'd add a filter), and you can thread them onto each other as well. Diopter values get added together, so screwing +1, +2, and +4 close-up lenses together would result in a large-magnification +7 close-up lens. That's why I

Figure 8-2   Tiffen's close-up lenses can be screwed onto several different digital cameras, including the Apple QuickTake, Epson PhotoPC, and Kodak DC cameras

recommend getting more than one close-up lens—get the set, and that way you can vary the magnification as needed (see Figure 8-3).

Does it matter in what order I combine close-up lenses?

Yes, it does matter. When you add lenses and filters to a camera, typically the best optic quality will still be the lens that came with the camera (though in some very inexpensive digital cameras, this is debatable). So when you're adding close-up lenses, you'd prefer to have the greatest magnification be the lens that has the highest quality. Always put the lens with the highest diopter number closest to the camera lens.

As an example, lets say that you're combining +1 and +2 close-up lenses on your camera to photograph a leaf in the park. First attach the +2 to the camera and then apply the +1 on top. There's an added advantage: If you discover you've applied too much magnification to the scene, you can reduce the magnification in smaller steps if the +1 lens is on top.

Figure 8-3   These images were taken from the same distance, but with different combinations of Tiffen close-up lenses

 Do I need to use a tripod when taking close-ups?

Absolutely. While you can get away with holding your camera in your hands most of the time, the extreme magnification provided by close-up lenses would make even the most subtle shake ruin the picture. In close-up photography, I wouldn't even recommend trying to use a monopod, which is often a suitable compromise between stability and mobility. You need three legs planted in the ground to make sure the camera doesn't jiggle or wiggle at all during the exposure.

TAKING CLOSE-UPS

 What are some interesting subjects for close-up photography?

The choices are so numerous; start by taking pictures of things that interest you.

Lots of subjects look radically different at close range and magnified than they appear from a human perspective. In

fact, some subjects take on an almost fractal appearance—that is, their underlying structure seems to have an infinite amount of complexity. That can make for some very exciting photos. Here are some subjects to consider trying your hand at:

- Hobby subjects like stamps, coins, and models
- Nature subjects like plants, flowers, leaves, insects, butterflies, and worms
- Found objects like rubber bands, paper clips, textured paper, and fabric
- Human subjects like hair and skin
- Snow, ice, and water

 If I want to take close-ups in my house, what kind of "studio" should I create?

Because close-up photography can be so challenging, creating your own "studio" for macro shots is a good idea. The key elements to any good close-up stand are to create a non-distracting background, include good lighting, and eliminate unpredictable air currents that can ruin a shot by making the subject move.

All you really need is a large piece of light-colored poster board to use as a backdrop. I prefer white because it doesn't draw attention to itself and it also reflects light well. You can also use colored paper for different styles of background, however. Get the largest one you can find—I use a piece that is about three feet on each side. Arrange the poster board so that it sits on a tabletop and the curls up in back to form a wall behind. Curl it gently to keep the transition from horizontal to vertical smooth.

Ideally, stand the subject you're photographing up and away from the background, so the poster board is out of focus. At macro distances, it only takes a few inches to ensure that the background is fully out of focus. Be sure to mount the camera on a tripod—you can use a full-size tripod or one of the small table-mounted units (see Figure 8-4).

Figure 8-4 A small macro studio is easy to set up, or you can shoot
these pictures outdoors

 **How close to or far away from my subject can I get
when taking close-ups?**

The distance from your subject at which you need to work
depends on the lens you're using. If you're taking pictures
with the lens that's built into your digital camera, then the
macro-focusing range should be clearly identified in the
camera's user's manual. Typically that focusing distance is
from about five inches to two feet.

If you're using close-up lenses, you can generally get
closer to the subject. Check the distance guide that came with
your lens kit. The Tiffen close-up lenses, used in conjunction
with the Epson PhotoPC, allow you to focus as close as two
inches from the subject.

Of course, you should check the focus visually—don't use
the distance measurements exclusively. On the other hand,
these distances give you a good indication of your focusing

capability, and they allow you to plan your shot. There are also circumstances in which you can't check the focus visually, in which case knowing the proper focusing distance can help out a lot.

Can I use close-up lenses with the telephoto mode on my camera?

Usually, yes. In fact, you can get some very close-up images using the digital zoom on your camera, turning on macro mode, and putting close-up lenses on top of all that! Since you don't usually have access to "real" macro lenses in the world of digital photography, it pays to experiment and use every means available to extend the magnification of your close-ups.

When I measure the distance to the subject, where on the camera do I start measuring?

With a 35mm SLR camera, exact distance-to-subject measurements are often necessary to ensure that you get a good focus in macro photography. The distance you need to measure is actually from the subject to the *film plane*—that is, the exact location of the strip of film buried deep inside the camera body. But where is the film plane? There's usually a mark on 35mm cameras to indicate the location of the film.

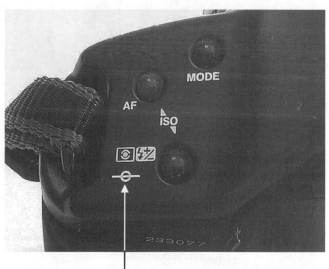

Film plane indicator on a traditional 35mm SLR

Knowing the focusing distance can be valuable in digital photography, too, such as when you can't tell if a picture is in focus because the LCD display isn't sharp or bright enough. Unfortunately, digital cameras never tell you where the "film plane" is—or, more specifically, where the CCDs are located. You can approximate this by measuring a half-inch back from the front edge of the camera. This is almost always accurate enough to yield in-focus pictures.

Do close-up lenses affect the exposure of my picture?

No, the auto-exposure system in your digital camera isn't affected by the presence of a close-up lens (or several close-up lenses, for that matter). You can take pictures normally.

On the other hand, you might want to experiment with the exposure of your camera—in particular, the exposure compensation control—if you need to adjust for the available lighting.

How do I avoid distracting backgrounds in my close-ups?

Luckily, close-up photography has a built-in weapon working against distracting backgrounds: shallow depth of field. As discussed in Chapter 5, the depth of field that your picture includes depends in part on your distance from the subject. Close-focus lenses that allow you to focus inches away from the subject offer very little depth of field, so you can use that to your advantage to blur distracting backgrounds, as seen in Figure 8-5.

In a nutshell, you can eliminate distracting backgrounds in these ways:

● Minimize depth of field by getting close to the subject.

● Lift the subject away from the background if possible—it only takes a few inches to completely blur the background at this close proximity.

● Use a flash. The flash can cause the background to appear black because it is much more weakly lit than the main subject.

● Use a plain background. You can insert a prepared background—like a piece of poster board—between the main subject and the distracting background. If the poster board is far enough away, it'll be out of focus and give a plain, diffuse look to the background.

Figure 8-5   Depth of field is shallow in macro photography, so you can isolate your subject using focus

My close-ups have such a small depth of field that important parts of the picture are out of focus. What can I do to get the whole scene in focus?

Usually, a limited depth of field is great for close-up photography—it helps focus attention on the subject. There are times, though, when the limited depth of field offered by a close-up can be a liability. Sometimes the depth of field isn't even deep enough to include the entire object you're photographing! Here are some tips for extending the depth of field:

● Move farther away. If your macro mode has a range of acceptable focusing distances, then move back to the longer end of the range. The farther away you are from the subject, the greater the depth of field.

- Turn up the lights. The more light you have, the smaller the aperture, which in turn increases depth of field. If you can take the photograph outside, that's ideal; if not, try using an electronic flash, shooting near a window, or placing lamps near the scene. Reflecting light into the scene can help as well.

- Compose the scene so that the subject doesn't extend as deeply into the foreground or background. In other words, it may be possible to change the angle at which the object is composed so that it is *in* the plane of focus, not *through* the plane of focus. In Figure 8-6, you can see that this long PC Card loses focus in the rear of the image. It should be photographed at a different angle for best results.

Should I use a large or a small aperture setting to take close-ups?

If you have control over the aperture of your digital camera—either directly or indirectly—then you can modify the exposure settings to get the amount of depth of field you need. In general, depth of field in close-ups is already narrow, and increasing the range of acceptable focus can help take a picture that's actually in focus. If that's the situation you find yourself in, then close the aperture as much as possible. Only open the aperture if you are sure the depth of field is too large, and you want to further isolate the subject.

Will my camera auto-focus in close-up mode?

That depends upon your camera. In most cases, if you have an auto-focus camera, it will continue to auto-focus in macro mode as well. If you have a fixed-focus lens, however, you'll need to manually set the focus in order to take the picture. The Canon PowerShot 350, seen in Figure 8-7, has a manual focusing lever.

Why do my close-up pictures never seem centered on what was in the viewfinder?

Most digital cameras are not through-the-lens devices in the same way that 35mm SLRs are. In a 35mm SLR, the viewfinder uses a mirror to see the scene through the same

Figure 8-6 At close range, the entirety of this subject doesn't stay in focus

optics that take the picture. At the moment of exposure, the mirror flips out of the way, simultaneously blocking the viewfinder and exposing the film.

Digital cameras work more like point-and-shoot cameras—the viewfinder provides a separate view of the subject that is only approximately the same as what the CCDs see through the actual camera lens. When you press the shutter release, the view through the viewfinder is not blocked, but the shutter exposes the CCD to the lens opening.

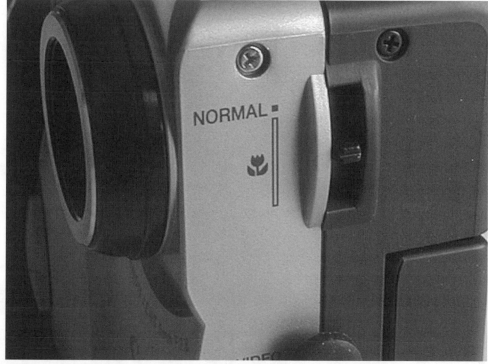

Figure 8-7 If your camera is fixed-focus, then the macro mode will have a manual focus control

All this usually has little effect on your picture taking. For most scenes at average distances, the fact that the viewfinder is displaced from the actual optics by an inch or two has no measurable effect on the final image. But as your camera gets closer to the subject, the displacement of the optics can begin to make the image that the CCDs see slightly different than the image that the viewfinder sees (see Figure 8-8). At the extreme—if you put a very small object right up to the viewfinder—the CCD won't be able to see the object at all, since it isn't in front of the picture-taking lens.

Close-up photography is particularly affected by this disparity between the two viewpoints, which is known as parallax. You can observe parallax by driving down a highway and looking at the passing scenery. The closest objects move by very fast, the farthest objects move more slowly. This is similar to the effect of placing the viewfinder and camera optics apart from one another in your

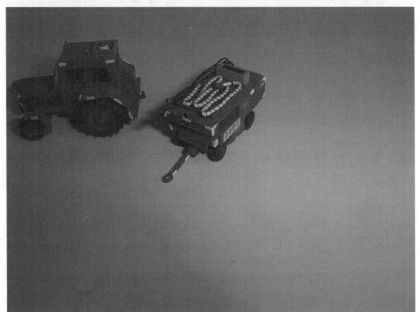

Figure 8-8   You can't trust the viewfinder when taking close-ups, since the viewfinder sees a slightly different scene than the CCD does

camera—the closer you get to the subject, the less accurate the viewfinder becomes. That's why you need to compose your picture a bit differently in close-up photography, and use one or both of these framing methods:

- Use the LCD display. The display on the back of your camera is seeing the scene through the eyes of your camera's CCDs, which means that you're seeing an accurate representation of the scene as it will be photographed.

- Use the correction marks on your camera's viewfinder to position your subject more accurately.

 ## How do I make sure my close-ups are in sharp focus?

Close-ups are tricky to do well with a digital camera, particularly if you've come to digital cameras from 35mm SLRs. There are two important problems with taking good close-ups:

- The viewfinder doesn't show you exactly what you're photographing, so you don't get any focus information from there.

- The LCD display on most cameras is rarely sharp, large, or bright enough to adequately inform you about focus.

Bottom line? It's hard to keep a close-up object in focus because you're operating blind. There are a few things you can do to try to keep the scene in good focus:

- If your camera has a video-out port and you're shooting indoors near a TV, connect the camera to a television. That way you can check the focus on a large screen in real time as you set up the shot. It's much, much better than trying to focus within the LCD display.

- Increase depth of field whenever possible by shooting from farther away or adding light to the situation.

- Learn the focus distance for your lens and make sure you're in the ballpark. Bring a tape measure or ruler with you to gauge your distance when you set up close-ups

Using the Correction Marks on Your Viewfinder

Your viewfinder probably has correction marks that indicate the difference between the position of your subject in the viewfinder and where the subject really is in the actual picture. You can think of these marks as the real viewfinder, and re-center your image to take this into account. On most cameras, the position of the viewfinder is above and to the left of the real optics, so the correction marks will force you to re-frame the scene slightly up and to the left.

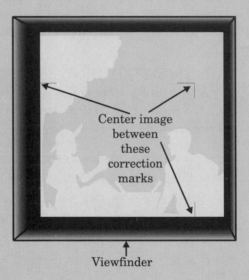

Center image between these correction marks

Viewfinder

There are some very important things to remember about correction marks:

- Correction marks are only approximate. Correction marks help you adjust for parallax when you compose an image at close range, but they're not perfect.

- They only work at close range. Parallax, by definition, diminishes with distance from the subject, so at ordinary distances you don't need to worry about the marks at all. In close-up, though, they become important.

- Whenever possible, use the LCD display as an alternative, since it shows you what you're really photographing.

 Sometimes pressing the shutter release is enough to jar my picture. What can I do to keep the image steady?

This can be a problem in normal photography, but it's even worse in close-ups. I recommend that you use the self-timer to activate the shutter release—that way, any jitter you give the camera will be gone by the time the picture is taken ten seconds or so later.

 It's hard to precisely position small objects in my picture. Is there an easier way than just nudging them with my fingers?

When your lens magnifies everything you do by an order of ten, it's hard to make subtle movements. Just try repositioning a leaf in a close-up composition by a small distance and you'll see what I mean.

For making small adjustments to objects in a scene, I keep a pair of modeling grabbers. It's like a miniature hand that I can use to rearrange things without causing a big mess. Likewise, tweezers are great for positioning things, or you can use a thin, long dowel to give objects a little shove without getting your big, clumsy hands in the way.

 What can I do to keep my subject perfectly still outdoors?

Outdoors, even a light wind can move light objects, like plants, around in your scene. I suggest setting up a large piece of poster board between the subject and the wind—as an added bonus, the poster board can act as a reflector. Another solution? Bring a big blanket or sheet and tie it to a nearby tree. If you need a larger area blocked from wind, this works well.

CLOSE-UP LIGHTING

 What can I do to improve the lighting in close-ups?

In most cases, natural sunlight is your best friend. Sometimes, though, natural light can't get the job done alone,

particularly if you're in uneven lighting or shooting when the sun is low on the horizon. Here are two light enhancers you can try:

● **Electronic flash**   Your flash has some advantages in close-up photography, chief among them being lots of light and the ability to make the background disappear into the, well, background. But be careful that you don't overwhelm your subject with an overly bright flash from too close. And check out what you got in the LCD display right away—the problem with a flash is that you can't see what you're going to get until after the picture has been taken.

● **Reflectors**   Use glossy white poster board or even aluminum foil to reflect natural light into darker portions of your image (see Figure 8-9). One common trick is to reflect light back up into a subject from below by putting a reflector on the ground.

Figure 8-9 A poster-board reflector is enough to cast light into these stones and brighten the image—notice that you can see detail in the shadows with the reflector

 If my flash is too bright, how do I reduce its brightness?

You can use any of the tricks discussed in Chapter 7 to reduce the impact of an electronic flash, but it's critically important to control your light in close-ups. Many digital cameras can't compensate for very close subjects, and overexpose the scene so badly it's not salvageable. Here are some of the best ways to use a flash at close range and get great results:

- Cover the flash with a layer or two of very thin fabric or tissue. Be sure it's white, or you'll color the subject.
- Bounce the flash if you can (most digital cameras can't).
- Underexpose the image with the exposure compensation control.

 If there's a sheet of glass between the camera and the subject, how do I avoid reflections and glare?

You might occasionally run into a situation where you want to shoot a subject that is contained under glass, such as at a museum. There are two tricks you can use to eliminate the resulting glare:

- Place the lens directly against—and parallel to—the glass. Then shoot the picture.
- Use a polarizing filter (see Chapter 9) to eliminate the glare, as seen in Figure 8-10.

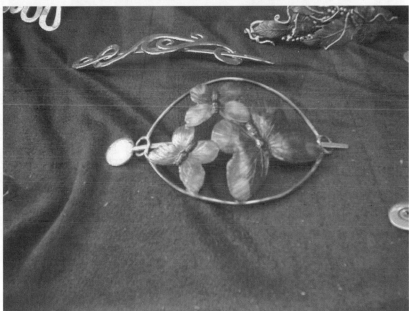

Figure 8-10 My legs are reflected in the glass on the top—but with a polarizer in the picture on the bottom, they disappear from the scene

Chapter 9

Using Peripherals and Accessories

Answer Topics!

Using Peripherals and Accessories @ a Glance

 A new digital camera brings with it many surprises—not the least of which is the fact that you'll go through batteries like water. Look here to find out what you can do to minimize battery consumption.

 Filters and additional lenses can enhance your photographs in many ways. They can help you achieve more realistic effects, such as truer colors, or fantasy effects like star patterns and soft focus. Look in this chapter to understand how to get the most out of these filters and lenses.

 Tripods aren't an essential accessory for every photographer, but many people will find them extremely useful. Tripods can help your camera deliver sharp pictures even in low light. But you need to know how to choose and use a tripod, or you won't be happy with the final results.

 There are other accessories you may find handy—like light reflectors and camera bags. Look here for the skinny on these add-ons for your digital camera.

 Need to know more? Look here for tips on which books, Web sites, and magazines you can use to learn more about the exciting world of digital photography.

ALL ABOUT BATTERIES

 Why do my camera batteries wear out so fast?

Digital cameras are battery hogs. You can't expect your camera's batteries to last very long, since there are a number of key functions they must power:

- The imaging system
- The LCD preview display
- The flash
- The image storage system

In other words, your batteries need to power the LCD so you can see the scene; then they need to provide power to the CCD and imaging subsystem to take the picture; at the same time, they may also need to fire and then recycle the flash; finally, they need to write the image to the storage media. If your camera has a hard disk, the batteries will also need to power the disk mechanism.

That's a lot to ask of a set of batteries, so it shouldn't be too surprising that you need to replace them often.

 When I remove the batteries, I lose my date and other settings. Shouldn't the camera remember this stuff?

That depends. Some cameras do, in fact, have a small watch battery that retains information like the date and time when the main batteries are removed from the camera. Others don't—look in your camera manual. If your camera doesn't have a small watch battery and asks you to input the date every time you remove the batteries for charging, you should plug the camera into an AC adapter before removing the main batteries, and leave it plugged into wall power whenever the main batteries are out.

 If my batteries die, can I lose the pictures stored in the camera's memory?

No, your images are stored in what is known as "nonvolatile memory," a fancy way of saying that it stores data even when there isn't power available, like a computer hard disk or the CMOS memory that remembers the date and time in your PC. Hence, a dead set of batteries won't affect the pictures you've already taken. You can think of it like a camcorder—if the battery dies, the video is already stored on tape, and it's safe.

What kind of batteries are best?

Unless you use your digital camera very, very infrequently, I recommend that you avoid using old-fashioned, disposable AA batteries. If you have to, use alkalines—they'll give you marginally better performance (refer to Chapter 3 for some background information on batteries).

If you use your camera at least somewhat regularly, though, you should definitely invest in a few sets of rechargeables. The oldest kind of rechargeable batteries are Ni-Cad (nickel cadmium) batteries. While cheap, Ni-Cads are prone to developing a "memory," which reduces their lifespan dramatically. Memory occurs when you use the battery a little and then recharge it. Over time, this process makes the battery "forget" about the capacity it has below the charging point, and it'll start to die and need charging far too soon.

A better alternative is either NiMH (nickel metal hydride) or LiOn (lithium ion) batteries. These newer rechargeables don't develop memories, and hence can be recharged anytime you like without fear of premature battery death.

Consult your camera manual to determine what batteries your camera can use. Given a choice, always avoid Ni-Cads in favor of newer, higher-performance rechargeables.

How many times can I recharge my camera batteries?

The manual that came with your batteries, the charger, or the camera itself will probably say, but you can tell for yourself when they're starting to die for good. If you typically get to take, say, 25 pictures with a single battery charge, the batteries are approaching the end of their useful life when they can only hold a charge for 20 or fewer pictures. Most rechargeables can be used over 100 times, so they're certainly worth the investment.

Get an AC Adapter

If you have a digital camera, you owe it to yourself to get an AC adapter. This is a unit that plugs into the wall and powers your camera, allowing you to use the camera without worrying about batteries. An AC adapter is handy for performing power-intensive tasks like copying images to your computer, and enables you to use the camera while the batteries are charging. Unfortunately, few digital cameras actually come with the AC adapter, so it's an option you'll need to buy separately.

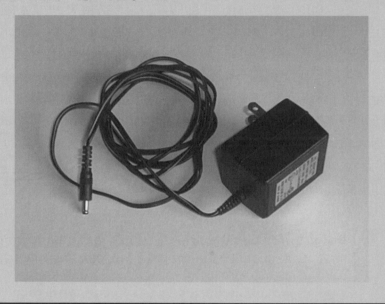

 How do I know when it's time to replace or recharge the batteries in my camera?

Most digital cameras have a battery strength indicator built into the status display or LCD monitor in the camera. All cameras use a slightly different method of telling you the battery status, but keep an eye out for the indication that your batteries are about used up. Usually, that's a half-battery icon that flashes or changes color.

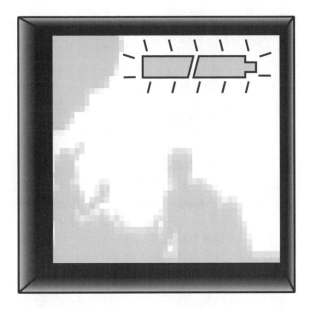

 Tip: *Even if your battery indicator shows that the battery is dead and the camera won't turn on, you might yet be able to eke a few more pictures out of the camera. Turn off your LCD display—without that tremendous load on the batteries, they can probably snap a few more pictures before you have to recharge.*

 ### What can I do to extend the life of my batteries?

Since so many different subsystems in your camera are drawing power from the same set of batteries (see "Why do my camera batteries wear out so fast?" earlier in this chapter

Pack Extra Batteries

Never go on a long trip without a spare set of batteries in your camera case. If your rechargeable batteries die, you're out of luck—unless you have a backup set of AAs. You'll never forgive yourself if your camera dies in the first few hours of your one and only trip to the Grand Canyon.

to learn more), it makes sense that you can extend the life of your batteries by taking a few simple precautions:

● Only use the LCD display when you have to, and turn it off when it isn't in use.

● Don't spend a lot of time reviewing pictures you've already taken in the LCD display. It might be fun to show people the picture you just took, but it eats up battery life like crazy.

● Disable the flash when you don't need it. Sure, there are good reasons to use the flash, even outdoors (see Chapter 7 for details), but each burst of light can be as much as 5% of the total battery life in your camera. Turn it on only when you need it.

● Don't turn the camera off after every single picture, especially if you're taking lots of pictures in a short time. You may think you're conserving battery life, but in reality, the initialization routines your camera runs every time it's turned on can use up a significant amount of battery life on their own.

My camera uses a small watch battery in addition to AAs. What is this watch battery for?

Some cameras use a small watch battery to keep track of certain settings, like the date and time, when the main batteries are removed. This battery has nothing to do with keeping your pictures in memory, so don't worry about losing images because all the batteries were removed. Not all cameras use this battery.

How long does the watch battery last?

The lithium battery that stores data in your camera is generally good for about five years, so it's considered a "lifetime" battery. Considering the rate of change in the computer industry, it's unlikely you'll still be using this year's digital camera in five years' time.

FILTERS AND LENSES

 ## What are filters, and why would I want to use them?

Filters are handy accessories for your digital camera. Usually, a filter is a translucent optical element that modifies the quality of the light that enters the camera. People use filters to improve the image by changing the characteristics of the light reaching the CCD. Filters can change the light's intensity or color, or add special effects.

You can use filters to get a special look from your pictures "in the lens"—that is, without post-processing on a PC.

 ## How do I attach filters or optional lenses to my camera?

In general, there are two ways to attach a filter to your digital camera:

- Some cameras have threads on the front of the lens that you can use to screw on filters.
- Sometimes you have to use a special adapter to mount the filter over the lens (see Figure 9-1).

Tiffen makes adapters for several consumer digital cameras that do not accept threaded filters on their own. You can contact your camera manufacturer or Tiffen for more details.

Either way, though, all you need to determine is what the mount size of the camera or adapter actually is. Digital cameras commonly use a 37mm mount, which is actually pretty small. Few camera shops carry filters this size, though you should be able to order what you need without too much trouble.

Adapter snaps onto
camera lens

Figure 9-1   The Epson PhotoPC includes an adapter that fits 37mm Tiffen
lenses and filters

 Tip: *If your camera uses an adapter to mount filters, get a
few spare adapters. They're pretty cheap, and that way you
can leave the filters you most commonly use connected to their
adapters, making it easier to get them on and off the camera.*

What filters are most useful for digital cameras?

Truth be told, most people don't use filters on digital
cameras. There are a few reasons for this. For starters,
digital cameras are often treated like point-and-shoot
cameras, which rarely use special filters. In addition, camera
manufacturers hardly make it easy to get filters on their
cameras. But if you want to experiment with filters, you'll
find you can get great results and make pictures that
approach 35mm quality. Bottom line: If you're a tinkerer or

an artist at heart, you'll want to try filters, even if you're just taking pictures for a Web site or your job.

These are the filters I'd recommend getting as a basic starter set:

- **UV filter**   The UV filter is a good general-purpose filter that reduces the bluish tint you can get in pictures. This is caused by an extra sensitivity to ultraviolet light, which a UV filter can eliminate from your pictures. And since many digital cameras have a tendency toward blue because of poor color balance, a UV filter is a good idea.

- **Close-up filter**   Not filters in the ordinary sense of the word, close-up filters are more like simple lenses. They provide additional magnification beyond the macro mode offered by your camera, and are great for getting very close to small objects. See Chapter 8 for more details on this kind of filter.

- **Polarizer**   A polarizer is one of the most all-around handy filters to use in different lighting situations. This filter can increase the contrast and color saturation in a scene, such as increasing the blueness of the sky. It can also eliminate (or at least reduce) glare and reflections from metal, glass, and water. It's a good idea to always have a polarizer handy when shooting outdoors in bright light.

 ## I've heard I should keep a filter on my camera to protect the lens. Is this true?

Think of it this way: Which would you rather ruin—a $10 filter or a $300 camera? Sadly, the optics in most digital cameras are permanently attached. That means that if something bad happens to your lens—like it gets scratched—then your camera is pretty much ruined. If possible, I recommend that you leave a filter on your camera all the time to prevent damage to the underlying optics.

Remember: Even cleaning the lens can scratch it if done improperly, so a filter is a good investment as a lens protector. Go ahead and clean the filter occasionally to keep it clean, and replace it periodically, especially if it gets scratched.

But what kind of filter should you use? Most photographers leave a UV filter on their cameras. The UV filter (see "What filters are most useful for digital cameras?" earlier in this chapter) has little noticeable effect on the image, only reducing the bluish cast sometimes apparent in outdoor photography by eliminating the ultraviolet. It's a good choice for general use.

What is a polarizing filter?

A polarizing filter, or polarizer, increases the color saturation and contrast in outdoor photography. It also reduces or eliminates reflections and glare caused by water, glass, and metal.

Most light in ordinary daylight conditions is unpolarized; that is, the constituent photons are emitted somewhat randomly. Some light, however—particularly light that reflects off a shiny surface—gets partially polarized. This is unwanted light that creates glare and reflections, and generally reduces the contrast in a scene. Polarized light can even make the sky look washed out, seeming less blue.

A polarizer looks different than many filters because it actually has a moving part—a flat lens with polarizing slits etched into the glass. By turning the polarizer, you can align the etchings so they are perpendicular to the polarized light and block it from reaching your camera's CCD (see Figure 9-2). The result is more saturated colors, a deeper blue sky, reduced glare, and diminished reflections.

How do you use a polarizer?

Using a polarizer takes a little practice, but the results are often worth it. The goal of a polarizer is to eliminate the polarized light reflected by shiny surfaces like water, metal, or glass. It also filters out polarized light in the atmosphere that robs pictures of saturated colors and full contrast. But since the angle at which polarized light reaches your camera is variable, you need to turn the filter until it is aligned properly (see Figure 9-3).

This is easier than it sounds—the LCD display (or TTL viewfinder, if your camera has one) gives you immediate feedback on the effect of the filter. In any given situation, the

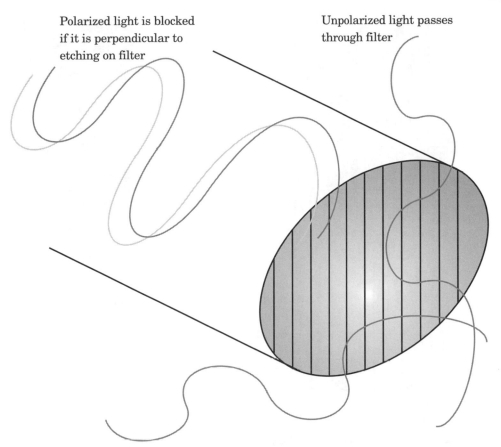

Polarized light is blocked
if it is perpendicular to
etching on filter

Unpolarized light passes
through filter

Figure 9-2 A polarizing filter blocks light that happens to be polarized
along a particular plane

polarizer works in two positions, 180 degrees apart. If you
turn the polarizer to any position in between, the effect of the
filter is diminished until, at 90 degrees from optimum, it has
no effect at all.

Here are some tips to keep in mind when using a polarizer:

● **Watch the position of the sun in the sky**   If you're
trying to enrich the blue in the sky, remember that a
polarizer works best when the sun is over one of your
shoulders. You won't get any results from a polarizer if
you shoot directly into or away from the sun (see
Figure 9-4).

Polarized has no effect

Polarized has maximum effect

Figure 9-3 You can see that by turning the polarizer 90 degrees, you go from zero effect to maximum effect

● **Avoid wide-angle lenses** If you use a wide-angle lens, it's possible that the picture will show a region of deep saturation in the sky surrounded by washed-out sections of sky. That's because the lens captures both parts of the sky that have polarized light and parts that don't.

● **Your angle relative to a shiny surface affects the amount of reflection** You can use a polarizer to reduce or eliminate reflections from shiny surfaces, like glass counters, water in a lake, glass buildings, or a metal frame. The polarizer works best when you shoot at about a 34-degree angle to the surface (see Figure 9-5); other angles of incidence have less depolarizing effect, like using a polarizer into or away from the sun.

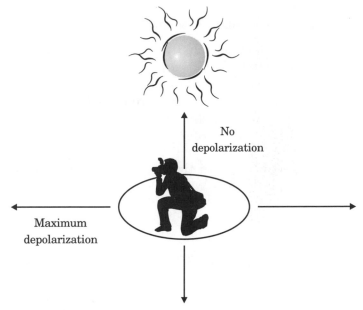

Figure 9-4   A polarizer is only effective at a right angle to the sun

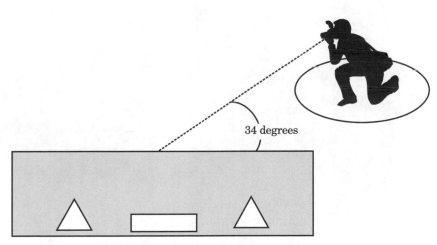

Figure 9-5   A polarizer is most effective at about a 34-degree angle from
a reflective surface

 ## Should I use a UV filter on my camera?

I recommend that you keep a UV filter on your camera most of the time, if your camera accepts filters. Not only does it reduce the bluish hue many cameras generate, but it protects the optics of your camera from dust, scratches, and damage. See "I've heard I should keep a filter on my camera to protect the lens. Is this true?" earlier in this chapter for more information.

 ## What other special filters might be useful?

Aside from the basic suite of UV, close-up, and polarizing filters, there are many other lenses available that can help dress up your photos. Here are some of my favorites:

● **Warming filter**   This is a good all-around filter, particularly if you take a lot of people pictures. It's an alternative to the UV filter, in fact; instead of adjusting for a bluish hue by eliminating UV, the warming filter adds a warm, golden hue to skin tones. The effect is subtle but appropriate. You can use this as your all-around lens protector if you want to.

● **Star filter**   This is a special-effect filter that turns any point light source in your picture, such as a candle, light bulb, or even a window opening, into a multi-point burst of light. Star filters use etchings on a flat lens to create the star pattern, and turning the filter adjusts the angle at which the star burst radiates away from the light. Star filters are available in a variety of "points," though four-point star patterns are the most common.

● **Neutral-density filter**   This filter reduces the amount of light entering the lens. It's great for very bright situations in which the camera simply can't cope with how much light is entering the lens, or where you'd like to slow down the shutter speed or decrease the depth of field. Neutral-density filters are available on their own or as part of another filter, like a soft-focus filter.

● **Soft-focus filter**   Also known as a diffusion filter, a soft focus filter can be used to flatter people's features in portraits or create dreamy landscapes.

 Tip: *Use special-effect filters like star filters carefully. They can easily overwhelm your image and, in fact, often look cheesy. Also, be selective about which filters you use in a given picture—you should use as few filters together as possible, as every layer between the optics and the subject reduces light and introduces imperfections into the picture.*

Can I make filters myself?

Absolutely. Before filters were generally available in camera shops, photographers made their own filters all the time. And since digital camera owners don't always have a large selection of filters to choose from, making your own is a good idea.

The easiest way to create a homemade filter is to begin with a clear—or nearly clear—commercial filter. If you want to experiment, I suggest you get a few UV filters that are compatible with your camera and work with those. Since a UV has no obvious effect on the image, you know that whatever you do to the filter will be obvious in the finished picture.

There are a lot of different things you can try. Here are some suggestions:

- Applying a very thin layer of petroleum jelly to the filter can create a soft-focus effect. Vary the thickness of jelly to get different effects. Use a Q-tip lightly coated with the jelly for best results.

- Apply petroleum jelly to specific areas of the lens to get a localized effect. You can diffuse just someone's face, for instance.

- Apply the jelly in a pattern to get star or flare effects. This takes some practice, but you can get better effects with this method than you'd get with a commercial star filter, since you can localize it to just a portion of the filter.

- Breathe on your filter immediately before taking the shot for a fog effect.

Even without a filter, you can get a diffusion effect. Tightly wrap a nylon stocking around the front of the lens—this can diffuse the scene in direct proportion to the number of layers and overall thickness of the stocking material.

 ## How do I take soft-focus pictures?

Get a soft-focus (or "diffusion") filter for your digital camera. If no such animal is available for your particular digital camera, try to make a substitute yourself—see the preceding section.

Note: *Soft focus is not the same thing as out of focus. Many novice photographers watched too much* Star Trek *and assumed that Yeoman Rand looked fuzzy because she was simply out of focus. Out of focus looks, well, wrong. It isn't a substitute for some kind of diffusion.*

Serious Soft Focus

Most soft-focus filters are flat lenses with diffusion etchings that slip over your camera's optics, though you can also get telephoto-like soft-focus lenses for SLR-based cameras. These lenses work like pinhole cameras, only with bigger apertures.

If the pinhole through which light enters the camera is very small, you can get a very sharp image. As the aperture in a pinhole camera gets bigger, though, the image is resolved less sharply. Soft-focus lenses take this principle to the extreme and offer huge openings in the front that render the subject in a fuzzy manner on purpose. You can even control the amount of fuzziness by changing the size of the opening. If your digital camera allows interchangeable lenses, you can get such a soft-focus lens.

 Is there a filter designed to reduce the amount of light entering my camera?

Yes, it's called a neutral-density filter, and you can use it to slow down the shutter speed of your camera or decrease

depth of field. For more information, see "What other special filters might be useful?" earlier in this chapter.

 Do I need additional lenses for my camera?

That depends upon what you want to photograph. Perhaps not. In theory, you selected your digital camera at least in part on the basis of what kind of focal length it offered. A fixed-focal-length, wide-angle lens is only good in certain situations—you can't use it to take portraits, action shots, or close-ups, for instance. But hopefully you knew that when you bought it.

If you find that there are things you'd like to photograph that your existing digital camera can't handle, then you might want to see about adding lenses. Contact your camera manufacturer to see what capability you may have for expanding your suite of lens options.

 What lenses are considered "essential" for general photography?

This is a matter of opinion, but I recommend that any half-serious photographer have access to:

● A normal lens for general-purpose photography; in all likelihood, this lens is part of your basic camera configuration

● A telephoto lens, like a 2x telephoto adapter that can attach to your existing lens

● A wide-angle lens, such as a .5x adapter

See Chapter 5 for a more detailed discussion of what lenses suit various kinds of subjects.

TRIPODS

 Do I need a tripod?

I'll be perfectly honest: Depending upon the kind of pictures you take, you may never need a tripod in your entire life. Your brother may have been taking pictures all his life with a point-and-shoot camera, and never have used a tripod at all, much less owned one. But ask yourself—does he have a collection of slightly blurred pictures? Or has he ever tried doing anything really interesting with his camera, aside from the normal assortment of people pictures at the Grand Canyon?

In my opinion, many photographers will need a tripod from time to time, usually when shooting pictures in low-light conditions, with a slow shutter speed, or when trying to capture a close-up (or macro) photograph. If you want to take your photos to the next level—increase their sharpness, get low-light images, that sort of thing—then you should invest in a tripod and use it occasionally.

 Will any tripod work with a digital camera?

In most cases, yes. Nearly all cameras accept the universal 1/4-inch tripod screw.

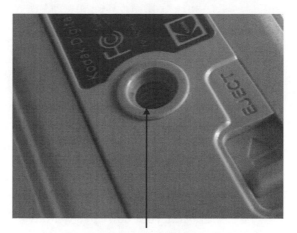

If your camera is threaded for a tripod at all (look at the bottom of your camera for a 1/4-inch threaded hole), your camera is almost guaranteed to accept this style of tripod.

Most digital cameras use a
¼-inch tripod mount

Some digital cameras just don't include a tripod socket, and there's not much you can do about it (I discuss the alternatives to a tripod later in this chapter).

Keep in mind that some tripods are threaded with a 3/8-inch screw. These tripods won't fit your digital camera, but that size is actually pretty rare.

 ## What kind of tripod works best?

There are many brands of tripod on the market, and they all work OK to varying degrees. I suggest you take your digital camera to the camera shop and experiment with the various units on display there. Stand the tripod up on its feet, mount and unmount the camera, play with its various degrees of motion. Only buy a tripod you're comfortable with, since a clumsy tripod design can cost you in time, aggravation, and missed photographs. Don't buy a tripod based on the ad copy on the box and assume you'll get the hang of it at home—make sure you like it, since what works fine for me might be a pain in the neck for you.

Keep in mind that you'll shop for a tripod for a digital camera somewhat differently than you would for a 35mm

SLR. Since there are fewer controls to fiddle with that might cause the camera to shake and a digital camera is lighter overall, the tripod doesn't have to be quite as heavy or robust.

Aside from these general recommendations about making sure a tripod is right for you, there is some fairly universal advice you might want to consider:

● Tripods can cost anywhere from $20 to $200. You probably don't need one from either end of the cost spectrum. I've found that many $50 tripods are great for general-purpose photography.

● Make sure the tripod is convenient. Play with all the controls and be sure it's easy to use in the field. Generally, the legs shouldn't have more than two telescoping sections, since three or more are difficult to extend and collapse quickly. Check the leg locks for convenience and security. You might have thumb locks, levers, or collars that hold the tripod legs in place (see Figure 9-6).

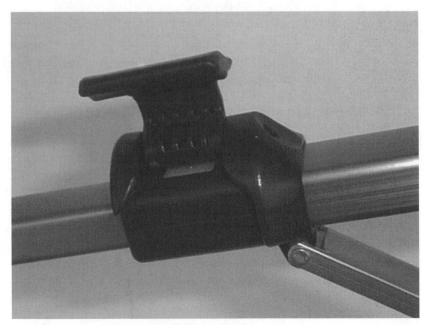

Figure 9-6 Check to make sure the legs are easy to lock firmly in place, such as with this lever system

● Make sure the tripod is sturdy, since that's the reason you're buying it. If you extend the legs and they wobble when they're locked, find another tripod.

● Be sure the tripod is a good compromise between strength and weight. A tripod made of cast iron would be pretty strong, but impossible to cart around easily. A papier-mâché tripod, on the other hand, would be hopelessly weak. In particular, round legs are very rigid due to their shape; U-shaped legs are not nearly so strong, and must be made of a heavier material to achieve the same relative strength.

● If you like taking landscapes, look for a tripod with a level. The level can help you keep your horizon level in the picture.

● Don't forget about the tripod's feet. If you take pictures outdoors, you may want feet with little spikes. Indoor shooting calls for rubber feet to grab the floor. And some tripods have spikes that screw out from within the rubber, making the tripod handy in all conditions.

How do I choose a tripod head?

The *tripod head*—that's the part of the tripod that actually screws into the camera—is an important part of the tripod. When choosing your tripod, you should look hard at the kind of head it comes with. Alternately, you can usually buy a head separately and add it to your tripod.

Note: *Not all tripods have removable heads, so if this is a feature you want, then shop for your tripod carefully.*

There are two kinds of heads: *ball heads* and *pan heads*. Ball heads are very easy to use—the camera rests on top of a ball that rests in a socket. You simply position the camera where you want it and tighten the socket lock; that holds the camera in place. A pan head, on the other hand, uses two handles to separately control the pan (horizontal swivel) and tilt (up and down angle) of your camera. It's more difficult to use, but provides a more secure lock (see Figure 9-7).

Figure 9-7 A pan head (left) uses more than one lock to hold the camera in position. A ball head (right) uses just one

In general, I recommend that people get pan heads for their cameras—ball heads are typically not strong enough to hold a heavy camera in position.

But with consumer-level digital cameras, I have a different opinion. Since these cameras are generally very lightweight and don't require you to fuss a lot with controls and settings, the ball head is ideal. Look for a ball head when you get a tripod for your digital camera.

Tip: *Make sure the ball head is tightly locked, or your camera can swing down unexpectedly and get damaged.*

Another convenient feature to look for in the tripod head is a quick-release mount. This allows you to screw the head into your camera and pop the whole head off the tripod with a single button or lever. When you're ready to take the picture, just snap the head back on the tripod.

 How do I use a tripod?

Using a tripod is mostly common sense, but a few recommendations can help you get the most out of this handy support:

- Set up the tripod in place before connecting the camera. If you screw the camera on first, you run the risk of damaging it as you try to extend the tripod legs.

- Drop the lower leg extensions first; that way you can still reach the other leg releases easily if you want to raise the tripod higher.

- Always try raising the camera via the tripod legs before extending the center post, since the higher you raise the center post, the less stable your camera will be. Only extend the post after the legs will go no higher.

- Whenever possible, set one leg in the direction the camera is pointing and work between the remaining two legs. That way you'll be less likely to trip on the legs and knock the tripod over.

Tip: *Always make sure you loosen the lever, knob, collar, or other control holding the tripod in position before moving anything. If you force the tripod to do something when it's tight and locked, you'll ruin the locking mechanism and shorten the life of the tripod. It might even cause the camera to fall and break.*

I need to set up shots very quickly, and tripods are too bulky and slow. Is there an alternative?

Yes, there are a few alternatives to the bulky old tripod (though if you haven't looked at tripods in a few years, I think you'll find they're much lighter and easier to use than they used to be).

Here are a few different ways to steady your camera:

- Get a monopod. This is a one-legged "tripod" (I know, it's an oxymoron). Monopods are telescoping poles with a tripod screw on the top. You can lengthen the pod so the camera stands at eye level, and often the stability offered by the pole, in combination with your hands, is enough to steady your shot. This kind of support is very popular among action photographers, who can move around quickly with the camera on a monopod and use it to pan and swivel rapidly to photograph fast-moving subjects.

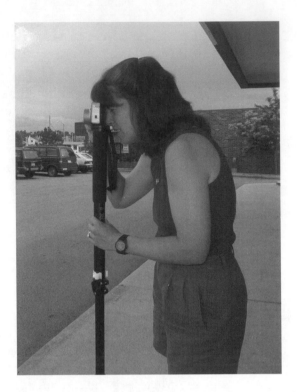

 Use a bean bag. You can place your camera on a large bean bag (in a pinch, I've actually used my kid's bean bag toys). If you nestle the camera into place, it's surprisingly effective at reducing camera movement.

 If you want to steady a shot without any equipment at all, look for something to lean against and steady the camera on. That can be a tree, window sill, fence, or anything else you can transfer your weight to.

What do you use those little tabletop tripods for?

These tripods are commonly used by point-and-shoot and digital camera photographers because they're exceptionally small and light. Just a few inches in size and weighing only ounces, they fit in any camera bag.

These tabletop tripods—also called mini-tripods—are handy for setting up a camera and then using the self-timer to take a portrait. You can also connect your camera to the tripod and place the legs on your chest for extra stability when you take pictures in low-light conditions.

OTHER ACCESSORIES

 Some photographers use exposure meters. Should I get one for my digital camera?

No, it really won't do you any good at all. An exposure meter allows you to fine-tune the exposure of your picture and requires your camera to include exposure controls similar to those on a 35mm SLR. If you take a reading with a meter but can't adjust the shutter speed or aperture of your digital camera, the knowledge provided by the meter will do you no good whatsoever.

 ## How do I shop for a camera case?

I suggest that you get some kind of case to hold your camera equipment. If all you have is a single digital camera, and nothing more, perhaps you don't really need much in the way of a case. Consider what a well-equipped photographer might have, however: camera, spare memory cards, cleaning supplies, additional lenses, a few filters, and a mini-tripod. Without a case, your spouse and kids will spend a lot of time carrying stuff around for you.

Cases come in a wide array of sizes, shapes, colors, and features. Some of the best cases are made explicitly for cameras and the manufacturers (like Tenba and Tamrac, for instance) have been doing it for years. Here are some things to consider when you shop for a camera case:

- Make sure it is big enough for all your equipment, but not too big. No one likes to carry a lot of junk around with them, and "my case is too big" is perhaps the biggest excuse for amateur photographers leaving their stuff at home on vacation.

- The inside of the case should be padded and configurable. Usually, you can move compartments around thanks to Velcro-edged walls. With a system like this, you can design the interior of the case to hold your stuff any way you like.

- The outside of the case should be rugged and water resistant. Ballistic nylon is generally considered to be the ultimate in strength for a camera bag. Make sure that there are flaps to protect zippers from rain, and that all the seams are cross-stitched for strength.

- Buy a style of camera case that matches the way you like to carry things. You can get shoulder bags, backpacks, handheld cases, and combinations that convert by moving a strap. Some photographers like the look and convenience of a photo vest. Instead of carrying your

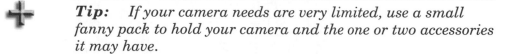

accessories over your shoulder, with the photo vest you have lots and lots of pockets for holding your stuff.

➕ ***Tip:*** *If your camera needs are very limited, use a small fanny pack to hold your camera and the one or two accessories it may have.*

Should I get a hard case or a soft case?

This is a matter of taste, but for a digital camera, a soft case is probably the way to go. I recently had the opportunity to test a hard case from Zero Halliburton, and while it's impressively strong (and gorgeous to look at), it's a thief magnet, and not particularly convenient to use. Soft cases are somewhat less secure from accidents than rigid cases, but if you travel around with your camera very much, you'll appreciate a soft case.

Should I get a reflector?

If you like to take indoor portraits and indoor or outdoor close-up photos, you might benefit from a reflector. You can make one yourself from a large sheet of poster board, or get a reflector from your local camera shop. I really like Photoflex Litediscs. These reflectors unfold into a variety of sizes, fold up into very small pouches (see Figure 9-8), stay very flat (important for making sure the light reflects the way you want it to), and you can mount them on optional stands.

What do I need to take care of my camera?

It's important to keep your camera clean—particularly the optical surfaces. A dirty lens can make your pictures blurry and ruin otherwise good photo opportunities. But be careful how you clean your camera. You should have some basic supplies:

● To keep the lens clean, get a special lens cleaning solution and cleaning paper. Don't use ordinary tissue, since that's

Figure 9-8 This Photoflex reflector folds into the small black case that my wife is holding, yet it unfurls into a large reflective surface

typically abrasive and will scratch your lens. Plus, tissue leaves lots of little fibers behind on the lens.

- When the camera's not in use, use a lens cover (if your camera comes with one) or keep the lens shuttered if your camera has such a feature. When possible, keep it in a closed camera bag to minimize the dust it collects.

- Get a can of compressed air or a lens brush to keep dust out of the corners of your LCD display.

- Consider equipping your camera with a UV filter from a supplier like Tiffen. The filter can improve your photos, but more important, it protects your camera's lens. It's a lot easier to replace a $10 filter every year than deal with a scratched lens.

SOURCES OF INFORMATION

 If I want to learn more about digital photography, what books do you recommend?

While I'd like to say that all you need is this book, photography is such a big field that you can always read more and learn more about the art of taking pictures. I think you should read up on traditional photography and apply those principles to the digital domain, so in addition to this book, you might want to investigate some of these others, which concentrate on 35mm photography:

● *The Basic Book of Photography* by Tom Grimm and Michele Grimm (Plume, 1997)

● *The Photographer's Handbook* by John Hedgecoe (Knopf, 1992)

If you want to learn more about PCs, such as how to troubleshoot connection problems or install hardware like scanners and hard disks, then definitely check out:

● *Upgrading & Repairing Your PC Answers!* by Dave Johnson and Todd Stauffer (Osborne/McGraw-Hill, 1998)

 Are there Web sites dedicated to digital photography?

Yes, there are plenty. For a list of camera manufacturers who have Web sites, see Chapter 2. Here are some sites that offer more than just marketing information, though:

● **http://www.photoflex.com/** The Photoflex Institute of Photography is found on the Photoflex Web site. For a subscription fee, you can take their online photography courses.

● **http://www.dcresource.com/** The Digital Camera Resource Page is full of news, reviews, and visitor messages about everything new in digital photography.

● **http://photo.net/photo/** This useful site is chock-full of product reviews, questions and answers, how-tos, and other photography articles.

- **http://www.dvcentral.org/** This site can tell you everything you ever wanted to know about digital video. DV camcorders, the topic of this site, are discussed in Chapter 18.

- **http://www.hyperzine.com/** This online magazine is dedicated to traditional and digital photography. Here you'll find articles, discussions, and product reviews.

- **http://www.radioguys.com** That's my Web site. Feel free to drop in and ask a question any time you like; if your question is interesting enough, I'll include it in the next revision of this book and make you eligible for a small prize as a thank-you.

What magazines should I investigate?

If you like your information about digital photography to arrive every month in your mailbox in print form, then check out these magazines:

- *Digital Camera Magazine*, (516) 349-9333
- *Digital Video Magazine*, (888) 776-7002
- *Imaging Magazine*, (888) 824-9792
- *Peterson's Photographic*, (800) 800-3686

Chapter 10

Storing Images

Answer Topics!

Storing Images @ a Glance

Your camera can only store so many images—that limit is determined by the amount of memory the camera contains. What are the different kinds of memory cards? Can you upgrade memory? Look in this chapter for the scoop on Compact Flash, SmartMedia, and the many other memory formats today's cameras use.

Your camera is a simple appliance. Right up until you try to connect it to a PC, that is. That's when you run head-first into terms like "COM ports," "FireWire," "USB," and "TWAIN." On the plus side, this chapter has the answers to all your questions about these confusing topics.

Once you get your images stored on a PC, the fun begins. Eventually, you're sure to run out of hard-disk space, and so this chapter covers alternate storage solutions and installing a second hard disk. You'll also find more mundane topics here, like estimating the size of image files and understanding the myriad file formats.

CAMERA MEMORY

 ### What kinds of graphics formats will my camera use to store pictures?

Most digital cameras store images in a format known as JPEG (pronounced "jay-peg"). On PCs, files stored in JPEG format have a file extension of .JPG. The JPEG format is a common and versatile one, and is usually used to store photographic-quality images as opposed to line art or hand-drawn graphics.

JPEG is a popular format because it compresses images significantly. This is great on a device like a digital camera that has limited space in which to store graphics. Since you can set the level of JPEG compression to 10:1, 20:1, or even 100:1 or higher, a 200K file might only be 20K—or even 2K—after conversion to the JPEG format.

JPEG has a downside, too, though: It is a "lossy" format (as opposed to "lossless"), since the compression process also reduces the file's data, making it an imperfect copy of the original. Usually, this reduction is hardly noticeable, but it is possible to compress a JPEG image so much that the resulting graphic is horribly distorted (see Figure 10-1).

If your camera lets you choose different quality levels when taking pictures, it is the level of JPEG compression that you are actually setting. The higher the quality, the less the image is compressed. In most cases you can set the camera to use high or medium quality without any obvious changes in the image. But avoid telling the camera to use the greatest level of compression—the lowest quality—unless you really need the storage space on your camera. Low quality is obvious since the edges in the image become jagged and you can sometimes even see large chunks of color instead of smooth changes from one part of the image to another.

While most cameras use JPEG compression, a few cameras use the TIFF format instead. TIFF is a format that can preserve every pixel of the original image without loss—but the files are large, too. You can find out what format your camera uses by looking at the specifications in your user's manual.

Figure 10-1 JPEG compression can create artifacts and distortion, so use low compression ratios when possible

 ## How much memory does my camera have?

This depends upon your specific camera—they're all different—but in general you can expect at least 2MB of memory. That'll get you a few dozen pictures at standard resolution, enough for most average photographers. Here's a short guide to the memory that comes with some popular cameras. Keep in mind that cameras that come with memory cards can always be upgraded to use larger cards.

Camera	Memory
Canon PowerShot 350	2MB card
Epson PhotoPC 700	4MB internal, memory card optional
Nikon CoolPix 900	4MB card
Ricoh RDC-300	4MB internal
Sony Mavica	1.44MB floppy disk

As you can see from this table, the real question is whether your camera has built-in memory, a removable memory card, or some combination thereof.

If your camera has internal memory only, then once you fill it up, you need to delete pictures or download them to your PC. If it's equipped with removable memory cards only, your camera can't take any pictures unless there's a card

inserted. Once it's full, you can pop out the card and insert another, like changing a roll of film, to continue shooting. The most versatile cameras, however, offer a combination of the two—you can use the internal memory till it's full, then pop in a memory card and use it. When that card is full, then you can swap another in its place.

Can I upgrade the memory in my camera?

Since the memory in your camera is like a film cartridge—the bigger it is, the more pictures you can take in a single session—it makes sense that you might someday want to install more memory in the camera. After all, it's no fun to always be tied to a 12-exposure roll of film!

If you have a digital camera with nothing but internal memory—that is, no ability to insert memory cards—then unfortunately, you're forever locked into whatever amount of memory the camera came with. No current camera manufacturer offers the capability to upgrade a camera's internal memory.

If your camera uses memory cards, whether they're in PC Card, Compact Flash, or SmartMedia format, then you're in luck: Not only can you swap out these memory modules in favor of fresh replacements (not unlike changing rolls of film), you can also get bigger memory cards. You may, for instance, have gotten a 4MB Smart Media card with your camera. But when you want to get another, there's no reason why you can't slide a 16MB card into your camera instead. The only limits are cost—large-capacity memory cards can get expensive—and the current limits of technology (the largest cards are about 64MB right now).

Can I damage my memory card by dropping it?

Not easily. If you're using the most common kinds of memory cards for digital cameras (like SmartMedia, Compact Flash, or floppy disk), then a drop from even six or eight feet won't affect it. I don't recommend that you drop it, step on it, and

jump up and down on it, of course. But the reality is that these memory cards are hard to damage.

The only kind of memory I'd be concerned about is the PC Card. Such memory systems aren't designed to be rugged, and you can break them if you're too rough. This is particularly true of PC Card hard drives, such as you'll encounter in high-end cameras. Be gentle.

 ### I have a PC Card hard drive and it gets very hot. Is this normal?

Yes, PC Card hard drives are exactly what they sound like: tiny little hard disks that have to spin very fast and be read by the same kind of read/write heads as the hard disk in your computer. Use a PC Card hard disk for a while and it'll get very, very hot—almost too hot to handle with your bare hands. The PC Card is okay, but be careful that the heat doesn't make you drop it, since you can damage the drive if you handle it too roughly.

How many times can I use my memory card? Does it wear out like a set of batteries?

Thankfully, your camera's SmartMedia or Compact Flash memory card will simply not wear out. You can read and write to it more times than anyone is ever likely to try and it'll keep on ticking, if you'll pardon the expression. So don't worry about overusing it; you can't.

The same can't be said for floppy disks and PC Card hard drives, which are mechanical systems (unlike memory cards, these storage devices have moving parts). They will, without a doubt, wear out. That's why I suggest that users of the Sony Mavica (the camera that uses floppy disks for storage) always carry a small collection of floppy disks. Even if you only expect to need a single disk, spares protect you from write errors.

A hard disk will last a long time—five years or more—but if you've had your current PC Card hard disk for several years and you use it frequently, it pays to replace it before you get stuck in the field with a failure.

The Mavica's floppy-disk storage looks very attractive. Is there a catch?

Of course. There always is. The Sony Mavica can store a dozen or so images on a floppy disk, and you can then insert the floppy into your PC and read the images immediately. On the other hand, as camera resolution improves, floppy disks quickly look unattractive. After all, a single high-resolution image can take up over a megabyte of space, the entire capacity of a floppy. Floppies are also slow, extending the lag between photo opportunities. If you can live with the compromises, floppy storage is convenient—but little more.

I've seen the term "SSFDC" used for some digital camera memory. What is it?

SSFDC is short for "solid state floppy disk card," and it's another name for SmartMedia memory cards. SmartMedia, together with Compact Flash, are among the most common storage media for digital cameras.

What's the difference between Compact Flash and SmartMedia?

There's a format war taking place right now between these two competing formats. These memory modules are both about the same physical size (see Figure 10-2) and come in the same capacities. So why are there two?

The fact is that they're very similar, though they're championed by different companies and work somewhat differently. Here is a comparison of the two formats:

SmartMedia	Compact Flash
Requires a special controller chip in the camera, making it slightly more expensive	Potential for higher capacity than SmartMedia
Thinner, with exposed connector pins—and thus more susceptible to damage	Thicker than SmartMedia
Installed base of existing digital cameras is large	Installed base of existing digital cameras is large

Figure 10-2   SmartMedia and Compact Flash memory are both used in today's digital cameras

The most compelling difference is the fact that SmartMedia is a "dumb" memory chip that requires the camera to include a controller chip. While that can make the memory itself cheaper, the result is that in some cases your camera can't read new, larger-format SmartMedia cards. Compact Flash, on the other hand, has its own controller chip in each card and is both forward- and backward-compatible. Compact Flash seems the smarter choice when buying a digital camera.

 Is there an emerging standard for camera memory? Should I get a camera with a particular kind so I don't end up buying the camera equivalent of a Beta VCR?

No, there's no clear winner emerging. Table 10-1 lists the kinds of memory used by 15 popular cameras. You can see that the field is mostly split between SmartMedia and Compact Flash, with just a few cameras using a different kind of memory.

Camera	Memory Type
Agfa ePhoto 1280	SmartMedia
Agfa ePhoto 307	Internal only
Apple Quicktake 200	SmartMedia
Canon PowerShot 350	Compact Flash
Casio QV-11	Compact Flash
Casio QV-300	Internal only
Epson Photo PC 600	Compact Flash
Fuji DS-8	SmartMedia
Kodak DCS 210	Compact Flash
Konica Q-mini	Compact Flash
Minolta Dimage V	SmartMedia
Nikon CoolPix 300	Internal only
Nikon CoolPix 900	Compact Flash
Olympus D600l	SmartMedia
Ricoh RDC-300	Internal only
Sony Mavica	1.44MB floppy

Table 10-1 Memory Types of Popular Cameras

This much is true: There are distinct advantages to each kind of storage medium, so buy the one that's appropriate for your needs. The Mavica, for instance, is ideal for point-and-shoot photographers who want an easy way to transfer their low-resolution images to a PC. Between Compact Flash and SmartMedia, however, Compact Flash seems to have an edge over SmartMedia since the former is more compatible (see "What's the difference between Compact Flash and SmartMedia?" earlier in this chapter). And beware of internal-only memory. I recommend you buy a camera that lets you grow.

TRANSFER METHODS

 ### How do I connect my camera to my computer?

Most digital cameras come with a serial connection. Since Macintosh computers and PCs have the serial port in

common, camera manufacturers know that they can make a
serial cable system for their camera and it'll work with both
kinds of computers.

To connect your camera to your PC, just find the serial
port on the back of your computer and plug in the serial cable
that accompanied your camera. The serial port is fairly
forgiving, but it's best if you turn your computer off before
plugging in the serial cable. Likewise, make sure the
computer is off before you unplug the serial cable.

Take the other end of the cable and plug it into the correct
port on your camera. You'll also need to turn your camera on
and set it to the correct mode; usually, that's either a special
"PC" setting or just the "Playback" position (see Figure 10-3).

Your camera may use a different kind of connection than
a standard serial port. Some cameras use a SCSI (Small
Computer Serial Interface) connector; SCSI is common on the
Mac but a fairly uncommon optional accessory on PCs,
though it's sometimes used on PCs to connect scanners and
additional hard drives. If your camera uses a SCSI connector,
it will probably come with the necessary SCSI card, which
you'll need to install in an empty expansion slot in your PC.

Other connection alternatives include USB and FireWire.
USB (universal serial bus) is a new connection found on many
new PCs. It's easy to use—just plug the cable into the USB
port and connect the other end to the camera. USB will never
generate the cryptic error messages that are too common with

Figure 10-3 You need to set your camera to the correct mode so it can communicate with your PC

other PC ports. FireWire (a FireWire connector is shown in Figure 10-4) is a close cousin of USB, but it is not built into new PCs—you'll need to buy a FireWire card and install it in your PC. From there, it works very much like USB.

 What if the camera's serial cable won't fit my serial port?

Get an adapter. There are two different kinds of serial ports: a small 9-pin port and a longer 25-pin one. They both work the same way, and it may be that your computer has the older 25-pin variety.

Most digital camera cables come with connectors for the newer 9-pin port, but it's entirely possible the camera included an adapter in the box—fish around and check. If not, drop into your local computer store and get a 25-pin-to-9-pin adapter. They tend to be inexpensive.

Tip: *You might even already have a serial adapter from another product you've bought, like a modem or mouse. Don't worry, they're 100% interchangeable.*

Your Computer's Ports

If you're not an old hand at working on your computer, the back of the PC may be a confusing and intimidating array of connectors. Use this diagram to find the serial, USB, and other important ports on the back of your computer. Remember that the ports may be in different locations on your PC, but their sizes and shapes will always be the same.

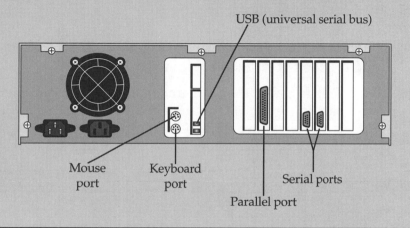

USB (universal serial bus)

Mouse port

Keyboard port

Serial ports

Parallel port

Figure 10-4 FireWire is a very fast connection method for high-end digital cameras

 Do I need to install the software that came with my camera?

Yes, you need to install the necessary drivers to transfer images from the camera to your PC. Without that software, your camera can't chat with the PC at all. However, not all the software you get with a camera is necessary: Some of it is graphics editing software, photo album software, or even Internet access programs. Read the setup screens carefully to tell which software is optional, particularly if you're low on hard-disk space.

 My camera's setup program wants to know what COM port it's using. How do I know?

This is easier than it sounds. Most digital cameras I've used can figure this out on their own, but in case they leave it up to you, here are some rules of thumb you can use to determine what COM port is available:

If you plugged it into:	It's probably using:
The small, 9-pin serial port in back of the PC	COM1
The only serial port in back of the PC, regardless of size	COM1
The big, 25-pin serial port in back of the PC	COM2

Your computer may also have a COM3 and a COM4; they're usually assigned to serial ports on expansion cards installed internally within your PC.

These are not universal, hard-and-fast rules—if all else fails, experiment and see what works!

 Tip: *Write down in your PC manual (or here in this book) what each of your COM ports is doing. That makes it easier to install new serial hardware like your camera later.*

 I connected my camera and tried transferring pictures, but all I got was an error message!

There are a few reasons why you might get errors. Check out all these possibilities, and you can track down the problem pretty quickly:

- Make sure the cable is securely connected to both the computer and the camera.

- Turn the camera on and be sure it is set to the correct mode for transferring images.

- Make sure there isn't another program running that's tying up the serial port. You might have a fax-modem program incorrectly set to control the camera's serial port, waiting for an incoming fax. Another possibility is that you have a PalmPilot with the Hotsynch software watching the serial port for a connection.

- If all else fails, quit the program that is trying to transfer camera images and restart it. If something had hold of the serial port, the program may need to be completely refreshed before it will work.

 Why do my pictures transfer to the PC so slowly?

This isn't the fault of the camera. Serial transfers in particular are fairly slow, and the camera may not take full advantage of the serial port's speed. If that's the case, transfers will be even slower. You can speed up your transfers in a couple of ways:

- If your camera uses removable memory cards, get a card reader (see "Is there a way to insert a memory card directly into my PC?" later in this chapter). They're usually faster than the serial port and have the added benefit of not tying up your camera throughout the transfer.

- If your camera is compatible with an alternative transfer method—like SCSI, FireWire, or USB—upgrade to that. They're all much faster than serial.

 How do I actually get the pictures into my PC?

The transfer process is similar no matter what kind of transfer system your particular camera uses. Most cameras use a TWAIN driver (see Chapter 4 for an explanation of TWAIN) to enable you to move images from the camera to your PC. Here's the process:

1. Turn your PC off.
2. Attach the cable to the camera and computer as described earlier in "How do I connect my camera to my computer?"
3. Restart your PC.
4. Turn on your camera and set it to the appropriate mode, if necessary. Sometimes there's a special PC mode; other cameras simply need to be in playback mode. If you have an AC adapter, connect it to your camera to conserve battery power.
5. Start the transfer software that accompanied your camera and choose the images you want to transfer.

Keep in mind that your mileage may very. If you use a Mavica, for instance, just insert your floppy into the PC and copy the images from the disk. Or perhaps your camera uses a PC Card memory system. If that's the case, you can probably remove the card, insert it in a notebook PC, and read the data from there.

 Do I have to use the graphics program that came with my camera?

No, usually not. Almost all cameras use a TWAIN driver to control the transfer process (see Chapter 4 for more about TWAIN), so any graphics program that understands TWAIN is compatible with your camera. Some common programs that work with most digital cameras include Corel PhotoPaint, Jasc Paint Shop Pro, Adobe Photoshop, and Adobe PhotoDeluxe. Here's all you need to do to switch to the program of your choice:

1. Start the program, like Paint Shop Pro, that you want to use.

2. Choose File | Select Source. The resulting dialog box allows you to choose the TWAIN driver for your camera.

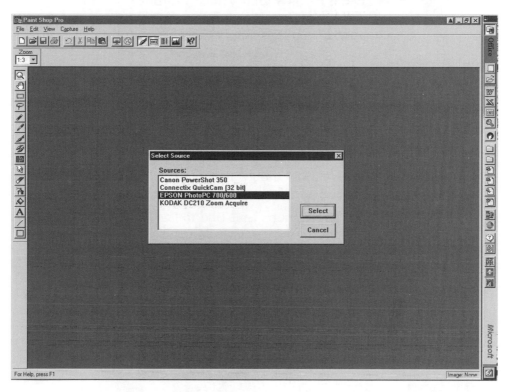

3. Double-click on the driver for your camera. There may be more than one driver in the list, particularly if you also have a scanner attached to your PC.

4. Choose File | Acquire. The transfer program for your camera will start. Choose the image(s) you want to move to the PC, and they'll open in your graphics program.

 Note: *A very few digital cameras use proprietary transfer software that is not compatible with Windows' TWAIN system. If that's the case with your camera, then you really are stuck with whatever came in the camera box.*

 Is there a way to insert a memory card directly into my PC?

One of the advantages of using SmartMedia or Compact Flash cards is that you can remove the media from your camera and read the data directly into your computer. Of course, you'll probably need some additional hardware called a *card reader* (see Figure 10-5). Card readers typically plug into your parallel port (see the sidebar "Your Computer's Ports" earlier) and accept one or more cards. By reading the cards through a card reader, you gain several advantages:

- Images are usually read faster than they are via the camera and the serial port.

- No more dangling cable from the serial port, freeing up the port for something else (like a modem or PalmPilot).

- The camera isn't tied to the computer; you can go take pictures with it while you're transferring images from the memory card.

- If you don't have an AC adapter for your camera, the card reader enables you to avoid draining camera batteries just to transfer images.

Figure 10-5   A card reader can transfer the data in a memory card through the parallel port more quickly than it can be transferred through the computer's serial port

There are numerous card readers on the market. The ActionTec CameraConnect has two slots, one for Compact Flash and the other for PC Cards (it can also read SmartMedia with an appropriate adapter). Likewise, SanDisk (a manufacturer of Compact Flash memory cards) offers the ImageMate card reader.

STORING PICTURES ON YOUR PC

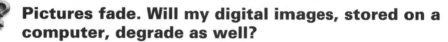

Pictures fade. Will my digital images, stored on a computer, degrade as well?

Yes and no. Digital data doesn't degrade in the same sense that print documents like photographs do, but data loss can occur. Depending upon the storage medium—like floppy disk or hard disk—your data will start to experience file errors after a number of years. That's why it's a good idea to make backups and not rely indefinitely on a single source for important data. You can generally get five to ten years of error-free data retrieval from a hard disk, and more (as much as 200 years) from a CD-ROM.

What graphics format should I save my pictures in?

The graphics format that you should use for your images depends in large part on how you intend to use your pictures. Most folks who have been working with computer images for a while have their own favorites, and they instinctively save their images in the correct format based on the project they're working on. Others have never really learned the right format to use, and tend to use the same format for everything even if it's an awful choice.

Don't stick to a particular format just for the sake of using the using same format all the time—you'll come to regret it. Here's an overview of the most common formats and what they're used for:

● **JPEG** This format was discussed in "What kinds of graphics formats will my camera use to store pictures?" earlier in this chapter. In a nutshell, JPEG is a lossy format that, when set to a high-quality compression mode,

balances image quality with file size. When compressed
too much, though, the image can look unattractive. JPEG
is commonly used on the Web and in e-mail since it
enables a colorful photo to be downloaded fairly quickly.

● **TIFF**   TIFF is a very popular image format because it can
easily be read by both PCs and Macintoshes, and because it
can be compressed without losing any image quality. To
compress a TIFF image, use the LZW compression option
in your graphics program when saving. TIFF's major
disadvantage is that uncompressed images can be
big—very big—and TIFF isn't used on the Web for that
reason. Use TIFF if you plan to work on an image later and
want to fully preserve all the image's details.

● **FlashPix**   The FlashPix format is a new standard that is
still gaining acceptance in the industry. To appreciate
why FlashPix was designed, you need to understand what
it's like to view images on the Internet and in other
electronic media. There's always a compromise between
image quality and file size, and to zoom in and view a
detail of a Web graphic, for instance, means you'll
generally look at a pixilated, ugly mess. FlashPix,
however, stores several versions of a graphic in the same
file: a low-resolution one that downloads quickly, and
successively higher-resolution versions underneath,
arranged like a pyramid, that can be displayed if the
viewer tries to see more detail (see Figure 10-6). This
same principle enables you to edit a large, detailed image
without loading a huge graphic into memory. Right now,
only a few programs use FlashPix (like LivePix and
PhotoDeluxe), and the image isn't supported by Web
browsers (though you can display FlashPix images with a
plug-in).

● **BMP**   This is the old standard format for Windows
users. It can be used for general-purpose storage, for
image editing, and as the wallpaper on your Windows
desktop, but it isn't always readable by Macintoshes, and
BMP files tend to be large. It isn't supported on the Web,
either. In general, the BMP format only makes sense

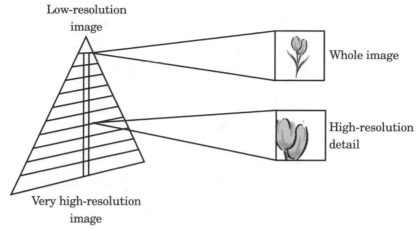

Low-resolution
image

Whole image

High-resolution
detail

Very high-resolution
image

Figure 10-6 FlashPix images store several versions of an image in
varying levels of resolution

these days for storing images that will be used exclusively
within Windows, such as for wallpaper.

- **GIF** Originally developed by CompuServe, the GIF
  format is commonly used on the Web, alongside JPEG.
  GIF has a few advantages over JPEG on the Web: You
  can make the background transparent, you can make
  your image display in "interlace" mode (that is, in chunks,
  so the viewer can get an overall impression of the picture
  before it's done loading), and you can reduce the image
  down to just a few colors. If your picture only has a few
  colors to begin with, saving it as a 16-color GIF can make
  it download very quickly.

How do I know what format my pictures are currently stored in?

Each graphics formats has a corresponding filename
extension. Every file on your PC has a three-letter extension,
like .DOC (a Microsoft Word file) or .TXT (a plain text file).
Graphics files typically end in .TIF, .BMP, .GIF, and .JPG. To
see the filename extension, right-click on a file and choose
Properties from the menu. You'll see the entire filename,
including the extension.

 ## How much space will my images take up?

Each graphic on your hard disk takes up a certain amount of space based on its overall size and the color depth it contains. To calculate the maximum file size of a graphic, use this handy formula:

$$File\ size = \frac{Width \times height \times color\ depth}{8}$$

In other words, multiply the number of pixels in your image by the color depth and divide by eight, as in this example of a low-resolution image from a typical digital camera:

$$\frac{640 \times 480 \times 24}{8} = 921{,}600\ bytes$$

That's just under a megabyte, though JPEG compression will reduce that file size significantly—probably down to about 70K or less. This equation tells you the *maximum* size any image can be before compression, a handy thing to know if you're low on disk space.

 ## What is color depth?

When we talk about color depth we're talking about how many colors any particular pixel in an image is capable of displaying. Color depth is usually measured in bits per pixel, as in a 24-bit image. A one-bit image is capable of displaying two colors: The pixels can essentially be turned on or off. Original Macintosh graphics are an example of one-bit imagery—rather than displaying true grayscale, each pixel could be either black or white and the impression of gray could only be achieved by "dithering" lots of pixels in a varying black-and-white pattern.

Two-bit color is actually four colors (in this mode, each pixel can have four states), and 24-bit color is the threshold of human color perception, with 16.7 million possible colors.

It's an important distinction that a 24-bit image doesn't necessarily show all 16 million colors—there aren't enough pixels on the screen to do that. Instead, when we talk about 24-bit color depth what we're saying is that each pixel has the

opportunity to display any one of the 16 million colors visible to humans, and that's what makes the image photorealistic. All digital cameras capture images in 24-bit color, but you can later reduce the number of colors in an image to save space or let the image download faster on the Web (see Figure 10-7).

Table 10-2 shows some common color depths and what they are used for.

Is there a way to save space so my pictures won't fill up my whole hard disk?

Running low on disk space? You can sometimes save some disk space by managing your images and their file formats. Try some of these tricks of the trade:

- Save your graphics in the most compact format possible. Compressed TIFF is okay, but JPEG will always be better. BMP is among the worst offenders for wasting disk space.

- Use a compression program like Zip to compress your images. This works well on "fat" file formats like BMP and uncompressed TIFF, but generates little or no space savings on files that are already compressed (like JPEG). You can zip a whole bunch of graphics together at once, or compress each one individually.

Figure 10-7 The left image was taken with a digital camera in 24-bit color. It was then reduced to 256 colors (center) and again to 16 colors (right)

Bits per Pixel	Colors	Application
1	2	Original Macs; line-art mode for faxes
4	16	Simple grayscale
8	256	256-shade grayscale or simple color; good for showing color photos on the Web
16	65,536	High-color mode; looks almost as good as true color; a common computer monitor setting
24	16,777,216	True color; generally the threshold of human perception
32	4,294,967,296	Beyond human perception; good for image editing and computer analysis

Table 10-2   Common Color Depths and Their Applications

 Search your hard disk for multiple versions of the same image saved in different formats. Often, you'll save an image from your camera first in JPEG, for instance, but later save it as a TIFF in your image editing program. You don't need both; delete one.

How much effort is it to add a new hard disk to my computer?

If you're always running out of hard-disk space, one option you may want to consider is actually installing a new hard disk. Hard disks are inexpensive, but they typically require you to crack open the computer case and work inside the guts of your PC. You can pay a computer shop a few dollars, or you can do it yourself—it's really not that hard. If you want to try it yourself, pick up a copy of *Upgrading & Repairing Your PC Answers!* (Osborne/McGraw-Hill, 1998) and refer to Chapter 8, which has detailed information on replacing and adding hard disks. For a brief overview of hard disk installation, check out the following section.

How do I add a hard disk?

You'll need to do a little PC surgery to install a hard disk, but it isn't that hard. After you install your new drive, you can have three to five gigabytes or more of virgin hard disk for storing digital camera images. But use common sense—work with the PC powered off, ground yourself, and work slowly and carefully.

Tip: *Always have an emergency boot diskette on hand before performing a hard-drive installation. If you don't have that diskette (or at least a boot diskette for DOS or Windows), you may not be able to boot your computer again to format, partition, or test the drive.*

First, here are some preliminaries you need to get out of the way before you install your new drive:

● Open the case and make sure you have a free drive bay, and that the hard-drive controller's ribbon cable will reach the new drive comfortably. (If you already have a hard drive installed, notice whether or not there's a drive bay that can accept the second hard drive near the first one.) If the currently available bay isn't a good fit, decide whether you're going to move the existing drive so it can be closer or get a new ribbon cable.

● Also, make sure the bay you choose for your new drive is the right size. Any new hard drive is probably a 3.5-inch half-height drive; if you're installing a 3.5-inch drive in a 5.25-inch bay, you'll need an adapter kit.

● Next, make sure you don't need any special rails or other devices to hold your drive in place. Most hard drives are installed in internal bays—since there's nothing to remove, it's best to keep hard drives in these interior bays so you'll have plenty of expansion room for removable drives, floppies, and CD-ROM drives.

● If this will be the second drive in your system, determine which jumper is the "master/slave" jumper on your new drive. Set the jumper on your new drive so that it will be the "slave," which should make it drive D in your setup.

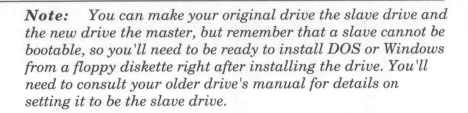

Note: *You can make your original drive the slave drive and the new drive the master, but remember that a slave cannot be bootable, so you'll need to be ready to install DOS or Windows from a floppy diskette right after installing the drive. You'll need to consult your older drive's manual for details on setting it to be the slave drive.*

● Finally, make sure you have an available power adapter for the new drive. If not, you'll need a splitter to allow one existing power adapter to be used for two drives.

Now, with the preliminaries out of the way, here's how you add a hard drive:

1. Shut down the computer and remove the case.

2. Ground yourself frequently by touching the computer's power supply cage.

3. If you're replacing a drive, remove the original drive. If you're not replacing an older drive, simply locate the existing IDE drive ribbon cable and an available power cable.

4. If your case requires rails, install those now. Take care that you install them in the right orientation on either side of the drive.

Note: *Your drive may also require a special cage or mounting kit to change it from 3.5-inches to 5.25-inches wide. Install that kit now if necessary.*

5. Slide the drive into the exposed bay. Stop sliding when it's fully in and locked (using rails) or until the drive is correctly positioned and aligned with the screw holes in the case (without rails).

6. Connect the ribbon cable and the power cable to the drive. If this drive is drive C, it should use the end connector on the ribbon; for drive D, use the middle connector.

Tip: *Usually, ribbon cables can only fit one way on the drive. If you find your cable will connect to the drive either way, examine the drive for little numbers at each end of the connector. The side with the low numbers should be connected to the side of the ribbon cable that has a colored stripe. Power cables only fit one way—if it doesn't seem it fit, turn it over.*

7. Screw the drive into place. If it's inserted correctly, the drive should line up with any holes in your PC that can accept screws to hold the drive in place.

8. Replace the case on the computer.

Now you're ready to test the drive. Turn on your computer. You should see both hard drives acknowledged during the boot process. If you don't, then restart the PC, bring up the BIOS setup program and enter the appropriate values for the new drive.

Once your computer gets through the boot process, you should get one beep as usual, followed by the configuration table that appears along with the "Starting Windows" message. Check that table and ensure that your drive appears.

If you've installed a new master drive, you may need to boot from a floppy diskette—either an emergency diskette or the first diskette for DOS or Windows. From there you can format and partition the drive, then install the operating system.

How do I tell my original hard disk that I've installed a second one?

This is done using the "master/slave" jumpers on your hard drives. Your C drive should be set to be the master, and any subsequent drives should be slaves. Note that only a master drive is bootable, so install DOS or Windows on a master drive. Consult your drive's manual for info on the correct jumper settings.

If you have a PC with two EIDE connectors, it can be confusing to determine whether you need to rig your drive as a master or a slave. Keep in mind that your new drive can be either a master or a slave depending upon which EIDE connector you connect it to. If you connect the drive to the same connector as the first drive using a single ribbon cable, then they have a master/slave relationship. If you connect the drive to the other EIDE connector, however, and it's using a ribbon cable all by itself, then both drives are masters.

Other Storage Options

You don't need to install a new hard disk to get extra storage space for your PC. There are a variety of removable media around these days that you can add to your computer. But this much is certain: You will, eventually, want more space. Even small 50K images from your camera will start to accumulate like sand on a beach in your PC, and expanding your storage options can help keep you from pruning them too severely. Here are some options to consider:

- **Zip** The Iomega Zip drive is perhaps the single most common removable storage solution on the market today. Zip drives hold 100MB of data on each cartridge, and they're easy to trade with friends and co-workers, since it seems almost everyone has one these days. The parallel version is slow, though, and 100MB is starting to look a bit limiting.

- **LS-120** Sometimes called the SuperDisk, the LS-120 is a 120MB alternative to the traditional floppy disk. It has slightly more capacity than Zip and the same drive can read both LS-120 and regular floppies. Downside: Few people use this format, so you can't exchange disks as easily.

- **Removable hard disks** The computer stores are packed with high-capacity drives that store 2Gb or more on a single cartridge. The Iomega Jaz 2, for instance, is a fast, convenient drive that falls into the 2Gb/disk category. You can also use these systems for hard-disk backup, making them useful for more than just storing your pictures.

- **CD-ROM** You can get a writable CD-ROM drive for just a little more than a plain, read-only CD-ROM these days. Since each CD holds about 650MB of data, you can pack a lot of images onto a single disc. Most of the disadvantages of CD-R are gone now, including formerly expensive blank discs. But watch out—some CD drives can't read CD-R discs, particularly early DVD drives.

Chapter 11

Image Editing

Answer Topics!

Image Editing @ a Glance

One of the principal advantages of using a digital camera is the flexibility it gives you in processing images. Don't like the composition? Change it. Too dark? Brighten it. All you need to turn good images into stunning ones is an image editing program and this book. But before you dive in, get your questions about software, computer requirements, and imaging terminology answered here.

Look in this chapter for tips on making some of the most common adjustments to your images, like cropping, size adjustments, and color depth changes.

This chapter also has tips on using your computer like a traditional darkroom for changes like color adjustments, dodging and burning, and sharpness improvements. Not only can you modify digital images, you can scan old photos and edit those, too.

It's rare that you need to make global changes that affect your entire picture. That's why tools like selection areas and masks exist. This chapter explains how to use them and when to use one instead of the other.

301

EDITING BASICS

 Note: *Almost any image editing software can accomplish the sorts of tasks discussed in this chapter. But since it isn't feasible to explain how to use all of the many programs on the market, I've chosen Paint Shop Pro from Jasc Software to answer questions in which a particular technique is demonstrated. I chose PSP for several reasons: It's inexpensive, you can download it from the Internet, and its features are representative of those in many other paint and editing programs. You can get a copy of Paint Shop Pro yourself from Jasc Software. Their Web site is at http://www.jasc.com.*

What kinds of changes can I make to a digital image after the picture has been taken?

Compared to what's possible in traditional, film-based photography, the power you have over your digital photographs is incredible. Not only can you change the composition of your picture by cropping it, you can brighten, darken, change the color balance, and perform a myriad of other, more obscure modifications on your pictures. You can add text, superimpose other pictures, add borders—the list goes on and on.

Sure, you could do a lot of this with your old film camera, but it would take a darkroom and a fair bit of technical know-how. Thanks to image editing software, you can edit your images in almost any way imaginable with little more than a low-cost image editor and this book.

What kind of software should I use to edit my images?

Almost any image editing program will do. Your camera probably came with a program that you can use to edit images; common ones include PhotoDeluxe, Photoshop LE, iPhoto Plus, PhotoImpact, and Canon Creative. Other imaging devices, like printers and scanners, also sometimes come with this sort of software. No matter what the source, these programs will work with your digital images.

If your camera came with such a program, try it out and see if it works the way you want it to. They will all get the job done, but as with any computer program, you may prefer something different. There are many graphics programs on the market, and some are easily downloadable from the Internet—at least in trial form. Unless you're perfectly happy with what you already have (and one way to find out is to experiment with its tools and features), there's no harm in trying alternatives.

 I run out of memory a lot when working with images. Do I need more than 32MB of memory?

You're probably being warned about insufficient hard-disk space, not random access memory (RAM). RAM is the

How Much Computer Do You Need?

While the computer industry would love to sell you the biggest, fastest computer around, odds are good that you don't need that kind of power just to do some image editing. We've reached the point where processor speeds are only making incremental improvements in your computer's overall performance, and today's software usually doesn't need 400 MHz Pentium II muscle anyway. But what do you need? Here's a solid image editing platform:

- 166 MHz Pentium processor or higher
- 32MB RAM (though I'd really recommend 64MB—you can double your memory for $100, and it's really worth it)
- Video display capable of showing 65,000 colors at 1024×768 pixels
- A PC with two external serial ports so you can connect a camera plus another peripheral

As for image storage, this is where I wouldn't compromise—if you really get into digital photography, you'll want a large hard disk (or two hard disks). 6Gb worth of hard disk is probably the smallest storage I'd want to work with.

memory—usually 16, 32, or 64MB—that your computer uses to store open programs, do calculations, and manage its housekeeping tasks. The hard disk, on the other hand, is like a filing cabinet that holds all your programs, data, and digital images.

While it's possible that you can run out of RAM, it isn't likely. Hard-disk space is a much more precious resource, since Windows uses empty space on the drive to serve as additional RAM. This is called a *swap file,* and if you run out of swap file space, your program can't complete its task. You can also run out of hard-disk space when saving new images on your computer or making changes to those images in an editing program.

The answer? Additional RAM is never a bad thing, but your hard disk is likely to give out first. Here's how to check on the health of your hard disk:

1. Open the My Computer icon on your desktop and right-click on your hard-disk icon.

2. Choose Properties. The Properties dialog box appears, displaying the amount of free space on the drive.

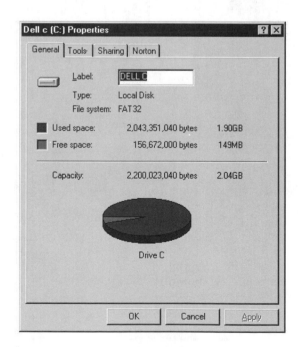

3. Repeat this process for any other drives or partitions on your computer.

 Tip: *When using any image editing program, try to keep at least 150MB of hard-disk space available at all times—the more the better, since image editors use lots of disk space while you work. Defragment the drive on a regular basis. Also close all your other applications to maximize your available memory.*

You can keep some free space on your hard disk by emptying the Recycling Bin often and discarding unused programs and data files. I explain in detail the many ways to keep your hard disk lean in *Upgrading & Repairing Your PC Answers!* (Osborne/McGraw-Hill, 1998).

 What if I make changes to an image and I don't like the result?

Experiment to your heart's content! If you do something you don't like, then you can always use the undo tool to go back to

Defragmenting Your Hard Disk

It's important to keep your hard disk error-free and fully defragmented, especially if you frequently work with large files like digital images. As you write data to your hard disk, the drive begins to run out of large blocks of empty space in which to store information. As a result, your drive gets *fragmented* and a single file might be broken up and stored in lots of little empty spaces all over your drive. The result is that your computer slows down—it takes longer to load files since they're broken up all over your hard disk.

Defragmentation software moves the data on your drive around to keep all the empty space in one place. That way you can store new files in a single place instead of in lots of little empty digital cubbyholes. You can learn a lot more about how to care for your drive by reading *Upgrading & Repairing Your PC Answers!* (Osborne/McGraw-Hill, 1998).

the state you were in before. Some programs have multiple levels of undo, and others only let you undo a single action. Either way, it's a failsafe to get you backward at least one step.

Of course, any change you make to your image isn't permanent until you save the file, so your original image is still safe on the hard disk even if you mangle the version you're working with in your image editing program beyond recognition; just close the image without saving it. (Some programs offer a Revert option to enable you to return to the saved version without closing.)

 Tip: *When you're making changes to an image, save the file with a different name. That way you'll still have both versions in the future.*

 Should I use the Wizards and one-step editing tools in my graphics software?

There's no harm in trying them out. Many programs have Wizards and other similar tools for fixing problems in your pictures. They work great for some purposes, like for eliminating red eye. But other processes don't quite do what you would expect, or introduce their own problems, like throwing your brightness and contrast out of whack. Bottom line: Try them, use them when they work, but don't rely on them. Learn the procedures explained in this chapter and Chapter 12 so you can do it yourself.

My graphics program has "layers" in it. What are they for?

Layers are described in more detail in Chapter 12. They add a three-dimensional aspect to your image by letting you stack images, text, graphics, and other elements of a picture on top of each other, like sheets of paper. With layers, however, you can vary the level of transparency in each layer, allowing certain ones to show through to varying degrees. It's a fun and powerful feature, but not all graphics programs have it.

Image Editing Glossary

Brightness	On the surface, the definition of brightness is obvious. But in a color image, different pixels can have the same brightness even if their actual color is different; that is, they'll appear equally bright even if one pixel is gray and another is blue. In this context, brightness is also known as luminance.
Contrast	Contrast is the range of brightness between different pixels. In an image, contrast is measured by evaluating how the pixels are spread out in a luminance distribution. A high-contrast image would have lots of bright pixels and lots of dark pixels.
Filter	A filter is graphics-speak for a tool that allows you to edit or manipulate your image. It's called a filter because a specific mathematical process is performed on your image, filtering the original data and delivering a modified image. An example of a filter is Sharpening, which adds contrast to the pixels in an image, increasing the apparent sharpness.
Gamma	Gamma adjustments have a greater effect on the midtones of an image than on the extreme bright and dark regions. Gamma is handy for brightening an image without washing out shadow regions, for instance.
Pixel	Pixel stands for "picture element." It's the smallest complete unit of information in a picture, and it appears as a dot on the screen or printed on paper. Each pixel is actually composed of three color registers. By combining some quantity of red, green, and blue, the pixel takes on a particular color.
Resolution	The resolution of an image is its size in pixels, expressed as, say, 640x480 pixels.
Selection	A selection is the part of an image you're currently working with. You can use a selection tool in your graphics program to isolate just one part of the picture.

THE DIGITAL DARKROOM

 Why are there so many options when I save a file?

Most graphics programs offer at least four or five different file formats in which to save your images; other programs

offer many more. When the time comes to save your file, you need to decide what format to use. This is usually based on what you intend to do with the image.

If you're still editing the image, you should save it in the program's native format, which usually preserves layers, marks, palettes, and other details so you can later load the image and pick up where you left off. If you're done working on the file and ready to save it in a form to be used elsewhere, consider what you intend to do with the image. Look in Chapter 10 for a guide to the major file formats and what they're good for.

Even if you decide to save the image in GIF format instead of JPEG, though, you're still not done making decisions. Often, you can control some options within the file format. In Paint Shop Pro, for instance, you can get to these options in this way:

1. Choose File | Save As. The Save As dialog box appears.

2. Choose the file type you want to use to save your image from the Save as Type drop-down menu.

3. Click on the Options button. Choose the option you want to set and click OK.

If you don't know what the options do—or if you don't care—leave the options alone. The defaults are fine. But here are some of the most important options you can set for popular file formats:

● **FlashPix** You can set the level of compression. This affects the image quality. Files can also be saved uncompressed.

● **GIF** You can specify that files should be interlaced or noninterlaced. On the Web, interlaced images are first loaded in low resolution and then refined as more information is downloaded. You can also set whether GIFs are saved with or without a transparent color. This option only works on GIF version 89a.

- **JPEG**   You can set the level of compression. This affects the image quality. The default is low compression.
- **TIFF**   You can choose the compression scheme. The most common is LZW compression; files can also be saved uncompressed.

I want to post an image on my Web site. How do I reduce the image's file size?

While you *can* take a 640×480 pixel, 24-bit image and post it to a Web site, it's not a good idea. Such an image might be 40K or more in size, and that takes a while to download from the Internet. Instead, try to save your visitors some modem time by reducing the file's size. Try some of these options:

- Trim the image by cropping away nonessential parts of the picture. See "How do I crop an image to change its composition?" later in this chapter.
- Reduce the image's physical size by lowering its resolution. See "How do I make an image bigger or smaller?" later in this chapter.
- Reduce the image from 24-bit color to 256 colors (see "Can I change the number of colors in my image?" later in this chapter) and save it as a GIF.
- Save the image as a JPEG and compress it.

I took my picture sideways—how do I turn the image so it stands up straight?

This is one of the easiest edits you can perform on your digital images. Most programs have a command that lets you rotate your image 90 degrees to the left or right. In Paint Shop Pro, you can select Image|Rotate and choose the desired action from the resulting dialog box.

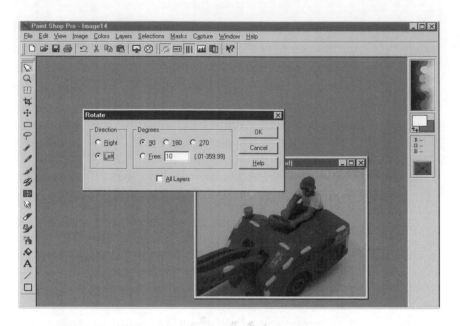

How do I make an image bigger or smaller?

Most image editors have a tool that allows you to resize an image, making it either bigger or smaller. To resize in Paint Shop Pro, do this:

1. Choose Image | Resize. The Resize dialog box appears.

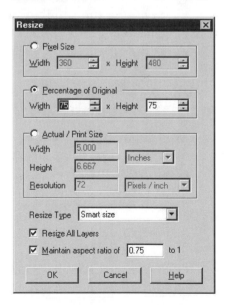

2. Make sure that the check box for "Maintain original aspect ratio" is selected. In most cases you'll want to keep the image's aspect ratio the same, or it will turn out stretched and distorted.

3. Enter the new dimensions for the image. You can enter it in pixels, as a percentage of the original image (like 40%, for instance), or in the actual print size (in inches, for instance). If you're keeping the aspect ratio the same, you'll only need to enter the new X or Y dimension, and the program will figure out the other dimension on its own.

4. Click OK.

Sometimes it can help to know what the actual size of your image currently is before you try to resize it. In Paint Shop Pro, that information is available from View | Image Information.

Tip: *Avoid increasing the size of your image. This reduces the resolution and makes your image look less sharp. If you increase the size too much, you can even see individual pixels in your image. Resizing works best when you need to make an image smaller.*

Can I change the number of colors in my image?

Absolutely! It's easy to drop the number of colors in an image, thus giving it a smaller file size. Likewise, there might be occasions when you want to take a 256-color image and save it in 24-bit format, making it easier to perform certain image editing operations on it.

Most image editors enable you to adjust the number of colors with a single menu selection. In Paint Shop Pro, you can reduce a digital camera image from 24 bit (16 million colors) to 256 colors by doing this:

1. Choose Colors | Reduce Color Depth | 256 Colors.

2. A dialog box appears that lets you decide how to reduce the colors. Choose Optimized Median Cut and Click OK. The Optimized option is almost always the best, but you can experiment with other settings if you want to.

   Tip: Want to know if your image will look acceptable at a lower color depth? Find out how many unique colors are actually being used in your picture by choosing Colors | Color Count Used.

 How do I zoom in and zoom out to work on my picture?

Sometimes you want to work on just part of an image, and it helps to be able to enlarge the display so all you see is what you're working on. Or perhaps you'd like to zoom out and see the entire image at once.

Either way, the zoom tool is a fairly universal feature in editing software. Just look for the magnifying glass in the toolbar, or look in the View menu for a zoom control. In Paint Shop Pro, you can select the magnifying glass and click on the image; every right-click zooms in and every left-click zooms out.

How do I crop an image to change its composition?

In the world of film photography, you'd have to make a trip to the photo shop and pay to make a new print based on your crop marks. Or just live with a picture you aren't perfectly happy with. But this is a digital image, and it's a piece of cake to cut away the parts of the image you don't like.

To crop your image, you'll need to use your image editing program's selection tool. Selection tools can often select

Using Cut and Paste

The cut and paste tools in your image editor work just the way you'd expect them to. Select a portion of your image and choose Edit|Cut, and that portion of the image is sliced out of your picture and sent to the clipboard. You can choose Edit|Paste to put the clip back somewhere else in your image, or into a new image of your choosing. Of course, you can also choose Edit|Copy to place a copy of the desired section in the clipboard, leaving the original intact.

circular, rectangular, or even irregular regions, but for a crop you'll want just the plain old rectangular tool. Follow these steps:

1. Choose the rectangular selection tool from the program's toolbar.

2. Click and drag the selection area (typically called a "marquee") around the region of the picture you want to keep (see Figure 11-1). You should see an outline of the area when you finish dragging.

3. Copy the selected region to the clipboard by choosing Edit|Copy.

4. Paste the cropped image back into your program's Edit window by choosing Edit|Paste. You may need to select an option like "Paste as a new image."

Your cropped image is now ready to be saved. You can discard the old image if you don't want it anymore.

 Tip: *Some programs simplify the process by featuring a crop tool. Instead of copying and pasting a selection into a new image, you can just choose the crop tool, drag the marquee to select the desired region, and click a button to crop the image.*

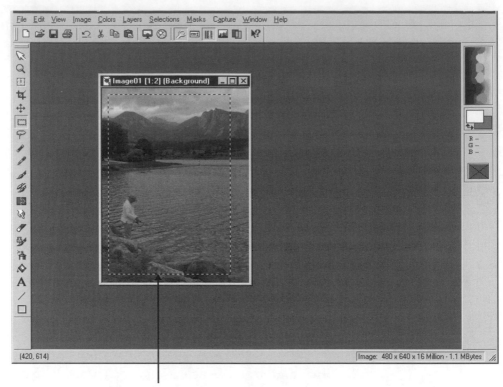

The marquee indicates the
selected area

Figure 11-1 To add the marquee to an image, click where you'd like to
place one corner and then drag the mouse to the opposite
corner

TWEAKING YOUR IMAGES

 My images are too dark. How do I brighten them up?

Everyone has a stockpile of too-dark images. The flash didn't
reach the subject, or perhaps the camera underexposed the
subject because of a bright background. Earlier chapters
discuss how to avoid those problems "in the lens" when you
take the picture, but you can also repair some of the damage
in post-processing.

There are two primary tools for adjusting the brightness
in an image:

● You can use the brightness control (sometimes called luminance). Brightness raises or lowers the entire image's luminance value indiscriminately in all areas, whether they need it or not. Of course, you can always change the brightness of just a portion of an image by selecting a region first, but brightness will still change within the entire region.

Tip: *Use the selection tool to add or remove brightness just to the selected area.*

● Alternately, you can use the gamma control. Gamma affects the midtones of an image more than the extreme bright and dark regions; that means you can brighten a dark skin tone without over-brightening a black shadow nearby. Gamma affects a specific range of luminance in the image, so you can better target your changes.

The procedure for changing brightness in an image is similar regardless of software; only the menu locations change. Alternately, you may find the brightness or gamma in a toolbar. In Paint Shop Pro, you can brighten up your image in this way:

1. Choose Colors|Adjust|Brightness/Contrast. The Brightness/Contrast dialog box appears.

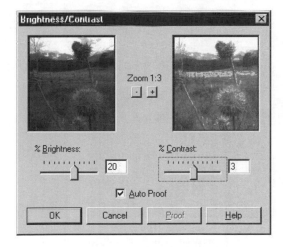

2. Use the Brightness slider to adjust the brightness in the image. You can see the effect of the change in your image immediately by clicking on the Proof button.

3. When you're satisfied with the results, click OK. Your image will be updated with the new brightness value, as in Figure 11-2.

 I keep increasing the brightness, but dark areas just get kind of gray. Why?

That's the ugly little secret of brightness control. You can only take brightness so far, because you can't add detail to an image that wasn't there when you originally took the picture. A black shadow, for instance, will only get gray as you continue to increase brightness—you'll never see the authentic Bigfoot creature that was hiding in the thicket of

Figure 11-2 This ominously dark picture of a tree looks completely different after being brightened up

trees. That's why it's important to start with the best exposure you can.

Which should I use when editing a picture: brightness or gamma?

I tend to reach for the gamma control first. I've found it's often the midtones in a picture that need enhancement, and the brightness control tends to wash out dark regions and increase the intensity of the highlights too much. So as a general rule, you should see if gamma gets the job done.

On the other hand, you may want to uniformly increase or decrease the luminance of an image. If that's the case, go ahead and try the brightness control. You can even use brightness to brighten an image overall slightly, then use gamma to bring up the midtones.

My image is flat or washed out. Is there a way to make the colors more vivid?

There are a few ways to add some life to washed out, flat, or bland pictures. One way is to use the contrast control. Since bland pictures are often a result of low contrast, you can increase the contrast in the image and make the scene look much "punchier." To do that, simply find the contrast control and try working the slider. In Paint Shop Pro, you can find the contrast control by choosing Colors | Adjust | Brightness/ Contrast.

Tip: *Contrast can work the other way to good effect as well. Want to create an artificial fog scene? Just reduce the contrast in a picture by about 50% and the image seems obscured by a dense fog.*

Another way to improve your image is via the saturation tool. Saturation increases or decreases the intensity of colors in an image, much like the saturation control on your television. Too much saturation can make the picture look like it was taken on Mars, but the right amount can add life to an otherwise bland picture.

> *Tip:* *Do you have a people picture that's a little too red? This doesn't happen often, but can occur when you take indoor pictures in artificial light. Back off on the saturation slightly to get a more natural skin tone.*

My images look too blue (or red). How do I adjust their color balance?

Quite often, the colors in your pictures won't come out quite right for some reason. In digital cameras, I've found that the whole image is often shifted at least slightly toward the blue end of the spectrum.

To fix these out-of-sync colors, open the color balance tool in your imaging program. In Paint Shop Pro, you can find it by choosing Colors | Adjust | Red/Green/Blue. You'll get a dialog box in which you can slide the three primary color controls to the left (less) or right (more) to bias the colors in your photo. For best results, use the color balance tool very conservatively and be sure to preview your work before clicking OK. You'll rarely need to change the colors in your image by more than about 15%.

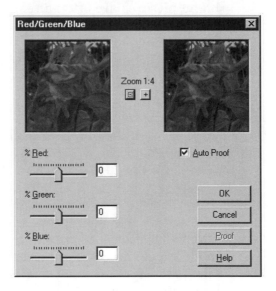

If your image is too blue, however, you won't necessarily get the effect you're looking for just by moving the blue slider to the left. Use the following table to fine-tune your image.

Problem	Solution
Too red	Decrease red, then increase both green and blue by half that amount
Too green	Decrease green, then increase both red and blue by half that amount
Too blue	Decrease blue, then increase both red and green by half that amount

 ## My image looks a bit out of focus. Is there a way to make it look sharper?

First, let me begin by saying that as great as digital imaging is, you can never add detail or information to a picture that wasn't there to begin with. That's why I'm always amused in movies at the way they can take a surveillance videotape and enlarge it enough to read the phone number on a piece of paper across the room. No matter how much they blow it up, the Hollywood computer can always seem to perfectly sharpen the focus. In reality, there's only so much you can do to improve an image; if the camera jittered badly while you took the picture, for example, no amount of sharpening will hide the result.

With that said, there are two ways to sharpen an image: a direct way, using the sharpen tool in your image editing program, and an indirect way, which amounts to blurring the background so your subject doesn't look quite so bad (see "What's another way to make my subject look sharper?" in the following section for instructions on the latter).

The easiest way to sharpen an image is with the sharpen tool. What this tool does is increase the contrast between pixels, making the image seem sharper (see Figure 11-3).

In most graphics programs, there are a few different kinds of sharpening filters available (in Paint Shop Pro, they're available from Image | Sharpen):

● **Sharpening** This affects all the pixels in your image indiscriminately. "Sharpen more" is a common alternative that is just more intense.

● **Edge sharpening** This only increases the contrast along edges in your picture, where a lack of sharpness is

Figure 11-3 This very blurry picture was taken indoors in poor light without a flash. Sharpening tools have dramatically improved it

most obvious. It is usually more effective than sharpening.

● **Unsharp mask** This is a variation of edge sharpening—it adjusts the contrast of pixels that neighbor an edge in addition to the edge itself.

Which variation should you use? Not all programs offer all three filters, but if you have a choice, edge sharpening is almost always more effective than the plain old sharpening filter. Unsharp mask works best of all, but it takes some tweaking on your part. You'll generally get to set at least three options:

● **Strength** This is the intensity of the sharpening effect.

● **Radius** This determines how many pixels around the edges are also affected by the filter.

● **Clipping** This determines how different adjoining pixels need to be before they're considered an edge.

 Tip: *Start with 100 for strength and 1.0 for radius and watch the way the filter changes as you change clipping. A clipping of 0 is the most harsh effect; beyond about 30, changing clipping has no real effect on your image. Likewise, raising radius beyond 1.5 rarely has an attractive effect on your image.*

 What's another way to make my subject look sharper?

Using the sharpening filter is certainly one way to make your image look sharper, but there's another, more "artistic" way to enhance the apparent sharpness of your image: by blurring the background.

To blur the background of your image, you'll need to isolate the subject so the blurring only happens to the background. You do that by selecting the subject using techniques discussed later in this chapter in "Working with Just Part of an Image." Once your subject is selected, you need to invert the selection so that the subsequent changes you make will happen to everything except the subject.

Then run the blur filter on your image. In Paint Shop Pro, you can find blur by choosing Image | Blur | Blur. In most image editors, you can choose from among options like blur, blur more, soften, and soften more. Both blur and soften have roughly the same effect on your image, so you can combine these filters in order to get the effect you're looking for (see Figure 11-4). Once you've blurred your background, turn off the selection and save your image.

 I'd like to reduce the depth of field to blur my backgrounds, but my camera is auto-everything. Can I simulate a lower depth of field afterwards?

Yes you can, using the exact same procedure discussed in the preceding section. Just blur the background—you probably won't be able to distinguish it from a picture originally taken with a large aperture setting.

What if even the plain old blur tool is too much blur?

There's no way to get less blur than you get with the standard blur—or is there? Actually, you can combine the blur tool with layers (discussed in Chapter 12) to fine-tune your image's appearance. Try this:

1. Load your image that needs blur help and immediately make a copy by choosing Edit | Copy.

Figure 11-4 The foreground is much punchier with a blurred background

2. Run the blur filter on your image.

3. Paste the non-blurred copy of your image into the one you're working with as a new layer by choosing Edit | Paste as New Layer.

4. Vary the transparency of the top layer until you get just the right amount of blur.

For more information on using layers in your image editor, see Chapter 12.

WORKING WITH JUST PART OF AN IMAGE

 ### How do I cause an effect to happen to only part of my image?

Most of the time, when you modify your image—whether with a filter, by painting it, or by changing the brightness—you tend to affect the entire image. That's not always what you want, though. Sometimes it would be nice to affect just one part of a picture. You can do this by creating a *selection*. A selection lets you isolate one part of your image from another. Think of a selection as a piece of paper that you punch a hole in. If you lay this over top of a picture and spray paint at it, the paint affects the picture only where you cut the hole. In

other words, no matter what you do to your image while a selection is active, it won't affect the unselected portion.

 ### How can I quickly and easily select parts of my image?

There are a few different ways to create a selection. The most common method of selecting part of your image is to use the almost universally named *selection tool*. In Paint Shop Pro, you can get to the selection tool by clicking on the dotted rectangle on the tool palette.

To create a selection, just click and drag the selection box across part of the screen; when you're done, part of the image should appear to be enclosed in an outlined box called a *marquee*. This is the selection area, and you can test it by taking a tool like the paintbrush and trying to paint through the image. The only place it will leave ink is inside the selection area.

The selection area is the only part of the image the paintbrush can affect

Note that you're not limited to creating rectangular selection areas. You can use different shapes as appropriate. In Paint Shop Pro, the kind of selection area you create is determined by the setting in the controls palette, the small dialog box that changes depending upon which tool you choose from the tool palette. Using the controls palette, you can change the selection area to an oval, square, or circle.

Note: *If you don't see it, make sure the controls palette is on. Choose View | Toolbars and click on the appropriate check box.*

What if the region you're trying to select isn't a simple geometric shape, but an irregular shape like someone's face? In this case, you'll need to use the *freehand* tool. This tool is also called the lasso tool, because its icon is usually shaped like a lasso. Just click and drag the lasso as you trace out the selection area. When you let go of the mouse button, the start and end points of your selection area will be automatically joined. While the lasso is handy for creating irregularly shaped selections, it is not easy to accurately draw a shape (the computer mouse is harder to control than a pencil).

The last method of selecting a region is the most powerful. Typically called a *magic wand,* this tool creates a selection area based upon color. When you click the wand in your image, the selection includes all the pixels with a similar color in the adjacent area. The magic wand is very powerful for digital camera images because photos have many subtle variations of color in the same region. You could click on a person's hat, for instance, and if the hat is various shades of blue throughout, the entire hat will be selected (see Figure 11-5). The wand will not select a similar blue glove elsewhere in the picture, because the blue pixels (even if they're roughly the same shade of blue) aren't adjacent to the initial region.

Most programs allow you to fine-tune the magic wand's selection parameters. Sometimes called the *tolerance*, this allows you to specify how much latitude the wand should use

Boundary of the selection created
by the magic wand

Figure 11-5   Just a few selections using the magic wand can select the
entire background in this image

when determining if a pixel is colored similarly enough to
include it in the region. In most cases, the default is fine;
make the tolerance too great, and you'll include parts of the
image that you don't want.

    Tip: *Some programs, like Paint Shop Pro, also feature a
feather option. By feathering the selection area, you blur the
line between selection and non-selection (based on the
intensity of feathering you choose).*

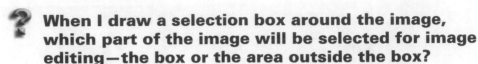

When I draw a selection box around the image, which part of the image will be selected for image editing—the box or the area outside the box?

It's not unusual to get disoriented when you first start working with images and lose track of which side of the dashed selection outline you're isolating from changes. But here's the scoop: The region inside of a selection outline is the part that you can change; outside the selection is locked and protected. If most of the image is selected except for a small unselected region in the middle, then you'll be able to see that the border of the entire image is outlined.

Is there a way to combine more than one region in a selection?

On occasion, you might want to create more than one selection area at the same time, enabling you to make the same modifications to all of them at once. In many programs, you can use the common SHIFT-select procedure to set up multiple selection areas. Just create the first selection area, then hold down the SHIFT key while you make your subsequent selections.

This technique can come in handy even when you're only trying to isolate a single area in your image. Take the example of a person, for instance. You may be able to use the magic wand to select the subject's clothing, but certainly their hair will blend in with a dark background, rendering the wand useless. So holding down the SHIFT key, you can next use the lasso tool to outline the face and hair. You can combine different selection tools and techniques as long as you remember to hold down the SHIFT key whenever you start a new selection.

What if I end up selecting exactly the opposite of what I want to work with?

No problem at all. Most graphics programs have a simple command to *invert* the selected region, making what was selected now unselected and vice-versa. In Paint Shop Pro, this command is available from the Selection menu.

Remember that you need to first create a selection area before this menu command will have any effect on your image.

I've made a selection, but it's too sharp. I'd like a graceful transition from selected area to unselected area. Is that possible?

Yes, it is if your image editor supports feathering. This is a technique in which the sharpness of the edge of the selected area is reduced to fade the effect of the selection over a short distance. A higher feather setting creates softer edges, and a lower feather value creates sharper edges. In any event, if you use feathering, the selection's borders will be expanded slightly to include the area necessary to fade the selection's edges. Alternately, you can use a mask (see the following section).

In Paint Shop Pro, feathering is available from the controls palette related to the selection tool, or from the Selection | Modify | Feather menu item.

What is a mask? Why would I use it instead of a selection?

A *mask* is similar to the selection tool you may have already used to isolate regions in an image. Just like the regular selection tool, a mask isolates the area that you want to protect from change when you apply color, filters, or other effects to an image.

Masks are significantly more powerful than ordinary selections, though. They have three attributes that selections don't offer in most imaging programs:

● A mask is a 256-level grayscale image. While a selection area is either on or off, you can use a mask to select the degree to which an effect will occur. Black parts of the mask block all edits; white parts allow changes to occur at 100% strength; and gray areas are something in between. It's as if you were spraypainting a model in your basement and using paper with holes to block unwanted paint, but different holes let varying amounts of paint through, as if you put thin gauze over the holes.

● You can fine-tune the mask with ordinary paint tools. While a selection area is only as accurate as your ability to draw with the mouse, when you create a mask, you can zoom in, paint pixel by pixel, and make sure it looks exactly the way you need it to.

● You can create a mask and save it to disk, meaning you can reuse it in many different images.

How can I get my selection to perfectly match an irregular object?

Unless your selection area is well-defined with a narrow range of colors conducive to using the magic wand (such as when you're trying to enclose a solitary object against a high-contrast background), a selection is only as accurate as your ability to draw with the mouse. So how do you get a selection area to perfectly match an underlying element in your image?

This technique relies on your imaging program's ability to turn a selection area into a mask (which most can do) and then turn a mask back into a selection area (which not all can do). Let's use Paint Shop Pro to show how this is done:

1. Load the image you want to use as the basis for your mask.

2. Using the lasso tool, draw a selection area around your subject. It doesn't have to be tremendously accurate.

3. Turn the selection into a mask by choosing Masks|New|Hide Selection.

4. Turn off the selection marquee by choosing Selections|Select None.

5. Enable mask editing by choosing Masks|Edit.

6. Choose a paint brush and edit the mask, pixel by pixel if necessary, until it perfectly matches the subject you're trying to duplicate. You can use the zoom tool to get a close look and alter the paintbrush's diameter to get just the right amount of detail.

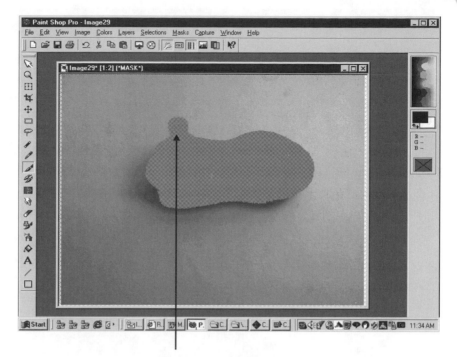

The paintbrush can
change the mask

Tip: *Regardless of the color your program uses to display the mask, the mask is really just a grayscale image and you need to paint with black, white, and shades of gray. Use white to erase the mask and black to paint the mask. If you want to manually insert various levels of transparency in the mask, use levels of gray.*

7. When the mask is just the way you like it, convert it back into a selection area by choosing Selections | From Mask.

8. Delete the mask by choosing Masks | Delete.

9. Now you have a selection area, but if you made the subject black, then it's exactly the opposite of what you want (everything but the subject is selected). To reverse this, choose Selections | Invert.

Replace Your Background

Why be satisfied with the boring background you had in the lens when you took someone's picture? You can get some cool-looking images by completely replacing the background of an image with a different picture.

This can be used to create special effects—like walking on the moon—or just to enhance a picture that had a lousy background. Here's how to do it:

1. Create a selection area around the entire subject that you want to transplant to another scene. Use any method to do this that was discussed earlier in this chapter in "Working with Just Part of an Image." You can feather the edges, but be sure you accurately cut along the edge between the subject and background.

2. Copy the selection by choosing Edit | Copy.

3. Open the image that you'd like to use as the new background.

4. With the new image selected, choose Edit | Paste as New Selection.

5. Position the subject in the new scene and left-click when you're done.

Chapter 12

Beyond Basic Image Editing

Beyond Basic Image Editing @ a Glance

- Most image editors come with a suite of painting tools, and for good reason. By painting, you can edit your images on a pixel-by-pixel basis, insert text, or replace the reality captured in the picture with your own digital alternative.

- Editing a single image is fine, but imagine what you can do when you learn to master multiple images. Through the magic of layers, for instance, you can easily make pictures that look like they came from a special effects studio. You can make double exposures, sophisticated "blue screen" effects, even wide panoramas that capture the entire Grand Canyon in a single frame.

- Ever get a tear or scratch on a cherished photograph? Using digital imaging, you can fix that and print out a new copy, good as new. You can also use your imaging software to improve on the reality you photographed by removing power lines, fixing the sky, and other little cheats.

- Now's your chance to become the next George Lucas. Try some of the projects in this chapter to make eye-popping images like black-and-white prints with a splash of color, sci-fi graphics, and aged images.

 Note: *Almost any image editing software can accomplish the sorts of tasks discussed in this chapter. But since it isn't feasible to explain how to use all of the many programs on the market, I've chosen Paint Shop Pro from Jasc Software to answer questions in which a particular technique is demonstrated. I chose PSP for several reasons: It's inexpensive, you can download it from the Internet, and its features are representative of those in many other paint and editing programs. You can get a copy of Paint Shop Pro yourself from Jasc Software. Their Web site is at http://www.jasc.com.*

 Note: *When working with your pictures in an image editor, be careful to save your work with a different filename. That way you can always go back to the original if you don't like what you've done.*

PAINTING

 ### What do all those painting tools in the tool palette do?

Using a full-blown image editor can be intimidating because of the wealth of options and tools that are available. Nowhere is that more apparent than in the selection of painting options. Most paint programs have an assortment of tools similar to those offered by Paint Shop Pro, which are listed in Table 12-1.

 ### How do I choose a color to paint with?

There are two important colors in any imaging program: the foreground color and the background color. These are usually displayed prominently (see Figure 12-1) for easy access and reference.

The foreground color is the color you'll paint with when you use the left mouse button. The background color appears if you use the eraser tool on your image, and in many programs you can paint with it using the right mouse button.

Icon	Tool Name	Description
	Paint brush	This is just what it sounds like—it lets you paint on the image much as you'd paint with a real brush. It's a lot more flexible than a real brush, though, since you can change features like the size and shape of the brush, as well as the amount of paint that you can spread at once.
	Clone brush	This tool lets you paint with pixels found elsewhere in your image, effectively cloning a part of your picture as you paint.
	Color replacer	This tool lets you replace a color currently in your image with a new one that you define. The color replacer also has a threshold control, allowing you to specify how close a color must be to the target color in order for the change to occur.
	Retouch	This great painting tool puts the power of many of the program's effects—like brightness and hue changes, effects filters, and more—into a brush so you can paint them on.
	Eraser	This tool allows you to paint with the currently selected foreground and background colors.
	Airbrush	You can configure this tool to splatter paint on your image like an airbrush.
	Flood fill	This tool pours paint into a region. The currently selected color will run right up to whatever color edges exist; as with the magic wand, you can set its color tolerance.
	Text	This tool lets you write text anywhere in your image, in any color and any font.
	Line	Use this tool to draw a perfectly straight line of whatever thickness you desire.
	Shape	Choose the shape and draw a filled or outlined geometric shape in your image.

Table 12-1   Paint Tools in Paint Shop Pro

The background color is also important if you save a GIF with the background color transparent—see Chapter 15 for more on this.

In Paint Shop Pro, you can choose a color from the color palette by moving the mouse over the palette and clicking on the color you like. A left click selects the foreground color; a

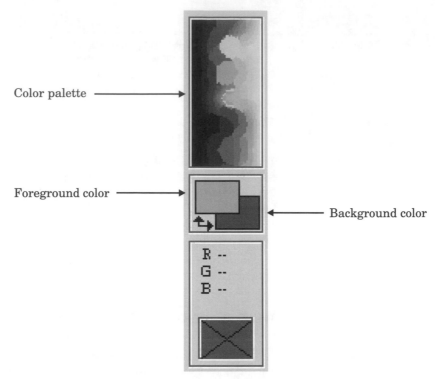

Color palette ————————————→

Foreground color ————————————→

                                                    ←———————— Background color

Figure 12-1   Use the color palette to select the foreground and
                   background colors in your image

right click sets the background. You can also choose colors
directly from an image; see the following section for more
information.

 ### I want to paint with a color already in my picture.
How do I figure out what color that is?

Use the eye dropper tool. To find the color of a specific pixel
in your image, zoom in far enough that you can actually see
it, particularly if it's a region in which the colors change a lot.
Then click on the eye dropper and click on the pixel. In most
image editors, clicking with your left mouse button makes the
selected color the new foreground; right-clicking makes it the
selected background color. The color palette window will
display the color you've closen as well.

What if I don't want to paint a single color, but instead spread a range of colors?

That's called a *color gradient*. If your program supports gradients, then you can paint with a color spread just as easily as with a single color (see Figure 12-2).

Usually, your imaging program will use the current foreground and background colors as the extremes of the color range. In Paint Shop Pro, you can paint a gradient in this way:

1. Select the foreground and background colors you want to serve as the extreme values in your gradient (see "How do I choose a color to paint with?" earlier in this chapter).

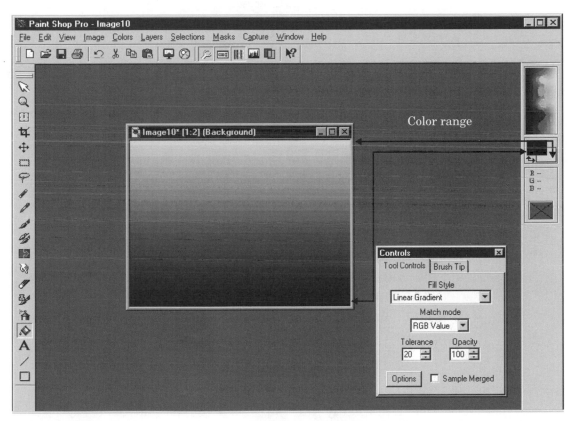

Figure 12-2 You can make a gradient between any two colors

2. Click on the flood fill tool, which in Paint Shop Pro can use gradient fills.

3. In the Flood Fill controls palette, select the Tool Controls tab.

4. In the drop-down menu for fill style, choose a gradient. There are several to choose from; pick "linear gradient" for now.

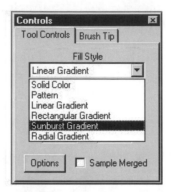

5. Click the flood fill tool in your image to pour out a gradient fill.

 How do I add text to my pictures?

If you're used to a word processor, you may be surprised to find that most image editors don't allow you to type directly onto the canvas. Instead, you need to type your text into a dialog box and then paste that text into the image. In fact, text plays by a few unusual rules:

● Make sure the currently selected color is the one you want the text to appear in, because that's what you'll get. Change the color if necessary before you start creating text.

● In most programs, text is an editable object when you first position it. That means you can position it, size it, and transform it, as well as change its color balance or perform any other operation you desire.

● As soon as you deselect the text, it is embedded permanently into your image and can no longer be modified separately.

In Paint Shop Pro, here's how you create text:

1. Make the foreground color the color you want to paint your text in.

2. Click on the text button in the tool palette.

3. When the Add Text dialog box appears, choose a font and font size and type your text into the space provided.

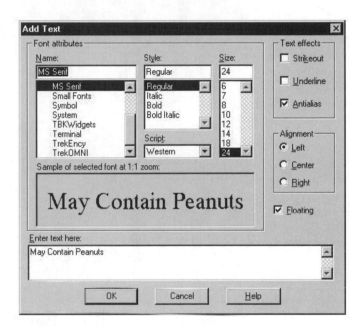

4. Click OK.

5. Position the text in the image and perform any other necessary edits now.

6. When you're satisfied with your text, choose Selections | Select None.

How do I make text have interesting fills?

Plain, single-color text isn't particularly interesting. You can use the tools built into your paint program to create much more compelling text. You can, for instance, make an image show through the letters of your text (see Figure 12-3).

Figure 12-3 You can make parts of images or color gradients show through text as if it were a stencil

Here's how you do this in Paint Shop Pro:

1. Open the image that you want to show through the text.
2. Click on the text icon and click in the middle of the image.
3. Enter the desired text, and set the font and size that you want the text to appear in.
4. Deselect the "float" option for the selected text.
5. Click OK. The text appears as a selection in the image.
6. Copy it to the clipboard by choosing Edit | Copy.
7. Switch to the image that you want the text to appear in and choose Edit | Paste.
8. Position the text and choose Selections | Select None.

 Can I make my text have a drop-shadow?

Drop-shadows are a cool embellishment that can really add to the visual appeal of your text—not to mention making it more readable, particularly on some kinds of images. Many programs come with a drop-shadow tool built in, making it a snap to add drop-shadows to your text. But if your program doesn't have a drop-shadow feature, you can achieve similar results simply by making two copies of the text in different colors and arranging them by hand so they look like text and shadow.

WORKING WITH MULTIPLE IMAGES

 How do I simulate the double exposures I used to take with my 35mm camera?

One of the most interesting kinds of picture, for me, has always been the double exposure. Getting the exposure right in each exposure, as well as composing the image and making it look interesting, is a considerable challenge. With digital photography, though, most of the difficulty is gone. You can get

the multiple exposure effect with most graphics programs, though it's easiest if you have a program that supports multiple layers. Paint Shop Pro is one such program, so here's a quick overview of how to make a multiple exposure with two or more images from a digital camera:

1. Open all the images you want to include in the final image.

2. Make sure the layers palette is visible. If it isn't, turn it on by choosing View | Toolbars and checking the appropriate box.

3. Select the first image. Note that the image is composed of a single layer named "Background." Right-click on the layer button and choose Properties. Rename the layer to something more meaningful and click OK. Repeat for all the images in your project.

4. Drag the layer button from one image into another. You should now have two layers in the same image. Repeat for as many images as you want to include.

5. Finish the image by adjusting transparency and moving your images around until they're composed to your liking.

Layering is a very powerful tool. Using the transparency sliders, you can adjust the "exposure" of each layer, making it more or less visible in the final image.

Can I get that "blue screen" effect used in movies to change the background of an image?

As you've already seen elsewhere in this chapter, it's easy to improve on reality with a digital photograph. You can cut out and throw away entire backgrounds, in fact, without preparing anything ahead of time.

In the movies, they need to film in front of a special color matte in order to know which pixels to eliminate from the final scene. Our lives would be easier if we could always shoot in front of a blue screen too—you could simply use the magic want tool to select the whole background with just a few clicks. But since we don't live on a sound stage, we'll make do with a slightly more convoluted process using Paint Shop Pro:

1. Create a selection area around the entire subject that you want to transplant to another scene (see Chapter 11 for more on making selections). You can use a combination of the freehand tool and the magic wand to get close to the edges of the subject, but don't spend too much time getting it exact. Just get a rough draft of the outline.

2. Convert the selection into a mask by choosing Masks | New | Hide Selection. A mask can be edited pixel by pixel using a paint brush, so you can get a perfect matte of the subject.

3. Enter Edit mode to change the mask and make the mask match the subject perfectly as described in "How can I get my selection to perfectly match an irregular object?" in Chapter 11.

4. Convert the mask back into a selection by choosing Selection | From Mask.

5. Copy the subject using Edit | Copy.

6. Open the new image that you want to paste the subject into.

7. With the new image selected, choose Edit | Paste as New Selection (you can also use layers if you prefer).

8. Position the subject in the new scene.

 ## How do I make a panorama from a set of photos?

A *panorama* is an image that's wider than the ordinary form factor of images produced by your camera.

Panoramas are typically used with landscapes, since landscapes provide the wide, sweeping vistas that look so impressive in a panorama. You can take a panorama of anything, though—a school play, the inside of your home, or some other subject. The key to making something a panorama with a digital camera is that you'll need to take two or more images and "stitch" them together in your image editing software. That means that the scene shouldn't change between photographs, or you won't be able to match them up. There are two steps to taking a panorama: photographing the scene and stitching the images together afterwards. When shooting the pictures, keep these tips in mind:

● You'll need to take a series of pictures that overlap. Try to get at least 25% of each image to overlap into the next picture to make it easier to stitch them together.

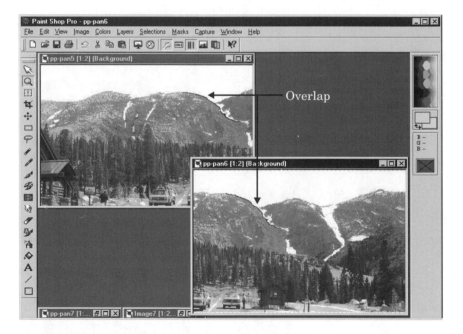

● In order to keep each image's perspective identical, you'll need to keep the camera's rotational axis the same. In plain English, that means you need to take all the pictures from the same location—don't drift a few feet as you photograph.

- All the images need to be taken level. For best results, use a tripod.

- Avoid using a wide-angle lens, since this can distort the images and make it difficult to line up edges.

Once you've got the individual images that will be your raw material, it's time to make the panorama. Once all the images are downloaded to your PC, load them in your image editing software. I'll use Paint Shop Pro in my example:

1. Determine image size of your individual images. They're probably 640×480, but if you don't know, choose View | Image Information.

2. Create a blank document by choosing File | New. To determine the width of the new document, multiply width of your individual images by the number of images your combining (for example, 640 pixels wide × 3 images = 1920 pixels). Make the new document's height about 10% bigger than the starting image height, such as 528 for a 480-pixel image. This gives you some room to maneuver if the images turn out to have some vertical offset. You'll want the image type to be a 24-bit (16 million color) image.

3. Add the first image to the panorama, working from left to right. In Paint Shop Pro, simply drag the layer icon for the first image into the blank image and it'll be added as a layer in the new file.

4. Take the next image and add it to your panorama document. As you add the images, line them up with the image to their left. If you use a program with layers, you can make the new image somewhat transparent to help see where to line it up with the previous image (see Figure 12-4).

5. Repeat this process until all your images are inserted and lined up.

6. When you're done, use the selection tool to crop the new panorama so that any irregular tops and bottoms aren't in the image.

7. Copy this selection by choosing Edit | Copy.

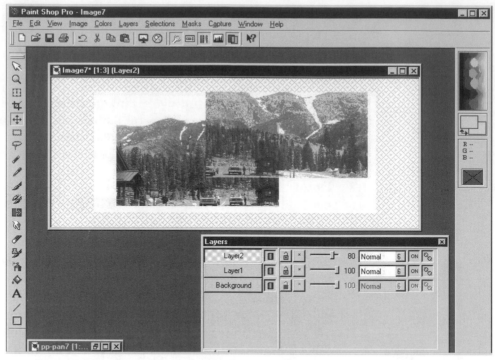

Figure 12-4 Using transparency can help you line up panorama images when you stitch them together

8. Paste the image into a new document by choosing Edit | Paste as New Image.

9. Save your file.

Now that I've told you the hard way to do it, let me add that there's an easy way as well. There are panorama-makers available that automate many of these steps. My favorite is Enroute Software's QuickStitch. Using this program, all you need to do is drag and drop the individual images in the proper order. The software matches up edges all by itself, and does a good job even with low-quality digital cameras, wide-angle lenses, and other technical difficulties.

FIXING IMPERFECT PICTURES

My picture isn't perfectly level. Can I fix that?

It isn't hard to do, but it may take some trial and error to get the angle just right. Most editing software includes an option to rotate an image by some arbitrary angle. In Paint Shop Pro, all you need to do is choose Image|Rotate. In the resulting dialog box, enter a number in the Free box and click OK.

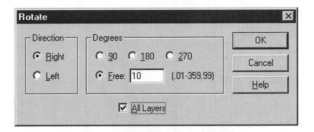

If you don't like the results, undo your action and try again.

Tip: *Don't add another rotation to the one you already entered in order to work your way toward the right angle! Since you're asking the imaging program to manipulate pixels in a very unusual way, each rotation introduces artifacts and compromises into your image. By adding rotations on top of rotations, you're compounding the error until the image looks visibly degraded.*

How do I eliminate red eye?

Many image editing programs come with red-eye reduction tools that automatically eliminate red eye from your pictures. You can do the same thing on your own, though—all you need to do is zoom in and select the eyes with the magic wand tool. From there, just adjust the color balance in the eyes to eliminate the obvious red glow.

Of course, it would be great if you could avoid red eye to begin with. See Chapter 7 for details.

 ## Can I "airbrush away" parts of my picture?

Yes, it's easy to eliminate unsightly parts of your image with the clone tool. This handy feature allows you to copy pixels from one region of your image to another. That means you can "airbrush away" distracting aspects of a picture, like power lines, hotspots, and so on, by duplicating a similar or nearby part of the image (see Figure 12-5).

To use the clone tool in your image editor just do this:

1. Click on the clone tool in the tool palette. Typically, it looks like a pair of paintbrushes.

2. You'll need to find a region in your image that is similar to the area you want to fix (see Figure 12-6). If you want to airbrush away a power line that runs through the air, for instance, you can look for a nearby patch of sky.

3. Clone a section of the image that contain the colors you want to work with. Usually, that means simply

Figure 12-5 The image on the right looks better without the tall lightning rod obscuring the view from the top of Pike's Peak

Figure 12-6 When airbrushing with the clone tool, be careful that you select a similar part of the image and work in small spurts

right-clicking on the area you selected in step 2. A target or some other symbol may appear where you clicked.

4. Move your mouse over to the area you want to airbrush and start painting. Don't try to cover the blemish all at once; paint a little, pick up the mouse, and paint again. This reduces the chances that a recognizable pattern will appear as a result of your painting.

The clone tool works best in small areas, since you can start to tell something is wrong with the area you're cloning to if you paint over too large a region.

You may have to repeat steps 3 and 4 several times. You may need to change the source region for your cloning operation if the areas you're trying to change vary dramatically in color or texture.

✛ *Tip:* *Cloning tools usually work in two different modes. In one mode, when you pick up the brush and paint elsewhere, the source of the cloning operation stays where you put it: This is called "non-aligned." If you pick up the brush and start painting elsewhere and the source moves the same relative distance from where you first started, this is the aligned mode. Some pictures work better with one mode or the other—experiment to see which is best in each situation.*

In the darkroom, I can "dodge and burn" to improve my pictures. Can I do that in a digital image?

Yes! *Dodging and burning* is a term used in traditional film-based photography to indicate that you're under- or overexposing images in selected regions on the fly as you develop the prints. You can do the same thing in the digital arena, with the advantage that it's easier to experiment and you don't waste paper if you goof up.

To selectively adjust the brightness, contrast, gamma, or even color balance of just part of a picture, select the region and then apply the desired filter or tool to just the selection. This is explained in detail in "Working with just part of an image" in Chapter 11.

How do I remove a scratch in a picture?

If you have a damaged print that has been sitting around waiting to be repaired, it's easy to use digital editing to fix the problem. One of my wedding pictures, for instance, had a few nasty scratches due to broken glass. The image was irreplaceable, so I turned to digital editing to make a repaired duplicate.

First scan the image into your PC at a resolution high enough to print at the size you want (see Chapter 4 for details). Then you can fix the damaged image using the same techniques described elsewhere in the book. There are two principal methods you can employ:

● In some cases, you can select and copy an undamaged area of the picture that is similar in color and overall texture to the damaged portion, then paste it over the

damaged area. This is particularly effective in fairly
uniform backgrounds such as the sky.

● Another alternative is to use the cloning tool. Select the
cloning tool (see "Can I 'airbrush away' parts of my
picture?" earlier in this chapter) and use a similar but
undamaged section of the image to paint over the mar.
Remember to use short, dabbing motions to paint, or
you'll introduce an undesirable pattern into the image.

There are annoying specks all over my picture. Can I get rid of them?

Yes. Specks can come from images that were taken on grainy
film, from bad scans, or from using a digital camera in very
low light. No matter how the specks got there, most image
editors have a despeckle tool that you can use to get rid of
them. In Paint Shop Pro, you can find it by choosing
Image | Noise | Despeckle.

SPECIAL EFFECTS

What are plug-ins?

Your image editor may be able to use something called
plug-in filters, or simply plug-ins. These are filters that were
originally designed for Adobe Photoshop. Photoshop filters,
however, have become something of a standard among image
editing software, and many programs can accept these filters.
You can download filters from the Web, purchase them in
stores, or get them with other image editors.

What do the filters and effects in my image editor do?

The best way to find out is to actually experiment with them.
I say that because it's one thing to read an explanation of the
filter—mathematical or physical—and it's quite another
thing to actually process a picture with each filter to see the
effect. In general, you probably won't use many of these
filters very often. But it pays to try them out, because you

never know when a certain effect will be just what you're looking for:

- **Blur**   Blur filters average nearby pixels to give the impression of blur, poor focus, or motion.

- **Deformations**   Deformation tools let you distort and skew part of an image. They're good for displaying an image in a different perspective. You can change the orientation of an image in three dimensions with the free deformation, or use some of the geometric deformations to distort images within circles, cylinders, and other shapes.

- **Edge**   Edge filters typically enhance and trace edges— regions defined by high-contrast borders between pixels.

- **Emboss**   This filter turns the image into a dull gray image that resembles a bas relief painting.

- **Erode**   This filter enhances the darkest regions in an image. It can actually help increase the apparent sharpness in the image, too.

- **Mosaic**   A mosaic filter reduces the resolution of your image by averaging the colors in large chunks, turning your image into a set of larger tiles.

- **Noise**   These filters can add or remove "noise" in an image. Noise manifests itself in digital images as specks of high-contrast color.

- **Sharpen**   Sharpen filters try to increase apparent sharpness in an image by increasing the contrast between pixels, either throughout the image or just along edges.

Is it possible to transform an image so that it looks like a framed picture in another image?

Sure, you simply need to use the free deformation tool. This is a feature that lets you take an image and rotate, resize, and skew it, changing its perspective. In general, all you need to do is copy the image you want to deform into the target image, then shrink and deform it. In Paint Shop Pro, you'd do it this way:

1. Open both images and select the region from the first image you plan to deform.

2. Choose Edit | Copy, then select the target image and choose Edit | Paste as New Selection.

3. Activate the free deformation tool.

4. Grab the image by a corner and drag to shrink it down to more or less the size you want.

5. Skew the image so it looks like it's lying on a tabletop by activating the skew mode (hold down the SHIFT key) and dragging the top-center handle to the left.

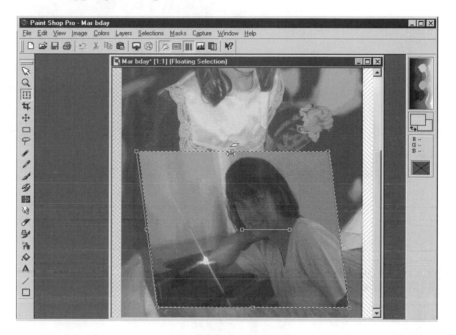

6. Fine-tune the position and appearance of the image using skew, rotation, and drag modes. When you're happy with the result, click outside the image to deactivate the deformation tool.

7. To complete the effect, draw an outline around the image with the chisel tool so it looks like a framed picture. While the image is still selected, choose Image | Effects | Chisel. Make the size about 10 pixels.

How can I make a black-and-white picture with just a splash of color?

This effect is a lot of fun. Surely you've seen television commercials in which everything is black and white except for one thing—a person, perhaps, or the featured product—that is in full color. It's an effective trick because your eyes are really drawn to the color image in a sea of gray.

And best of all, it's not very hard to do. It's particularly easy if your image editor supports layers. The basic idea is this:

1. Stack two copies of the image in separate layers.
2. Make the one underneath grayscale.
3. Select most of the image in the color version.
4. Delete the selection, leaving a small color subject on top of the grayscale image.

Specifically, here's how to do it in Paint Shop Pro:

1. Open the image you want to use and make a copy of it by choosing Edit | Copy. Don't paste it anywhere yet; just let it stay in the clipboard.

2. Select the image and convert it to a grayscale picture by choosing Colors | Grayscale. Then turn the image into a 24-bit file by choosing Colors | Increase Color Depth | 16 Million Colors.

3. Rename this image's layer "Grayscale" so it's easier to keep track of (right-click on the layer icon and choose Properties).

4. Now add the color image on top of this one by selecting the grayscale image and choosing Edit | Paste | As New Layer. You can prove that it worked by sliding the transparency control on the top layer until you can see the grayscale image peeking through.

5. With the new color layer selected, use the selection tool to trace out the subject you want to keep in color. Trace as carefully as possible—if you need to, create a mask to fine-tune the area and convert the mask into a selection.

6. When you're done, choose Selection | Invert to select everything *except* the color subject.

7. Choose Edit | Cut to cut the unwanted part of the color image away.

8. Choose Selection | Select None to finish.

How can I make my own science-fiction shots?

When I was in college, I took my love of "Star Trek," added a dose of photography, and came up with a hobby that could pretty much only be done around 3 A.M. While it didn't help my grades very much, it was a lot of fun to create special effects like phaser blasts and disintegration halos. The best part? It was all done "in the lens," so you can try it yourself if your camera supports very long exposures. Here's how I did it in college (this is the world premiere of my secret recipe for taking special-effects shots):

1. Set the camera up on a tripod in the dark and start a long exposure.

2. Using a flash, expose the subject (like someone holding a phaser) and the target person.

3. Get behind the subject and, pointing a flashlight directly at the camera, walk to the target of the phaser blast.

4. Outline the target with the flashlight, again pointing it at the camera.

5. If you want to make the target look like he's disintegrating, let him leave the scene and flash the wall behind him.

6. Stop the exposure.

That's a lot of work, and the results are often hit-or-miss. Against all odds, you can sometimes get a half-decent one, as in Figure 12-7.

With a digital camera and a program like Paint Shop Pro, though, you can do it a lot more scientifically. Here's an alternate way to create a similar image:

1. Take a picture of two people posed to be the aggressor and the target. "Star Trek" clothing is optional.

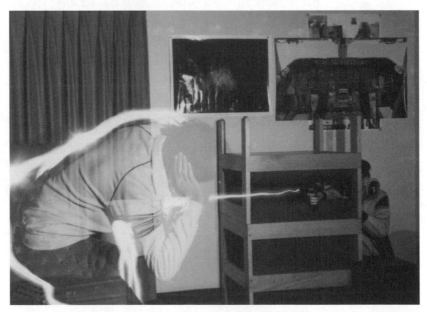

Figure 12-7 One of the better special-effects shots from my grab bag of "phaser tricks" using a 35mm camera

2. Load the image into Paint Shop Pro and immediately store a copy of the image in the clipboard by choosing Edit | Copy.

3. To make the target glow, create a selection around her and then expand it. Choose Selections | Modify | Expand and select perhaps 10 pixels. You can add a feather effect in the same way.

4. Convert the selection to a mask. Choose Mask|New|
   Show Selection so the rest of the image is protected.

5. Now add an effect to make the subject glow. I suggest
   adding the maximum amount of brightness or gamma.

6. Delete the mask by choosing Masks|Delete. When
   the dialog box appears, do not merge the mask into
   the image.

7. Next, add the copy into your image as a new layer.
   Choose Edit|Paste as New Layer.

8. Play with the layer's transparency until you get the
   effect you like. If you want a stronger image of the target
   person, go back to the original image and copy the target
   to the clipboard. Then paste her into the image as yet
   another new layer, position her in place in the middle of
   the halo, and reduce the transparency slightly.

You can also do variations on this: To get the target to disintegrate, take two pictures using a tripod so you have identical framing. In one image, include the target; in the other image, remove her. Then combine the images and use transparency to make her look like she's evaporating.

What about the phaser blast? Using a flashlight is a very inexact science (it's hard to get a straight line, as you can see in Figure 12-8). With a paint program, however, you can get a perfectly straight beam. In some paint programs, holding down the SHIFT key while you draw a line locks the brush into following a perfectly straight path.

In Paint Shop Pro, click for the starting point and move the brush to the end point. Then hold down the SHIFT key as you click, and the program draws a perfectly straight line between the two points. To make it look like a beam of light, make the color a bright white, red, or yellow and add a touch of feathering to the effect.

How do I "age" a digital image?

You can make a photo you took just a few days ago look like it has been in your dad's attic for 50 years. It's easy to do: Simply add some film grain and blur, change the color to look

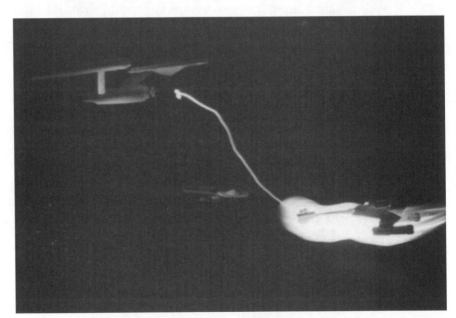

Figure 12-8   It's fiendishly difficult to "draw" a straight line through the air doing this the old-fashioned way, with a flashlight

like a well-aged, sepia-colored print, and you're done. Using Paint Shop Pro as an example, here's the process:

1. Load your picture.

2. Add noise to the image; this will create speckles that look like film grains. Choose Image | Noise | Add. Choose a number between 10 and 25. If it looks like too much, don't worry. It'll be diffused a bit shortly.

3. Now convert the image to grayscale (choose Colors | Grayscale).

4. Set the image back to 24-bit (choose Colors | Increase Color Depth | 16 Million Colors).

5. At this point, most images need to have their contrast increased. Choose Colors | Adjust | Brightness/Contrast and set both to about 20. Click OK.

6. Now we'll give the image its distinctive aged-color tone. Choose Colors | Colorize and choose 30 for hue and 50 for saturation.

7. Finally, to finish the image, choose Image | Blue | Blur.

Colorize an Image

You can create an interesting work of art using the colorize tool. Colorizing converts your image into a picture with uniform hue while maintaining the original brightness levels—that means you get a monochrome image that isn't grayscale. Instead, it's bluescale, redscale, or whatever-scale-you-happen-to-choose. That's how we managed to get an old-looking picture in "How do I 'age' a digital image?" and it can be used for a lot of other effects as well. Want to get an image that looks like it was photographed through night vision goggles? Try colorizing it with a hue of 75 and a saturation of 80. But keep experimenting—some images can look very dramatic when rendered in just a primary color.

Figure 12-9 Each passenger on the see-saw has had a different deformation applied to their face

 ## How do you warp and deform people's faces to make caricatures?

Use the deformation tools and filters that come with your image editing program. First select your subject's face—with either a simple oval or the magic wand—and then try the various geometric deformation tools (see Figure 12-9).

Tip: *If you can get your hands on a program like Kai's Power Goo, you're in for a blast. You don't need to muck around with filter names or tricky magic wand selections with these programs—just choose from a library of effects designed expressly for creating caricatures.*

Chapter 13

Projects for Your Digital Images

Answer Topics!

Projects for Your Digital Images @ a Glance

There's a place you can display your digital camera handiwork that's as close as your desk. Windows itself has a few virtual picture frames, just waiting for you to hang your newest images in them. Both the Windows desktop and (if you're using the newest versions of Windows) individual folders can be set to show your images. Find out how in this chapter.

Want to take your digital images to the next level? You can include them in projects of almost any kind, from business cards to PowerPoint presentations to T-shirts. Look here for details on how to make some of these exciting and productive items.

Sometimes your projects can benefit not just from your own handiwork with the digital camera, but also from stock images you can get from the Internet and other sources. Find out more about stock imagery and clip art in this chapter.

 Note: *Almost any image editing software can accomplish the sorts of tasks discussed in this chapter. But since it isn't feasible to explain how to use all of the many programs on the market, I've chosen Paint Shop Pro from Jasc Software to answer questions in which a particular technique is demonstrated. I chose PSP for several reasons: It's inexpensive, you can download it from the Internet, and its features are representative of those in many other paint and editing programs. You can get a copy of Paint Shop Pro yourself from Jasc Software. Their Web site is at http://www.jasc.com.*

 Note: *In this chapter I explain how to make a lot of common documents like business cards, stationery, and brochures. I use Microsoft Word to explain these projects, but you can take the general instructions and apply them to almost any word processor. My examples use Word 97, though almost any version of Word—even Word 2.0—will do.*

PROJECTS FOR WINDOWS

 ### How do I turn an image into Windows wallpaper?

If your Windows desktop still has that tired old blue background, you can use an image from your digital camera to brighten things up. Your desktop—the basic Windows screen on which all your applications, folders, and icons appear—can display any kind of image you desire, as long as it has been saved in GIF or BMP format.

To display your image on your desktop, do this:

1. Start by saving your image in either BMP or GIF format. Open a graphics program like Paint Shop Pro (or whatever program you like to use) and choose File | Save As. Select one of those two formats and save the image somewhere on your hard disk.

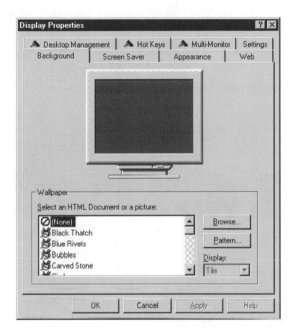

Tip: *If you like to switch among different background images on your desktop, then store them either in the Windows folder or, even better, in a specific folder like C:\WALLPAPER.*

2. Right-click on the desktop and choose Properties from the context menu. The Display Properties dialog box appears.

3. On the Background tab, click on the Browse button to choose the image.

4. If you want the image to be centered in your display, choose Center in the Display drop-down menu. If you'd prefer the image to be tiled on the display, choose Tile instead.

5. Click OK to close the dialog box.

❋ ***Note:*** *To later turn off the image in your desktop and get back to a plain green display, open the Display Properties dialog box and choose None from the list of images in the Background tab.*

When you save your image for the Windows desktop, decide how you want it to look. You can fill the entire display with your image, for instance, but you'll need to make sure the image's resolution matches the resolution of the display. Your display may be running at 640×480 (a common camera resolution), 1,024×768, or some other setting. To resize your image to fit, see Chapter 11.

If your image is too small for the display, it'll either be *tiled* (repeated) to fill the screen or will be centered in the display with a border around it. For photographs, I think the border looks good—tiling photographs is just too busy and annoys me (see Figure 13-1). Of course, you can experiment and arrange your display any way you like.

What is the Apply button in the Display Properties dialog box for?

This button lets you actually display the selected image on the Windows desktop without closing the dialog box first. It's handy if you want to "try on" a few different images before making your final decision. You don't ever need to click the Apply button; it's just there as an option for previewing your images.

How do you make an image tile on the desktop without seam lines?

One of the problems with selecting the Tile option for your desktop image is the fact that a tiled display has all those abrupt seams caused by the top of one image bumping into the bottom of another and left edge of one meeting the right edge of the next. One way to make these seams less abrupt is to vignette your image with a border so that the borders meet each other and blend together.

Figure 13-1 The same image shown centered and tiled

You can try this in almost any graphics program. In Paint Shop Pro, do this:

1. Load your image and choose the oval selection tool. Set the feather to at least ten pixels.

2. Select an oval that goes almost all the way to the edge of the image on all four sides.

3. Since the subject is selected, you need to reverse the selection region. Choose Selections | Invert.

4. Now paint the selected region of the image any color you like—this will be the border.

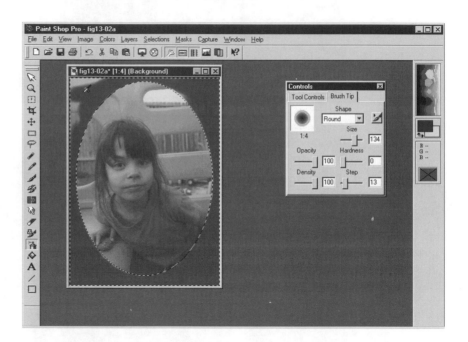

5. When you're done, save the image in BMP or GIF format.

Another, more automated solution exists. Many image editors have a tool that modifies your image so all the edges blend together when it's tiled, as shown in Figure 13-2. The image on the top looks very nice when tiled on the desktop. In Paint Shop Pro, select some part of your image and choose Selections | Convert to Seamless Pattern. When you use this

Figure 13-2 Converting an image to "seamless borders" with your image editor can make it much more attractive for tiling

tool, you can't select the entire image, since Paint Shop Pro uses pixels beyond the marquee to create a pattern with no discernible edges.

How do I display an image as the background in a Windows folder?

If you're using Internet Explorer 4 or higher, you have a new option: You can set up specific folders to display images when you open them (see Figure 13-3). Every folder can have a

Figure 13-3 One disadvantage of this feature is that folder contents are harder to see

different image, and some folders can open the normal way, without an image. It's all up to you.

Not sure if your computer has Internet Explorer 4 installed? To find out if your system supports this feature, just open a folder on your desktop and open the View menu for the folder window. If there's a menu item called Customize This Folder, you're in business.

Here's how to display an image from your camera as the background in a folder:

1. Start by saving your image in BMP, GIF, or JPEG format. Open a graphics program like Paint Shop Pro (or whatever program you like to use) and choose File | Save As. Select one of these formats and save the image somewhere on your hard disk.

2. Open the folder you want to display your background image in and choose View | Customize This Folder. A dialog box appears.

3. Select Choose a Background Picture and click OK.

4. Click on the Browse button and select the image you just saved.

5. Click Next and then Finish.

If you later want to turn the image off, follow steps 1–3 and then choose Remove Customization.

PROJECTS FOR FUN AND BUSINESS

 What kinds of projects can I make using my digital images?

These days, you can do pretty much anything with your PC, a digital camera, and some design or layout software. With just a little practice, you can make business cards, labels, stationery, greeting cards, posters, brochures, entire newsletters, and even specialty items like T-shirts and coffee mugs.

One way to think about digital imaging is that if the local store can do it, so can you. Don't be intimidated by projects that require special supplies, like T-shirts. You'll find that complete kits are readily available at your local computer shop (see Chapter 17 for more information). So be bold, and give away baseball caps with pictures of your kids on them next Christmas!

What software do I need to create projects using images from my digital camera?

There's a wide variety of project-oriented software on the market for digital camera owners. Odds are good, in fact, that you got something along those lines with your camera. Some programs, like Arcsoft's Photo Fantasy, are targeted at families that want to use special effects to create portraits in a wide variety of settings and virtual costumes. Some programs are specifically for creating greeting cards; others are more general purpose. Of the general-purpose programs, my favorites are LivePix's LivePix and Ulead's Photo Express. Both of these programs allow you to create a mind-boggling array of projects—everything from greeting cards to calendars to business cards.

On the other hand, you don't have to have a program like that to make some really interesting and useful projects with your images—a word processor like Microsoft Word will do quite nicely. In fact, many of the projects demonstrated in this chapter require only Word.

Can I add my own image to my personal letterhead?

Absolutely! Creating personal letterhead with your digital images is easy. You can do this in many different programs, but we'll work in Microsoft Word. Here's what you should do:

1. Open Microsoft Word. If you don't already have a new blank document open, click on the new document icon in the toolbar.

2. Design the letterhead any way you like. You should set your formatting to single-spaced and try to keep your text around 11-point or smaller.

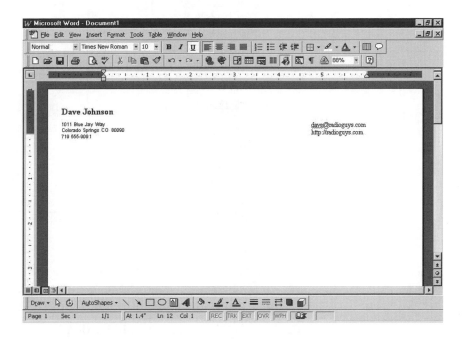

3. To insert an image, choose Insert | Picture | From File and locate the image you want to include. The image will appear in your document.

4. To make the image easier to move around and position on the page, you'll need to put a frame around the picture. Right-click on the image and choose Format Picture.

5. On the Position tab, choose Float over Text. Then click on the Wrapping tab and choose Both Sides and Tight, which tell Word how to make text wrap around your image.

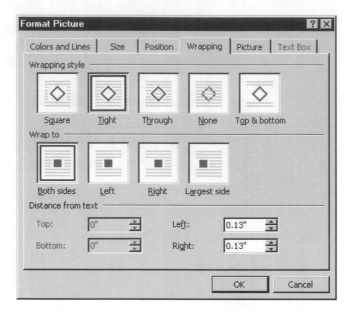

6. Click OK.

7. Position the image somewhere in the letterhead region of your document, such as to the left of your name. Notice how the text moves to accommodate the image.

8. Finish off the letterhead by drawing a thin horizontal line under the text and image (see Figure 13-4). To do that, activate the drawing tools by clicking on the drawing icon in the toolbar. Then click on the line tool and drag out a horizontal line while holding down the SHIFT key. The line will snap to the horizontal automatically.

9. Now you need to save the document as a template, so you can create new documents while keeping your blank letterhead intact. Choose File | Save As and change the Save As type to Document Template. Give your letterhead a name and specify which template folder you'd like to save it in.

Tip:　*Images in letterhead often benefit from feathering, which enables them to blend smoothly into the background. Figure 13-4 shows an example of this effect.*

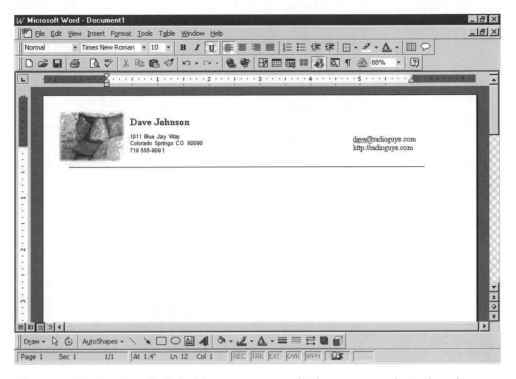

Figure 13-4 Small digital images can really jazz up your letterhead

In the future, when you want to write on the stationery you just made, choose File | New and choose the letterhead template from the list that appears.

 ## How do I make an image appear as a "watermark" on my stationery?

Have you ever wondered how to simulate a watermark in your Word documents? It's a simple thing to do, really, and you can make any digital image in your portfolio the mark behind your text.

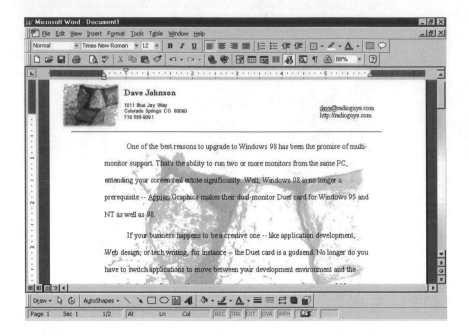

Here's what you need to do:

1. Open the document to which you want to add a watermark.

2. Insert your image by choosing Insert | Picture | From File. The image will appear in your document.

3. Now you need to turn the image into a watermark. Right-click on the image and choose Format Picture. The Format Picture dialog box will appear.

4. Click on the Picture tab and choose Watermark from the Color drop-down menu.

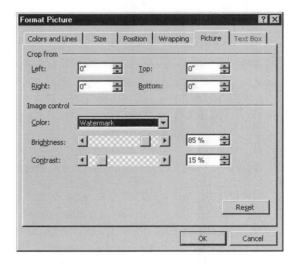

5. Switch to the Position tab and enable Float over Text.

6. Click on the Wrapping tab and select None.

7. Click OK to exit the Format Picture dialog box.

8. You're almost done. Now right-click on the picture and select Order | Send Behind Text.

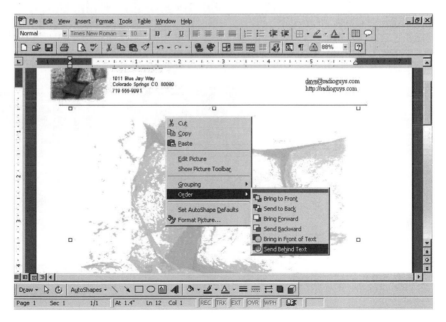

The text in your document should now flow on top of the image, which looks like a watermark.

 Tip: *If you plan to use this image as a watermark often, save the document as a template. That way you can get started faster without converting the image to a watermark every time.*

How can I make my own business cards?

You can create business cards (and similarly sized labels) with Microsoft Word, but most people don't even realize the capability is in there because the tools for creating them aren't near the surface. Both business cards and labels are great canvases on which to put images taken with your digital camera. Include your own picture, or if you're an architect, for instance, include a picture of one of your designs.

To create your business cards or labels:

1. Open Word and create a new, blank document by clicking on the new document icon in the toolbar.

2. Choose Tools | Envelopes and Labels. The Envelopes and Labels dialog box will appear.

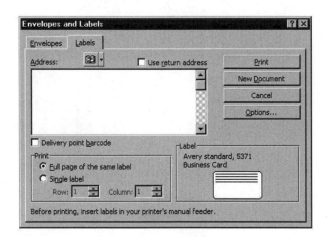

3. Switch to the Labels tab if it's not already selected.

4. Click the Options button. The Label Options dialog box appears.

5. From the Label Products menu, choose the kind of business card sheets that you will be printing on. If you don't see your brand, choose the brand that's recommended by the instructions that came with your business cards, or try Other, which may include your product.

6. In the product number listing, find and select the type of business card (or label) you're trying to print. Click OK.

7. In most cases (that is, assuming you're printing to a sheet of cards or labels that's fed through a laser or inkjet printer, instead of to a dedicated label printer) you'll click the New Document button in the Envelopes and Labels dialog box.

8. Now you have a new document that has been broken up into boxes that correspond to the business cards you're creating. In the top-left box, design your business card, as shown in Figure 13-5.

9. To insert an image into your card, choose Insert | Picture | From File.

10. When you're finished designing the card, move the mouse pointer to the left edge of the card. Notice that it turns into a right-facing pointer. When it does, click to select the entire card. If you go too far and select the entire row or column by accident, try again.

11. Choose Edit | Copy and then place the pointer in another box. Choose Edit | Paste. Repeat this process until you've pasted the card into all the other boxes on the page.

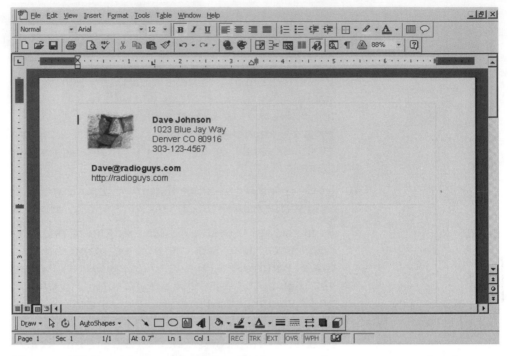

Figure 13-5 After creating your business card once, you can simply duplicate it throughout the page

How do I make brochures?

Tri-folded brochures are a great low-cost marketing tool for your business or even just a garage sale. You can make a brochure in Word very easily. Here what you need to do:

1. Open Word and create a new, blank document by clicking on the new document icon in the toolbar.

2. You'll need to change the document to a landscape orientation. Choose File | Page Setup. The Page Setup dialog box appears.

Optimizing Your Business Cards

When you create your own business cards, you have more creative control than you would if you let a print shop do it for you. More important, you can print them as you need them, so you never come up short right before a business trip. But it's easy to make silly or cheap-looking cards, so consider some of these tips:

● Don't print display elements—like text and graphics—too close to the edge, since they may end up right on the cut line.

● Use the heaviest paper your printer can feed. Look for at least 65-pound card stock.

● If your printer gives you a choice, choose the straightest paper path through the printer.

● For a splash of color, get card stock with preprinted designs and print the cards on a laser printer. Typical inkjets can't deliver the same level of sharpness in text as a laser, so you might want to avoid color inkjets for professional business cards.

● Print a test page before you print out reams of cards. That way, you can see what the cards look like and make adjustments as necessary.

3. Click on the Paper Size tab and select Landscape from the orientation section. Click OK.

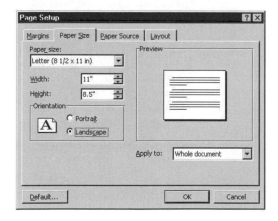

4. Now you'll give the document multiple columns. Choose Format | Columns.

5. In the Columns dialog box, select Three and click OK.

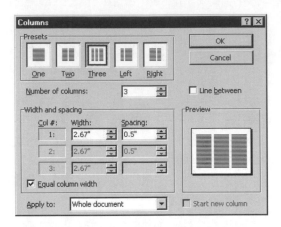

6. Now you can enter the text of your brochure. Insert images as you wish using the Insert | Picture | From File menu item. Layout is simple: You can drag and drop the images around the brochure as needed.

How do I make my own greeting cards?

There are two ways to make greeting cards using your computer: the easy way and the not-as-easy-but-still-not-very-hard way. The easy way is by using one of the many greeting card software packages on the market. Your digital camera or color printer may even have come with a greeting card program; if so, feel free to use it. Not only can you import your digital camera images into these programs, they come with a considerable collection of clip art and preformatted card templates.

If you don't have one of those programs, then you can still make your own greeting cards in a page layout program or even Microsoft Word. Since Word is the lowest common denominator—almost everyone has it—let's create a card in that. Before we get started, though, it's worth pointing out that there are two common methods for making a greeting card on the PC: the one-fold and two-fold techniques.

One-fold cards are simply made from 8.5×11-inch paper or card stock folded once down the middle so that it measures 5.5×8.5-inches. This is a slightly oversized card, but it's a good size and the one I most commonly make. The alternative is a two-fold card that is folded once lengthwise and again widthwise, for a card that measures 5.5×4.25-inches. The disadvantage to this kind of card is that it's a bit small and it has a potentially amateurish double fold on one edge (see Figure 13-6).

You can't really make double-fold cards in Word, since that kind of card requires one of the panels to be printed upside down. So Word is best at single-fold cards, as in this example:

1. Open Word and create a new document.

2. You'll need to change the document to a landscape orientation. First, choose File|Page Setup. The Page Setup dialog box appears.

3. Click on the Paper Size tab and select Landscape from the orientation section. Click OK.

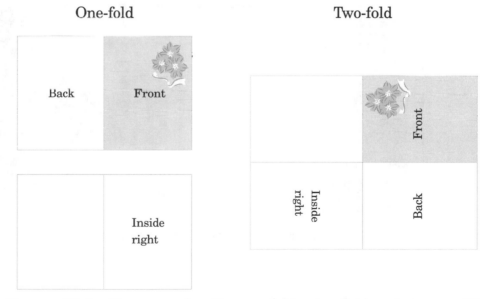

One-fold   Two-fold

Figure 13-6 You can make either one-fold or two-fold cards on your PC with the right software

4. Now you need to give the document two columns. Each column will be a panel on the finished card. Choose Format | Columns.

5. In the Columns dialog box, select Two and click OK.

6. Now you can enter your text. The left column on the first page is actually the rear of the card. If you want to, you can add something to the bottom of the rear panel as commercial greeting cards do. Just press ENTER enough times to get to the bottom of the page.

7. Now it's time for the front of the card. That's the right column on the first page, so press ENTER to get there. You'll probably want to insert an image there using the Insert | Picture | From File (see Figure 13-7). You can place text above or below the image, or integrate the text with the image in a program like Paint Shop Pro first.

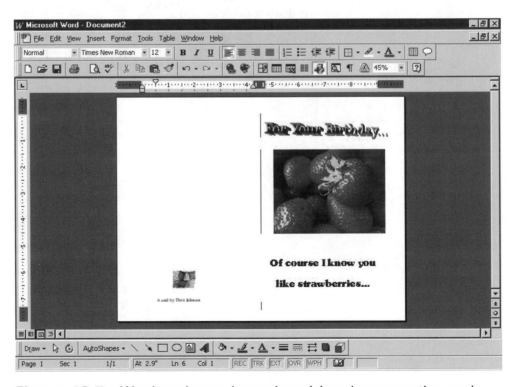

Figure 13-7 Word can be used to make quick and easy greeting cards, though a dedicated card program is a better bet

Be sure to experiment with large and stylish fonts for your card.

Tip: *Microsoft's WordArt is a great choice for dressing up a greeting card in Word. It lets you turn plain text into a fancy, 3-D piece of art, as seen in Figure 13-7. Choose Insert | Picture | WordArt or Insert | Object to insert WordArt into your project.*

8. The inside of the card is the second page of the Word document. The left inside panel is the left column and the right inside panel is the right column, so enter text and images as necessary to lay out the card you want to create.

9. When you're done, you'll need to print your card manually so you can print on both sides of the sheet of paper. To do that, you have two choices:

● Only load a single sheet of paper in the printer. When the first side is printed, turn the paper over and load it back in for the second pass.

● Change the printer settings. In Word, choose File | Print. Choose Properties to open the Printer Properties dialog box and change the printer's paper source to manual.

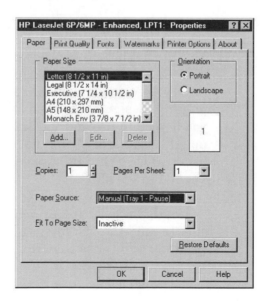

Tip: *If you're printing on an inkjet printer, make sure you wait for the first side to dry before turning the paper over and printing the second side. Also, see Chapter 17 for more tips on printing.*

Can I make a newsletter without expensive software?

Certainly, it might help to have a nice expensive page layout program to create a newsletter, but if your needs are fairly simple, you can create a pretty nice newsletter, complete with images from your camera, in Microsoft Word. Word even includes a Wizard that helps you. Just choose File | New and look for the Newsletter Wizard. Follow its instructions, and then substitute your own images for the placeholders that you'll find in the document (see Figure 13-8).

 Tip: *If you happen to have the Microsoft Office Small Business Edition, you also have Microsoft Publisher on your hard disk. Publisher is a much better tool for creating newsletters, and I highly recommend that you use that program instead of Word. Like Word, it's Wizard-driven, so all you need to do is follow the Wizard to get a spiffy-looking newsletter.*

How do I make a T-shirt with a picture on it?

You can get a T-shirt program like Hanes T-Shirt Maker, or do it yourself. There's not that much to it, really—in fact, there's only one important requirement. If you're not using a program designed expressly for T-shirt iron-on transfers, you'll need to use your editing program's flip tool to flip the image backwards. You'll need to print onto the transfer paper backwards so that it'll appear forward when it's finally applied to the shirt.

You can find T-shirt iron-on transfer paper designed expressly for color inkjet printers at most computer stores. Be sure to read the instructions that come with the paper carefully to be sure that you have the iron at the right

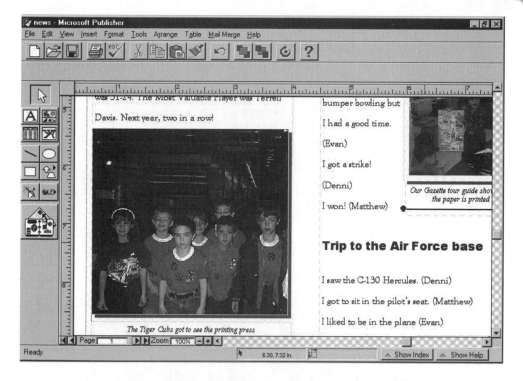

Figure 13-8 Newsletters can be easily made in either Word or Microsoft Publisher

temperature and that you're running the paper through the printer the right way.

How do I insert images into PowerPoint presentations?

If you commonly create Microsoft PowerPoint presentations, you may find that adding some digital camera images can brighten up even the most dull topic. Instead of being satisfied with run-of-the-mill clip art, for instance, you can include pictures of the actual people you're discussing, or shoot images of the buildings, equipment, or locations you're talking about.

Getting images into PowerPoint is a piece of cake. Here's all you need to do:

1. Open your presentation to the slide you want to include an image on.

2. Insert the image by choosing Insert | Picture | From File.

3. Position the image by dragging it anywhere on the screen you need it to go. You can also resize the image by using the handles in the image's corners.

4. Edit the image if necessary using the Image toolbar. You can add and remove brightness and contrast.

5. If the image isn't cropped well, you can do it within PowerPoint. Click on the Crop button on the Image toolbar and drag the resizing handles of the image. Rather than being resized, the image will be cropped.

 Tip: *Try to keep your images small, or your PowerPoint presentation can get large and sluggish.*

USING CLIP ART AND STOCK IMAGES

 ### What is clip art? How is it different than stock photography?

Clip art is any collection of canned images that are available for inclusion in word processing, page layout, Web design, or other applications that use graphics. Clip art is almost always line art or some other kind of simple hand-drawn image.

Stock photography, on the other hand, is actual photographs—people, landscapes, objects—that you can use in your graphics project. Stock photography is less common than clip art because it is more expensive and the files are larger.

 ### Where do I get clip art and stock photography?

Most creative software, like presentation packages, word processors, art software, and so on, comes with at least a small collection of clip art. Microsoft Office, for instance, has an integrated collection of clip art that you can use in any Microsoft application. You can get to it by choosing

Insert | Picture | Clip Art (see Figure 13-9). You can also purchase clip art collections in stores and over the Internet. Corel, for instance, has several inexpensive collections of clip art that you can investigate.

DeMorgan's WebSpice is a collection of clip art for Web pages. WebSpice Animations, for instance, includes over 35,000 "3D" animated GIFs in categories like words, objects, buttons, and arrows. You can sort through the art in a Web browser and easily drop it into your Web page. DeMorgan also has a 1,000,000 Page Design edition of buttons, graphics, page templates, and more.

For stock photography, an online source of imagery is Publishers Depot, found at http://www.publishersdepot.com. The site's 400,000 digital images can be easily searched, licensed, and downloaded in a matter of minutes. How do you find what you need with that many images? The site uses a natural language search engine—more efficient than keyword searches—that speeds up your hunt for specific kinds of images. The site even offers free research assistance.

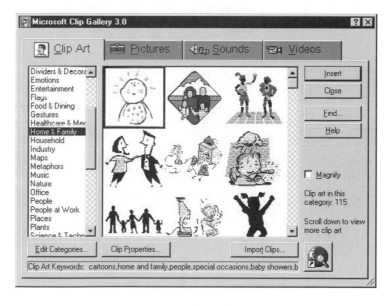

Figure 13-9   Microsoft has integrated a clip art tool into all the Office applications so it's available no matter which program you're using

Other vendors sell their stock images and clip art on CD-ROM. Both Artville (www.artville.com) and Adobe (www.adobe.com) have extensive catalogs.

How do I know if I have permission to use a piece of clip art or stock?

If clip art or stock photography is sold as such, it typically comes as "royalty free" art. That means you can use it in any application you want, since you've already paid for non-exclusive use of it. The license should clearly authorize you to use the art in this way, however. Be sure the images you're using are, in fact, authorized for such use or you may be in violation of the owner's copyright. For more information, see Chapter 16.

Chapter 14

Distributing Images

Answer Topics!

Distributing Images @ a Glance

How can you get digital images into the hands of friends and family? The easiest way is actually by printing hard copy, and you can look in Chapter 17 for details about that. After printing, the easiest solution is often sending images on disk or via e-mail. Look here for answers to questions about file formats, compatibility, and the easiest ways to distribute your images.

The World Wide Web is the ultimate printing press. Moments after you publish something to the Internet, it's available to the world. You can take advantage of this instant digital publishing to post your own images for the world to see. You can use other people's Web sites or create your own.

Multimedia is the synthesis of more than one kind of medium, like images and sound or video and text. You can take advantage of multimedia to publish images in compelling ways, like a video slideshow with music or within a PowerPoint presentation. Look here to find out how.

DISTRIBUTION METHODS

 Can I send images via e-mail?

Yes, you can use e-mail as a way of sending digital images from your PC to someone else's. It's simply a matter of including one or more images as *attachments* to your mail message. Attachments are binary files—as opposed to plain text—that your mail program can deliver to another person's mail system.

Most of the time, attachments work just fine. Occasionally, though, you'll run into problems sending images as attachments. That's because the original Internet didn't really have a method for sending binary files via e-mail, and encoding schemes were "tacked on" after the fact. Here are some snags you may run into:

● **Watch out for files that are too big.** Most e-mail systems can't deal with a single attachment that's bigger than about 2MB (or 2,000K). If you send a very large file to someone, it can get "stuck" in their mail server. Check the file size of your attachments (see Figure 14-1) before sending them.

● **America Online can only handle a single attachment.** Even though most mail systems can accept several attached files in each e-mail, AOL doesn't quite know what to make of that kind of message. Only send AOL users a single attachment at a time.

● **Not all mail programs are compatible.** You can send a plain text message between virtually any two Internet mail programs in the world, but if you want to send an attachment, sometimes it won't work. Your mail program may allow you to change the way your attachment is encoded. If that's the case, then you can experiment with different ways of sending the file to the recipient.

In addition, there are programs around that create "multimedia e-mail" messages for you. Often, you'll get such

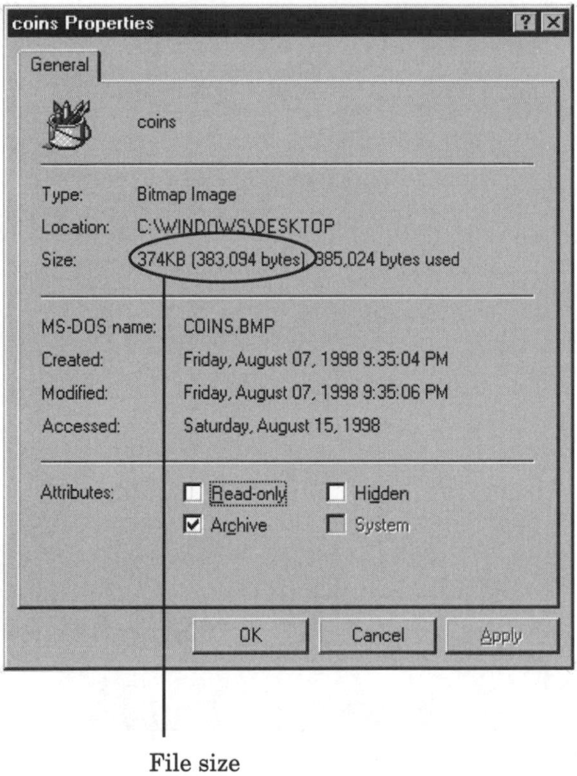

File size

Figure 14-1   Right-click on a file and choose Properties to see how big
it is

programs with digital cameras or bundled with image editing
software. Programs like Novita LiveLetter and Media
Synergy's Aloha help you create a complete multimedia
experience with sound, graphics, and text, and then attach
that to an e-mail message and send it to someone else (see
Figure 14-2). The recipient merely double-clicks on the
message to see the show.

How do I attach an image to an e-mail message?

While the procedure varies somewhat from one mail system
to another, it isn't terribly different in most programs. Almost

Figure 14-2   Novita LiveLetter comes with LivePix and can be used
to create multimedia e-mail messages to send to friends
and family

all mail software has an attachment button indicated by a
paperclip icon. Clicking that button usually brings up a
dialog box that you can use to specify files for inclusion in
your e-mail (see Figure 14-3).

 **How do I get to an image that someone has attached
to an e-mail message?**

In most e-mail programs (like Netscape Messenger, Microsoft
Exchange, Outlook, and Outlook Express), the attachment
appears as an icon that you work with like any other icon. In
other words, right-click on the icon to save the attachment to

Attachment button opens
an Insert File dialog box

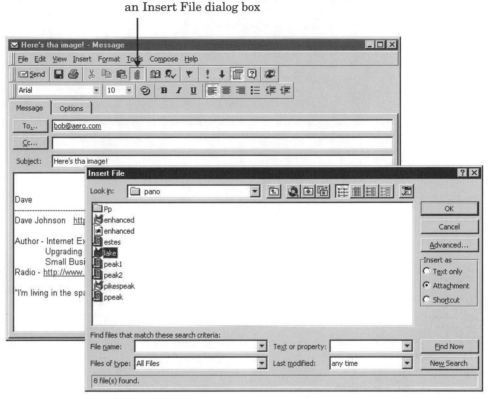

Figure 14-3 You can easily add images to your e-mail messages

another location on your hard disk, or double-click on the icon
to launch it in the appropriate application (see Figure 14-4).

Does it matter what file format I use? Can everyone read my images?

If you're sending an image to a Windows 95 computer, almost
any file format is fair game. To be on the safe side, you should
send Mac users files in TIFF or JPEG format, and Windows
3.1 users should get BMP or JPEG files. Since JPEG is a very
efficient file format for sending photographic images, sending
images in JPEG format exclusively is a good choice.

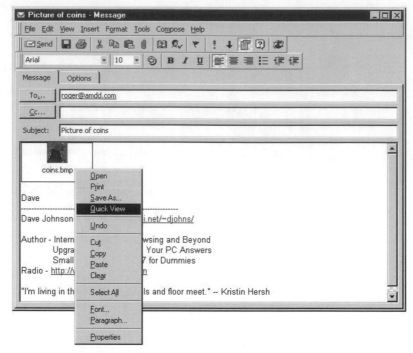

Figure 14-4   You can save attachments to your hard disk or open them
in the appropriate application right away

Can a Mac read a PC floppy or Zip disk? What about the other way around?

If you want to distribute an image on a floppy disk and you
are a PC user with Mac associates, you're in luck—the
Macintosh floppy drive can read PC disks just fine. That
means you can copy a few JPEG images to a floppy and give
it to a Mac user and they'll be able to read the images
just fine.

Going the other way is more problematic, though—PCs
can't read Macintosh floppies. So Mac users need to be sure
the disk is formatted for a PC before doing the handoff. The
same is true of Zip disks. A Zip disk made on a Mac cannot be
read on a PC.

Creating This Book

For this book, I used Zip disks to send the images and screen shots to my editor. That's a first for me, since artwork for books is generally sent by e-mail. But since I had so many high-resolution digital images in this book, some chapters had over 30MB worth of images! Sending that many images over the Internet or by floppy disk would have been impractical.

 How do I compress images so they don't take up so much space?

You have two primary tools at your disposal for reducing the file size of your images for distribution:

- Use the compression feature in the JPEG format to reduce file size. With many images, you can compress the image significantly before you start to see any obvious degradation due to compression. This is great if you're just passing images around among friends, though I'd be more careful about compressing images you are planning to print. Use a graphics editor like Paint Shop Pro (see Chapter 11) to save images in JPEG format.

- Use pkzip to compress images. If your image files are already compressed (such as if you use the JPEG or compressed TIFF formats), then pkzip won't do much for your total file size. But if you are trying to send uncompressed images via floppy or e-mail, then this compression program can be a lifesaver. I suggest that you get a version of pkzip that has a friendly Windows interface, like WinZip. Zip compression programs are readily available for download via the Internet—just go to a Web site like download.com or shareware.com and search for "zip" to find a suitable program.

 ### Can I distribute my images on PhotoCD?

Not exactly. PhotoCD is a format developed by Kodak that allows you to store very high-resolution images on CD, but they typically start out as 35mm negatives and are transferred to CD by a photo developer. PhotoCD is a great format for working with images, because each picture on the CD is stored in five different resolutions, so you can use the one that best suits your needs.

But digital images can also be stored on CD. You simply need a CD recorder, and CD recorders have become quite inexpensive in the last few years. You can store over 500MB of images on a single CD, so the capacity is tremendous.

 ### What's the most efficient way to send someone a lot of images at once?

If you're sending lots of images, use a Zip disk. Since the Zip disk holds 100MB of data, you have an awful lot of room to work with. It's certainly more efficient than the Internet, on which you're limited to a total file size of about 2MB and the download time is slow.

If you don't have that much data to send, however, e-mail is a very convenient way to send one or two images at a time. Just watch out for that file size so you don't overload the recipient's server (see "Can I send images via e-mail?" earlier in this chapter).

USING THE WEB

 ### Are there Web sites where I can post images to show off my work?

Yes, I've encountered several Web sites that allow you to post your handiwork for free so others can appreciate your photographic genius. Here are a few:

● **The Computer Artist's Forum**   Visit the forum at http://www.geocities.com/SoHo/3103/. Here you can view others' work and submit your own for display.

Faxing Your Images

Have you ever heard of color fax? Probably not; it's not very common yet. Color fax technology is a great boon for digital photographers, though. Using the right software, you can scan a color image and fax it to someone else's computer. The actual image being faxed looks like gibberish because it's a graphic representation of the image after processing and encoding. At the other end, software decodes the page of gibberish and prints out a color image on the recipient's color printer.

Even better, color fax technology allows you to send huge graphic files via a fairly compact, efficient fax. Images that would be far too big to send via e-mail or a floppy disk can be sent via color fax. At the other end, the page of digital gibberish is transformed back into a fully editable computer file that represents the original image. That means you can convert a JPEG image, for instance, into a fax and then back into a JPEG again at the other end.

Interested in trying this out? The InfoImaging Color Scan and Fax is a flatbed scanner that includes this unique conversion software. Just remember, though, that the recipient needs to have the same software in order to be able to decrypt the data.

- **i/us**   Found at http://i-us.com/, this site allows you to post images. It also is a comprehensive community of online digital artists and photographers.

- **Virtual Exploration**   Visit this site at http://www. virtualexploration.com. It's a virtual world atlas filled with pictures from around the world. You can submit your own images for specific cities.

How do I create my own Web site to showcase my images?

If you want to show off your digital creations to the world, one easy way to publish your images around the world is by

creating a Web page. Creating a Web page is easy, particularly if you use a WYSIWYG Web page designer, since you don't need to know any HTML at all to create interesting-looking pages. You can even get this kind of page design software for free—both Netscape Navigator and Internet Explorer come with free Web design software. See Chapter 15 for details on creating a Web presence.

Once your site is posted, however, how do you let the world know about it? You can advertise your site on search engines, but there is an easier answer: Join a group of Web sites that are all dedicated to the same thing as yours—photography. *Web rings*, which are groups of related and interconnected Web sites, are a popular approach to this community concept. You can get a list of all the Web rings at http://beq.webring.com. Or, you can investigate specific rings dedicated to photography (there are over 100 different rings). Some of the rings that may appeal to you include:

● **The Ring of Photography** http://www.best.com/~gazissax/paths/ring/index.html

● **The Amateur Photography Ring** http://home.earthlink.net/~troise/ring.htm

● **The PC Photography Ring** http://www.mgisoft.com/webring/webring.html

● **The Digital Art Ring** http://pluginhead.i-us.com/digring.htm

● **The Sony Mavica Web Ring** http://www.fortunecity.com/skyscraper/data/440/

USING MULTIMEDIA

 Can I distribute images on videotape, like in a slideshow?

Yes, you can. There are two ways to do this:

● Use the video-out jack on your digital camera to play back images on your television and capture them to VHS with your VCR.

● Transfer your images to the PC. Then use video editing software or a nonlinear editor to arrange and edit your images, add sound and fancy transitions, and finally output the results to video via the video-out jack on the video capture card in your PC.

Obviously, the first solution is easier, but the results may not be as good as you'd like. Transferring images from your camera to video is fraught with compromises. There's usually no way to precisely time the transition from one image to another in your slideshow, for instance, so you can't synchronize images to music. Also, images tend to roll slowly onto the screen as they are read from memory. It can look cheesy, particularly if you're used to seeing pictures "snap" rapidly onto the screen.

The second solution—using your PC and a video capture card—is a lot more elegant, though it requires more work and a video capture card, which you may not already own and would then need to purchase. On the other hand, using this setup allows you a lot more control over your images, particularly if you use a nonlinear editor like Adobe Premiere. For more information on this kind of solution, see Chapter 18.

How do I make a digital slideshow I can show on my PC?

Sometimes it's important to be able to show a series of digital images in sequence on your PC or a video projection system. I've had to display and explain digital images both in corporate meeting environments and in the classroom as an instructor. A common way to do this is using presentation software like Microsoft PowerPoint (which you may already own if you're a Microsoft Office user).

 Note: *You can make a digital slideshow with a wide variety of presentation programs, though I've selected PowerPoint as an example in this chapter. It's powerful, easy to use, and most important, most people already have it—it comes with many new PCs in Microsoft Office Professional.*

To create a slideshow using PowerPoint, do this:

1. Start PowerPoint and choose Blank Presentation in the main PowerPoint dialog box.

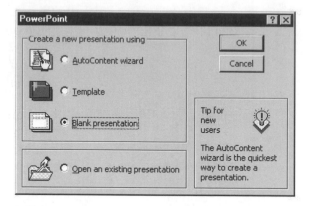

2. You need to choose a slide style for the very first slide from the New Slide dialog box. The best choice is typically the first one, which displays a title. Choose it.

3. To add a title to your presentation, just click in the text box (it's a placeholder containing sample text for you to type over) and type in a name for your presentation.

4. Now you're ready to add another slide. Click on the New Slide button in the Common Tasks dialog box.

5. In the New Slide dialog box, select one of the slide formats that include both text and a graphic, such as the two at the bottom left.

These layouts include placeholders for both text and graphics

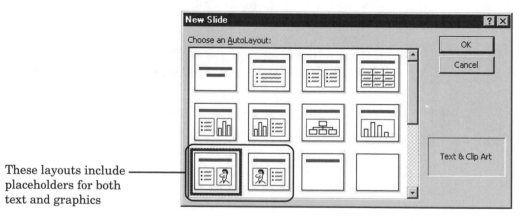

6. Enter information in the placeholders for the title and any text that will accompany the image.

7. Choose Insert | Picture | From File. Find the image you want to add to the slide.

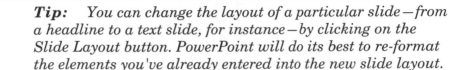

Tip: *You can change the layout of a particular slide—from a headline to a text slide, for instance—by clicking on the Slide Layout button. PowerPoint will do its best to re-format the elements you've already entered into the new slide layout.*

8. When the image appears on your slide, position it over the clip art placeholder. The image will "snap" into position and the placeholder will "absorb" the image so it's properly positioned on the slide.

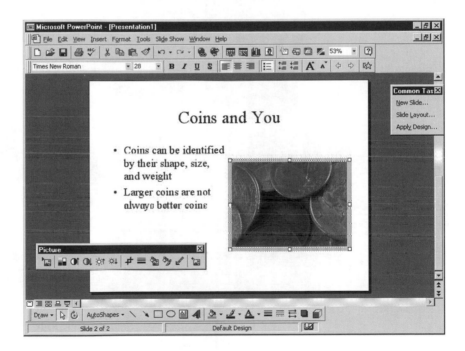

9. Save your presentation by choosing File | Save As.

10. Continue adding new slides and new images until your presentation is complete.

 ## How do I add interesting effects like wipes, fades, and animations to my slideshow?

A plain-vanilla PowerPoint presentation—even with digital images—just isn't all that interesting to look at. If you want to add some pizzazz, like animation effects or text that fades into view, you can tap into the power of PowerPoint's multimedia tools.

To try out some of PowerPoint's animation tools, create a page with some text and an image and try this:

1. Click on a text box and choose Slide Show | Preset Animation | Dissolve.

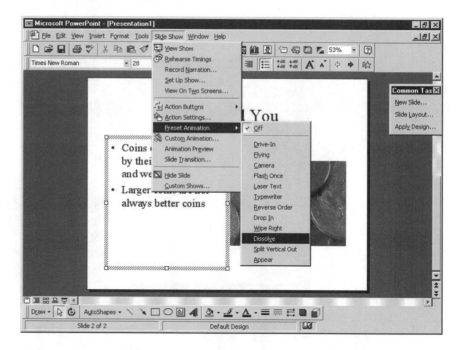

2. Click on another text box and choose Slide Show | Preset Animation | Camera.

3. Preview this new, animated slide by choosing Slide Show | Animation Preview. A thumbnail of the slide will appear and the animations you assigned will be

demonstrated in the order you entered them. Click on the preview window to play the animation over again.

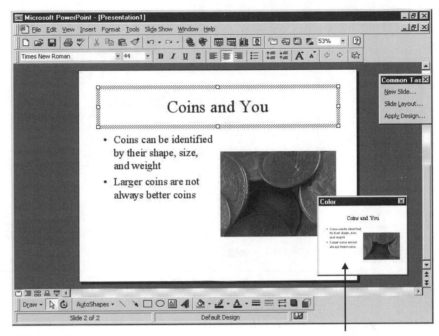

The animation preview window lets you see the effects you've chosen

Unfortunately, you can't assign these animations to digital images, though you can assign animation to line-art graphics.

Tip: *Experiment! There are a lot of cool animation effects in PowerPoint, and the best way to learn what they do is by trying them out.*

Now that you've created some animation on a slide, you might want to add transitions between slides. To add a transition to your slide, just choose Slide Show | Slide Transition. A dialog box appears in which you can select the

kind of transition you want, the speed, and a method for advance (such as a mouse click).

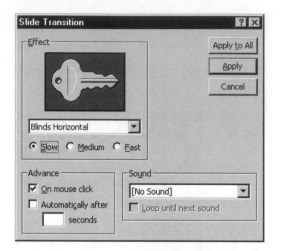

 Tip: *In the Slide Transition dialog box, you can Apply transitions to a particular slide or Apply to All the slides at once. In my opinion, slideshows that use a different effect for every transition, have a decidedly unprofessional look. I suggest you stick with a subdued single-transition approach throughout the entire presentation.*

How can I set up PowerPoint to cycle through a set of slides all by itself?

It's easy to configure PowerPoint to run autonomously, so it can cycle through your images on its own. Just follow these steps:

1. First you need to configure PowerPoint so it knows how long to display each slide. Choose Slide Show | Rehearse Timing.

2. The slideshow begins playing. Use the left mouse button to advance through the presentation at whatever rate you want it to play at.

3. When you're done, PowerPoint asks if you want to save the timing settings. Click Yes.

4. PowerPoint asks if you want to review the timings in the Slide Sorter. Click No.

5. Choose Slide Show | Set Up Show. The Set Up Show dialog box appears.

6. Make sure that the options "Loop continuously until 'Esc.'" (under "Show type"), "All" (under "Slides"), and "Using timings, if present" (under "Advance slides") are selected.

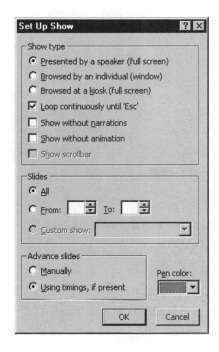

7. Click OK.

8. Now you can run your presentation. Choose Slide Show | View Show. The presentation should play by itself until you press the ESC key to stop it.

I'm giving a PowerPoint presentation that's packed with digital images and it's too big for a floppy. How do I get it to my destination?

You can use a Zip disk, since it can hold 100MB. But if the computer you need to use doesn't have a Zip drive, then try a

tool that is built into PowerPoint called "Pack and Go." To use it, create your presentation the ordinary way. But when you're ready to transport the presentation, follow these steps:

1. Choose File|Pack and Go. Step through the Pack and Go Wizard with the Next button.

2. Pick the files that you want to "pack." You can choose between "Active presentation"—which is the currently open presentation—and "Other presentation(s)." Choose the latter if you want to pack several shows at once.

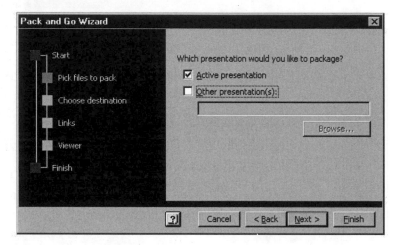

3. Pick the drive that you want to copy the files to. You can put them on floppies or copy them to a folder on your hard disk and move the files to a portable drive later. Click Next.

4. Choose whether to include linked files and embedded fonts. Including these ensures that the presentation will play properly on the other system. You can save space in the packed file, though, if you don't include these items. Click Next.

5. Choose whether to include the Viewer. If you know there's a PowerPoint program or Viewer on the destination computer, you can save space by leaving the Viewer out of the Pack and Go file. Click Next.

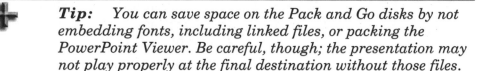

✛ ***Tip:*** *You can save space on the Pack and Go disks by not embedding fonts, including linked files, or packing the PowerPoint Viewer. Be careful, though; the presentation may not play properly at the final destination without those files.*

6. When you reach your destination, insert the Pack and Go disks and run the file called Pngsetup. It will extract the PowerPoint files so you can run your slideshow.

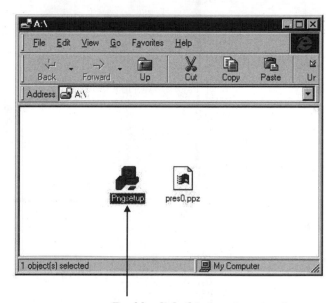

Double-click this icon to extract
and run your slideshow

❓ How can I customize my display during a presentation?

PowerPoint gives you a few different tools for customizing your display during a presentation. Here are your options:

● **Draw with a pen.** This is a great tool for pointing out aspects of images or drawing people's attention to a particular part of the side. Right-click on the screen and choose Pen. The pointer will become a highlighter that you can use to draw and write on the screen. To change

the pen color, right-click and choose Pointer Options | Pen Color. To resume your presentation, right-click and choose Arrow or just press the SPACEBAR.

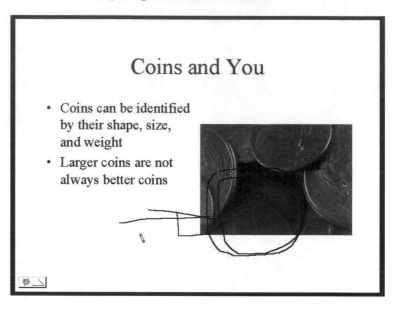

● **Blank the screen.** If you need to step outside your presentation for a moment and don't want to distract the audience with what's on the screen, you might want to blank the display. Right-click and choose Screen | Black Screen. Resume the slideshow by choosing Screen | Unblack Screen.

● **Take notes.** If you need to record comments during the slideshow, right-click and choose Meeting Minutes. You can take freeform notes on the Meeting Minutes tab or add structured action items. PowerPoint automatically creates an Action Items slide and appends it to the end of the slideshow. You can also export the action items and minutes to Word.

Chapter 15

Using Your Digital Photographs on the Internet

Answer Topics!

Using Your Digital Photographs on the Internet @ a Glance

Getting your digital images onto the Web isn't difficult, though you do need to plan ahead. This chapter explains image resolution and format issues that any Webmaster—someone who designs or administers Web sites—needs to understand. You'll also find out how to modify your images so they have greater impact on the Web, such as with transparent backgrounds and virtual-reality-type interaction.

America Online 4.0 has some new features designed for working with digital images. This chapter explains how to use AOL for sending and receiving images.

PUTTING DIGITAL IMAGES ON THE WEB

 Is the file format used by my camera good enough for posting on the Web?

Most digital cameras tend to use the JPEG format, and as you can see from other questions in this chapter, yes, JPEG is often just fine for placing images on the Web. However, if your camera uses an oddball file format that isn't supported by the Web, or if you want to do something special with your images, then you'll need to load the images into an image editing program and convert the images to the desired format. Your camera probably came with an image editor, or you can use a program like Paint Shop Pro (discussed in Chapter 11). For more on file formats, see "What file formats can the Web recognize?" later in this chapter.

 What size should I make my images for use on Web pages?

Many digital cameras take pictures that are 640×480 pixels in size, but this is overwhelming for a Web page. Not only does an image that big take a long time to download, it consumes a lot of space on the screen, making it difficult to lay out your page.

I recommend that you restrict your digital images to about 200 pixels across (see Figure 15-1). To learn how to resize an image, see Chapter 11.

Also, don't pack too many images on a single page. If you fill up a Web page with a dozen closely spaced images, the page is still going to be large and take a long time to load. In a nutshell, if you add together the file size of all the graphics on a Web page, they shouldn't be over 50K.

Tip: *Even if your Web design program lets you "shrink" an image just by dragging the picture's corner, don't do it this way! The file size of your image hasn't actually changed, so it'll take just as long to load in a Web browser.*

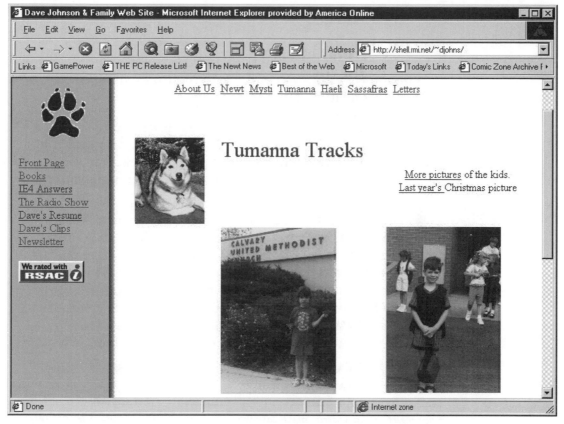

Figure 15-1   If you keep each image on your Web page fairly small, it'll load faster

What file formats can the Web recognize?

There are three file formats commonly recognized by Web browsers: GIF, JPEG, and PNG.

GIF

CompuServe originally developed the GIF format, which stands for Graphic Interchange Format (making the term GIF format somewhat redundant). GIF is a compact file format that is commonly used on Web pages. The major disadvantage of GIF, however, is that it limits images to just

256 colors (or less, depending upon the settings you use when saving the file). That can affect the quality of the image onscreen, though it's generally not significant.

Usually, Web designers like to use GIF format 89a. This is the newest iteration of the GIF file that supports three important features:

- **Transparency**   Transparency allows you to specify a color in the image that will be treated as transparent. That way, you can make the image's background or border transparent and there won't be an ugly seam or frame around the picture.

- **Interlacing**   An interlaced image downloads to a Web browser first as a chunky, low-resolution image, then increases in quality as more information is retrieved. A non-interlaced image would normally load a few lines at a time, so you'd see the top of the image displayed before the bottom. Interlacing isn't faster than the alternative, but it gives the viewer something to look at while the image loads, so it can seem subjectively faster.

- **Animation**   An animated GIF is really just a sequence of individual images played one after the other. Not really fast enough to give a real sense of cinematic motion with large images, animated GIFs are usually used to slowly display one image after another like a slideshow.

Though GIF is extremely pervasive, its future is uncertain—the format itself is owned by CompuServe and the compression scheme is patented by Unisys. That means that GIF may not be forever available for Web developers to use with abandon.

JPEG

The JPEG format was created by the Joint Photographic Experts Group to be a scalable file format that could be compressed to yield a small file size or be left uncompressed for higher quality. Unlike GIF, JPEG images can display a full 16-million-color palette. Depending upon how much you compress a JPEG image, however, the image quality can vary from nearly identical to the original all the way down to unrecognizable.

When saving a JPEG file, you can specify the level of compression to use. Most programs default to a fairly low compression level, preserving image quality. In reality, though, you can often compress the image much more aggressively than the default and still get adequate quality for a Web page.

PNG

The newest of the Web file formats, the PNG (Portable Network Graphics) format is similar to JPEG in that it displays full-color images, but it doesn't use compression that reduces image quality. It was designed specifically for the Internet, so PNG has lots of other features. PNG files support built-in color and gamma correction, for instance, as well as the ability to display at a low resolution but print at a high resolution.

PNG is brand new, however, so few people currently use it.

Understanding File Extensions

The three letters that appear after the period in a filename, like the "GIF" in PICTURE.GIF, describe the kind of file format the file is saved in. In other words, if you see a file that ends in .JPG, you immediately know that the file is in JPEG format; .GIF indicates a GIF file; and .BMP tells you it's a BMP format image.

Because it's standard to use three-letter file extensions to identify the kind of file, most programs automatically attach the right file extension to a file for you when you save it. If you choose to save an image as JPEG, for instance, most image editors automatically add .JPG to the filename whether you remember to or not.

Unfortunately, Windows isn't perfect. You can manually rename a file from PICTURE.BMP to PICTURE.JPG, for instance, and Windows won't try to stop you. You haven't changed the file format—it's still in the JPEG format—but programs that try to figure out how to display images based on file extensions will get confused when they try to read it. Remember: You need to convert a file in an image editing program to change its format. Just renaming the file won't do anything except change its name.

 What file format should I choose?

You can use whichever one best suits your needs. It's perfectly all right to mix JPEG and GIF images on a Web site, even on the same page. Use this chart to help decide which is the appropriate file format for your needs (I didn't include PNG in this chart because I don't recommend using it at the moment).

Use **JPEG** when you need:

- Full-color photographs compressed to very small file sizes

Use **GIF** when you need:

- A transparent background
- To interlace the display of an image
- To display an image with just a few colors

 How do the file sizes of PNG, GIF, and JPEG images compare?

In general, JPEG will produce the smallest file size, followed by GIF. A PNG file is usually a bit larger, though still smaller than an uncompressed image saved in, say, TIFF format. Table 15-1 shows typical file sizes for an image taken on a digital camera and reduced to 200×200 pixels for a Web page.

How do I make my image's background color transparent?

A transparent background can add a very elegant look to an image, particularly an irregularly shaped one. By making the background transparent, you can make the border of the image blend into the background of the Web page, no matter what color the Web page might be.

To make the background transparent, you'll need to save the image in GIF format. You can't have a transparent

File Type: Uncompressed
Size: 125K

File Type: PNG
Size: 65K

File Type: GIF (256 colors)
Size: 33K

File Type: GIF (16 colors)
Size: 10K

Table 15-1   Relative File Sizes of JPG, PNG, and GIF

File Type: JPEG (default compression)
Size: 12K

File Type: JPEG (moderate compression)
Size: 6KB

File Type: JPEG (heavy compression)
Size: 4K

Table 15-1　Relative File Sizes of JPG, PNG, and GIF (*continued*)

background using JPEG or PNG. Look for the file options and set the desired color to transparent. In Paint Shop Pro, you can do it in this way:

1. Open the image you'd like to edit. In this example, we've got a vignetted portrait with a plain white border.

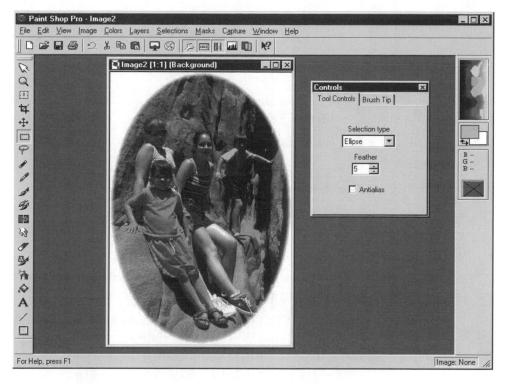

2. Convert the image to 256 colors by choosing Colors | Decrease Color Depth | 256 Colors.

3. Make the color you'd like to be rendered transparent the background color. Do this by selecting the eyedropper tool and right-clicking on the color in your image.

4. Choose Colors | Set Palette Transparency. The Set Palette Transparency dialog box opens.

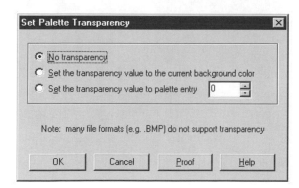

5. Click the radio button next to "Set the transparency value to the current background color" and click OK.

6. Choose File | Save As and choose GIF from the list of formats.

7. Click on Options and make sure you're saving in format 89a.

8. Save the file.

As you can see in Figure 15-2, a transparent background makes for a much more attractive image. No matter what color your Web page is, the transparent image on the right will blend in, while the unedited opaque border on the left works only on a background that's the same color.

How do I reduce the number of colors in an image to make my Web page more efficient?

Since the JPEG format is designed to always save 16 million colors, you'll need to save your image in GIF format. But you'll need to reduce the number of colors in the image first—in Paint Shop Pro, as in most programs, it's pretty easy to do. Just choose Colors | Decrease Color Depth | 256 Colors.

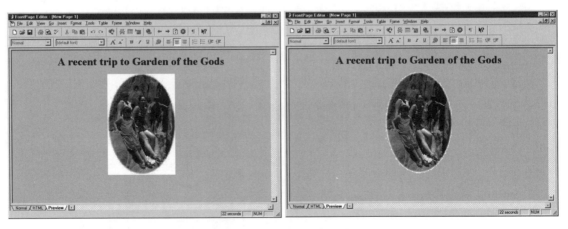

Figure 15-2 A transparent background can make irregular images blend into your page

Your image, particularly if it's a typical shot from a digital camera, may start with significantly more than 256 colors. If you have a choice, allow the image editor to choose "optimum" colors. The results will be better and may not even be substantially different than if you left it in 16 million color mode.

How can I make a slideshow out of my images?

Let's say you've taken a few pictures and you'd like them to appear on a Web page one after the other, like a slideshow. You don't need to do any fancy programming; all you need is to save your images as animated GIFs. Each image in your animation is referred to as a *cell*, and each cell can simply be a photograph from your digital camera.

There are many programs around that can do this for you. I've had success with both Jasc's Animation Shop (included with Paint Shop Pro) and Ulead's GIF Animator.

Both of these programs make it very easy to create an animation. But for the best animations, keep these tips in mind:

- Make sure all the cells in your animation are exactly the same size.

- Keep the images small. Animations with large cells take a long time to load and don't animate smoothly.

- Some animations benefit from transparent backgrounds, but most—like photo slideshows—should probably have opaque backgrounds of the same color.

- Tweak the animation speed settings. You can vary the delay between cells.

- Don't put too many cells in your animation. Remember that you'll want the animation to load and start running pretty quickly, or visitors may not even realize there was supposed to be an animation and leave before it finishes loading.

How do I turn images into a 360-degree scene you can move around in?

You can use your images to create a QuickTime VR movie. A QuickTime VR movie isn't really a movie in the conventional sense at all—it's a series of connected images that are stitched together so that you can pan from one image to another and get a sense that you're inside a large scene. QuickTime VR can be used to place Web visitors in the middle of a room, for instance—as they pan through the VR image, they can see the scene from any angle.

QuickTime VR movies are easy to make with stitching software similar to the kind mentioned in Chapter 12. If you've ever tried photographing a wide panoramic shot by taking a few pictures and connecting them, then you have the basic skills necessary to make a VR image. But instead of making a wide panorama, you're making a panorama that actually connects at the ends. It isn't easy to do this kind of thing without specialized software, so get an inexpensive

stitching package like Enroute's QuickStitch 360. Remember these tips:

- You'll need to take a series of pictures that overlap. Try to get at least 25% of each image to overlap into the next picture to make it easier to stitch them together.

- Most software requires you to rotate in a particular direction, such as left to right (clockwise).

- In order to keep each image's perspective identical, you'll need to keep the camera's rotational axis the same. In plain English, that means you need to take all the pictures from the same location—don't drift a few feet as you photograph. A tripod is handy for keeping your camera rooted in one location.

- All the images need to be taken level. For best results, use a tripod.

- Avoid using a wide-angle lens, since this can distort the images and make it difficult to line up edges.

 ### Can I use QuickTime VR to show different sides of a statue or building?

Yes, you can use QuickTime VR to walk around a stationary object as well as to spin around inside a large scene. As viewers pan through your image, the object can seem to rotate in place. This is a hard thing to shoot, however. It's important that the distance from the camera to the subject stay the same throughout the shooting. If your subject is small enough, set the camera on a tripod and place the subject on a center-mark. Take a picture, rotate the image on the mark, and shoot again. If you have a rotating platter—like a lazy susan—and the object is small enough to fit on it, then you can use the platter to turn the image between photos.

If your subject is too big to shoot this way, use a measuring tape to ensure that as you move the camera around the subject, your distance to its centerpoint stays the same. Also, try to keep the camera pointed directly at the subject's center; if you change the axis along which you're shooting, the impression that the object is spinning in place will be lost.

How do I insert the QuickTime VR file into my Web page?

You can add a QuickTime VR movie to your Web page as easily as you'd add an ordinary image. You'll need to use the EMBED tag, such as in this example:

```
<EMBED SRC="QTVR.MOV" height="400" width="400">
```

Simply substitute the actual QuickTime VR filename where it says "QTVR.MOV". Also change the height and width values to whatever dimensions you want the movie to play within. Don't use a bigger number than the actual size that you saved the movie in to begin with.

You have a few other options available as well. The simple line of HTML above doesn't display the QuickTime VR controller. The controller is a narrow panel that appears under the movie and allows viewers to use the mouse to zoom in and out, as well as to modify other settings. To turn the controller on in your Web page, just add CONTROLLER= "TRUE", as in:

```
<EMBED SRC="QTVR.MOV" height="400" width="400"
CONTROLLER="TRUE">
```

The controller uses 16 pixels, so be sure to add that number to your height value. It's also important to use the SCALE parameter to tell your browser how to resize the image, particularly if you're using the controller and the width or height are set smaller than the size of the controller. So, the bottom line is that the most useful way to use the EMBED tag for a QuickTime VR movie is this:

```
<EMBED SRC="QTVR.MOV" height="400" width="400"
SCALE="TOFIT" CONTROLLER="TRUE">
```

Figure 15-3 shows a QuickTime VR movie added to a Web page. Using your mouse, you can pan around in any direction to see more of the scene.

Figure 15-3   A simple Web page with a QuickTime VR file embedded

---

   Tip: *If you don't include the controller on your Web page, then visitors will need to use keyboard shortcuts to zoom in and out (the SHIFT and CTRL keys). Keep your page convenient and always include the controller.*

How can I learn more about QuickTime VR and using this format on my Web page?

Visit Apple's Web site at http://www.apple.com/quicktime/. This site is loaded with helpful tutorials, specifications, and examples, allowing you to get the most out of this really fun file format.

 ## What software can help me create a Web page?

Don't want to get your hands dirty writing Web pages from scratch? You can easily use one of the many Web design programs that look and behave like page layout programs. You can enter text, drag and drop graphics, and then edit and format the document's appearance with simple toolbar and menu controls. Many HTML purists don't like this method because HTML is still evolving, so a Web page made in such a program can't take advantage of the newest and most interesting innovations in Web design. Nonetheless, there's nothing wrong with using a WYSIWYG Web editor, particularly if you're a casual user just trying to make a family Web page (see Figure 15-4).

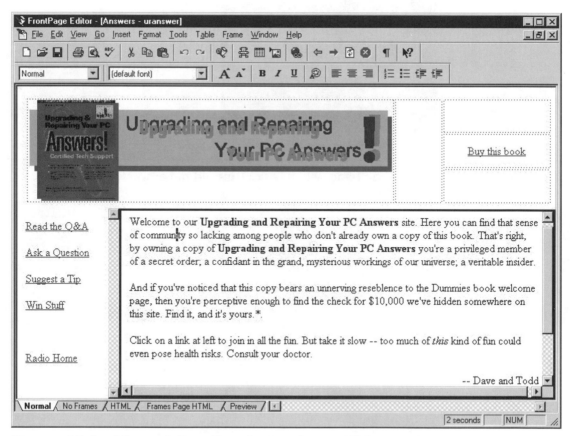

Figure 15-4 Microsoft FrontPage is one of many Web page designers that you can use to drag and drop your way to a Web site

There are many good HTML editors on the market. Some are free and some are retail products. Here's a rundown of the editors I recommend:

Editor	Where to Find It
Adobe PageMill	www.adobe.com
HotDog Pro	www.sausage.com
HoTMetaL Pro 4.0	www.softquad.com
Microsoft FrontPage Express (part of Internet Explorer 4)	www.microsoft.com/ie
Microsoft FrontPage 98	www.microsoft.com/frontpage

Can I start a Web page with WYSIWYG software and then edit it by hand?

Yes, you can. A lot of people start Web pages in programs like FrontPage, in fact, to get the basics done quickly and painlessly. Then they open the file up in a text editor and edit or add to the page by hand using their knowledge of HTML. You can do the same thing.

Do I need to learn HTML to create Web pages?

While most people prefer to get a Web page editor that automates much of the process, some people like to "code" a Web page by hand. Either method works just fine. For more on the automated solution, see "What software can help me create a Web page?" earlier.

I'm a big fan of learning to write some HTML yourself, so let's talk about that for a moment.

You can learn the essentials of HTML in an afternoon. Like playing the guitar, learning the basics of HTML is easy; learning to do it well is the hard part. HTML is a simple script language that, for the most part, is little more than a set of style "tags" that surround text for formatting purposes. You would bold a word in a sentence in this way, for instance:

```
This is an example of <B>bold</B> text.
```

The result of this line of HTML in a Web browser is shown in Figure 15-5.

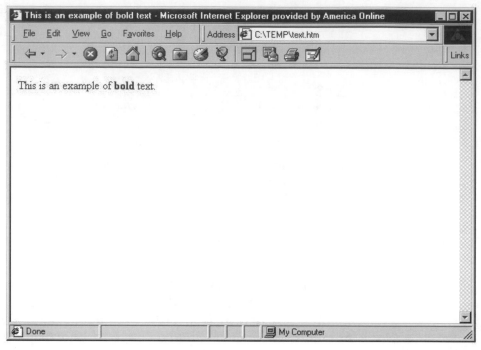

Figure 15-5 Tags are used in HTML to change the formatting of text, as in this example of a word in boldface

Most of the programming you'll do in HTML is simply a case of adding tags to your document. There are two major types of tags:

● **Document structure tags** These are tags that define the major parts of the Web page. They divide the page into the header, where you insert information like the name of the page, and the body, where pretty much everything else goes. The document structure tags define the skeleton of your Web page, and once they're done, you generally don't have to fool with them.

● **Markup tags** These are the commands that you'll use most often. They define how the document will be formatted and what information will appear on the page. There is a large variety of markup tags to choose from, and many good reference books explain how to use them.

You can think of tags as containers—they typically enclose text, telling the browser what to do with the text within. Most tags take this basic form:

```
<TAG>The tag will affect this line of text.</TAG>
```

The tag is always enclosed in angle brackets (<>), and the closing tag uses a forward slash to indicate the end of the command. If you omit the closing tag, it is like forgetting a closing parenthesis: The browser will continue to do whatever the <TAG> started all the way through to the end of the document or until another tag interferes, creating a potentially messy display.

All Web pages take the following form:

```
<HTML>
<HEAD>
<TITLE>Your Web Page</TITLE>
</HEAD>
<BODY>
This is the body of the Web page. Any text that appears
here will be drawn in a Web browser. You need to add
special tags to format this text and include images,
however.
</BODY>
</HTML>
```

Notice that the entire page is enclosed in an <HTML> tag. Within that giant container, the <HEAD> and <BODY> containers live. The <HEAD> container includes the equivalent of "administrative" data about your Web page, and the <BODY> container has all of the "guts" of your page. If you wanted to, you could simply dump the contents of your great American novel between the <BODY> and </BODY> tags and be done with it—though, without any formatting, it would be pretty ugly (see Figure 15-6). But it would work.

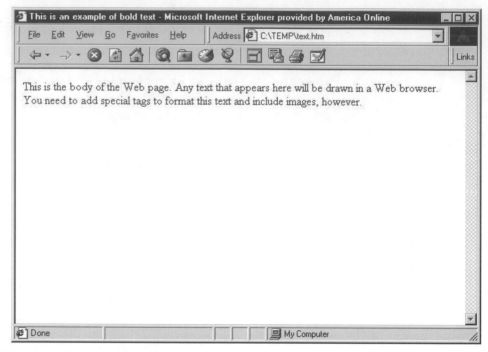

Figure 15-6   A Web page with no formatting

World Wide Web Glossary

● **Bandwidth**   Bandwidth is a measure of the capacity of a communication system. Because it is measured in kilobits per second, bandwidth is also directly related to the speed of a system. The Internet community is preoccupied with bandwidth because it determines how many users can use the Net and at what speed they can connect.

● **FAQ (frequently asked questions)**   A FAQ is usually a Web page, newsgroup post, or some other kind of file that answers questions commonly asked, particularly by beginners. This book is, in a sense, a huge FAQ—but most Internet FAQs are short enough to read in one sitting.

- **FTP (File Transfer Protocol)** FTP is a protocol that predates the Web for transferring files among computers on the Internet. You can download an FTP program to directly access downloadable files on the Net without loading a comparatively slower browser.

- **HTML (Hypertext Markup Language)** HTML is the scripting language used to format Web pages on the Internet. If you want to create a Web page for yourself, you need to either learn HTML or get a program that creates the HTML while you work in a WYSIWYG page creation environment.

- **HTTP (Hypertext Transfer Protocol)** This is the protocol used by your PC to request Web pages from a remote server somewhere on the Internet and then retrieve those pages. You precede Web page requests with the http:// identifier, though most Web browsers now assume you are using HTTP unless you specify another protocol, like ftp://.

- **PPP: (Point-to-Point Protocol)** PPP is the standard kind of Internet account available today from most ISPs. It allows you to directly enter the Net, linking your PC to the vast web of nodes on the Internet.

- **VRML (Virtual Reality Markup Language)** Similar to HTML, VRML allows your browser to navigate through simulated 3-D environments instead of just text. While VRML has yet to gain widespread acceptance because it is so slow, it is sure to become more popular as Internet connections and modem technology improve. To use VRML, you need the appropriate VRML plug-in for your Web browser (visit Netscape's or Microsoft's Web site to get the file).

How do I get my finished Web page out there on the Internet?

Sure, you can write a Web page on your PC, but when you're done with it, what then? Getting the finished Web page to the Internet is often the most perplexing part of the process, and that's why Web design companies are always trying to improve and streamline the process. You'll need to start by

having an Internet service provider (ISP) that provides server space for you to post your pages. If you don't yet have an ISP, see the following section.

The traditional method for getting finished Web pages on the Internet is via FTP (File Transfer Protocol). You'll need to install an FTP client on your PC—such programs are often available from your ISP's Web site. Using FTP, you transfer the finished HTML pages to your server space, usually using an interface not unlike File Manager (see Figure 15-7).

There's a newer method that avoids FTP altogether, however. If you have a Web page editor like Microsoft FrontPage or Adobe PageMill, you can use a built-in tool that automatically uploads the pages to a destination Web server from within the program. That's a good reason to use one of these programs, since it also keeps track of which pages

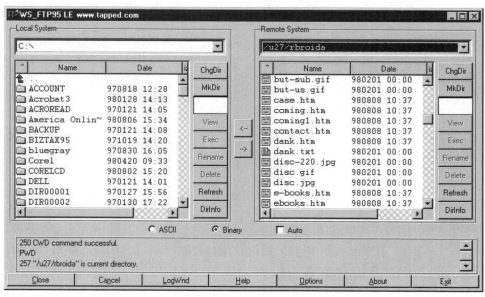

Figure 15-7 Using an FTP client is the most common method of transferring Web pages from your PC to the Web server

change when you edit your site, and only uploads changed pages instead of transferring the whole site every time.

Where do I find a list of Internet service providers, or ISPs?

You can find ISPs in a variety of places, including:

- **The phone book**　Look in your local Yellow Pages under "Internet Services."

- **Search engines**　If you have access to the Internet, check out Yahoo. This site has a comprehensive list of ISPs divided, among other ways, by state. Visit www.yahoo.com/Business_and_Economy/Companies/ Internet_Services.

- **ISPs.com**　CMPnet maintains a comprehensive, searchable database of Internet service providers at www.isps.com.

How do I create and publish a Web page for free?

You can publish a Web page by learning rudimentary HTML or by getting an HTML editor; many are free, available with products such as Netscape Navigator and Microsoft Internet Explorer. But is there a way to post your creation without spending any money?

You bet. Most ISPs and online services, including America Online, offer some server space for you to use. Or you can rely on the services of Web communities that offer the necessary resources to create and post free Web sites, usually in return for the advertising revenue they get for your traffic. There are many such communities on the Internet; here are a few of the most popular:

- **GeoCities**　http://www.geocities.com/
- **Tripod**　http://www.tripod.com/
- **Amazon City**　http://www.amazoncity.com/
- **Delphi**　http://www.delphi.com/
- **CyberTown**　http://www.cybertown.com/

How do I display images on my Web page?

Displaying an image on a Web page is very easy to do—the tag simply looks like this:

```
<IMG SRC="image.jpg">
```

where image.jpg is the name of the image file you want to display. This tag has to go in the <BODY> section of your Web page, of course.

Don't forget that you should specify the dimensions of your image to improve the browser's speed when loading the page. Do it by using the tag in this way:

```
<IMG SRC=image.gif WIDTH=x HEIGHT=y>
```

where x and y designate the size of the image in pixels.

 ## How do I make the images on my Web pages load faster?

You can help the visitors to your Web page by keeping your page fast and efficient. Here are a few easy ways to speed up the loading of images. While one of these suggestions requires changing HTML code, it's not difficult and well worth the effort:

Use the most efficient file format for each particular image. If you're including line art or clip art on a Web page, use the GIF format and reduce the number of colors. But for digital camera photographs and other full-color images, use JPEG unless you need a special effect like a transparent background.

● Resize your images to the smallest size that's practical. Don't stuff full-sized 640×480-pixel images into your pages.

● Tell the browser how big each image actually is. Include HEIGHT and WIDTH parameters within the <IMG SRC> tag, as in:

```
<IMG SRC=image.gif HEIGHT=200 WIDTH=170>
```

How do I make graphics clickable, so they take you to another Web page when you click?

You can use an image as a gateway to another Web page or to a different location on the same page. This in known as making the image *clickable*. Suppose, for instance, that you display an image of your new home. You can set up your page so that when someone clicks on the house, they're taken to a new page with more pictures of the home, as well as a description of your harrowing moving experience.

To make an image clickable, you need to use a different kind of tag, like this:

```
<A HREF="URL"><IMG SRC="image.jpg"></A>
```

In this case, URL is simply the page or site you want the visitor to go to when they click on the image, and image.jpg is the name of the image. For instance, you might have a line of HTML that looks like this:

```
<A HREF="house.htm"><IMG SRC="movevan.gif"></A>
```

in which clicking on the moving van image (movevan.gif) would send the browser to the page called house.htm.

Use Thumbnails

One common way to improve the performance of your Web site—especially if it's an online photo album that has lots of pictures—is to use thumbnails. A *thumbnail* is a small representation of your picture. If you make them very small (no more than 50 pixels across), then you can display a lot of them fairly quickly. If visitors want to see the entire picture, you can make the thumbnail a link that takes them to another page that loads a larger version of the image.

 Can you give me some tips for creating an efficient, attractive Web site?

Have you ever visited a Web site that crams everything onto a single page? It's easy to make a page like that, but visitors will need to scroll—and scroll and scroll—to see the whole thing. That's not the right way to design a site. Here are some tips for making your site look less like your 8-year-old kid made it (even if she really did):

● Instead of making your site a single large page, break it up into logical sections (see Figure 15-8). Establish a map for the information on your site and make that the template for the various pages.

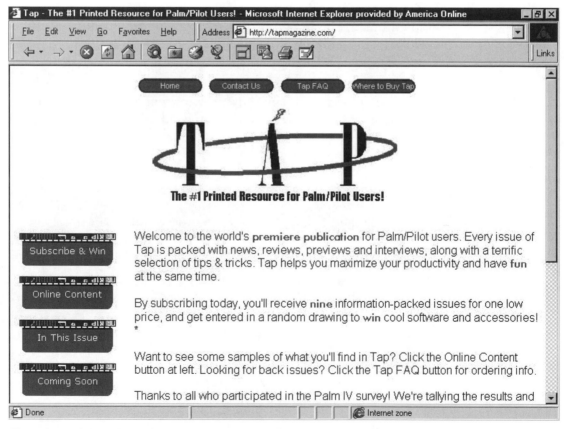

Figure 15-8 The buttons on the left side of the page take you to other pages on this Web site

● Provide good site navigation—put the navigational links in the same place on every page.

● Don't make stuff too hard to find. Some Web sites use something called the "two-click rule," which means that your visitors should be able to get where they want to go in two clicks.

● Keep the pages small. Every moment it takes for your page to load is an eternity in Web time, and many visitors won't sit around patiently until your navigation bar appears. Try to make sure your Web pages—particularly the front page that visitors see first—are no more than 40K in size. You can find the total size of a Web page by adding the size of the HTML file and the file size of any graphics the page needs to load (see Figure 15-9).

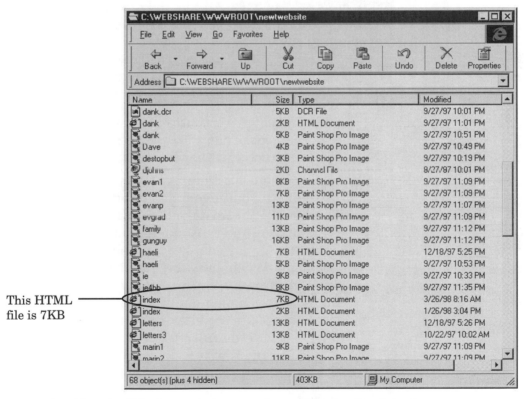

Figure 15-9 Use the Windows desktop to determine the file size of your pages. Don't forget to add graphics file sizes to the HTML file size for an accurate total

- Make your navigational choices obvious. Don't give pages on your site mysterious names; what, for instance, is "The Forum" or "The Depot"? It's anybody's guess, and visitors will probably need to actually go to the page to figure out what it actually does. Say exactly what the page does in the navigational tool.

- Use frames. These days, most Web surfers use browsers that can handle frames, and frames have some big advantages. They allow you to keep static information—like navigation bars—in the same place on the screen no matter where you go on the site. And they're faster. Using frames means that you don't need to make entire pages reload every time someone clicks on a link—only the part of the page with new information needs to change (see Figure 15-10). Frames are also easy to create these days. All the major Web design programs have a frame wizard or some other drag-and-drop method of laying out frames on the page.

- Make the pages interesting. Use different but complementary looks for each section of your site.

- Increase the padding inside tables to add extra white space. In fact, most Web sites don't make very good use of white space—check out a magazine to see how pages can look more attractive if they have less on them.

- When you design your site, remember that not everyone has the same computer you do. In fact, many Web designers make the mistake of thinking everyone has a $3,000 super-PC and thus alienate much of their potential audience. Smart designers write Web pages for the "lowest common denominator"—a 640×480-pixel display in which the browser consumes only about 2/3 of the screen. Lowest-common-denominator Web design also means making sure the site works just as well on a Mac as on a PC, that it downloads smoothly on a slow 28.8 Kbps modem, and that it looks good in as few as 256 colors to boot.

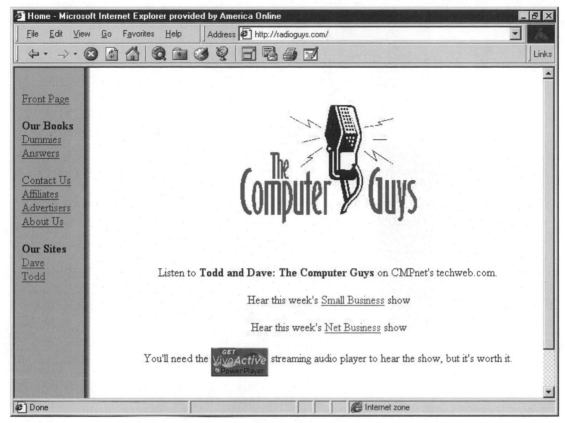

Figure 15-10 Because this page uses frames, only the right side changes when you click on a link

- Think you're done? You're probably not. After your site is complete, be sure to spell-check everything. There's nothing worse than finding an egregious typo on an otherwise interesting site; it makes the whole thing look amateurish.

- Avoid orphaned sites. Don't forget to go back later and keep the site up to date. Establish a schedule to keep the site current, and update it frequently. Visitor feedback is a great tool for knowing what to change. If you're motivated, provide a form visitors can fill in to tell you what they think.

USING DIGITAL IMAGES ON AOL

 How do I send someone pictures using AOL?

If you're using AOL 4.0, it's easier than it used to be. Just do this:

1. Choose File | Open Picture Gallery and find the image you want on your hard disk.

 Tip: *You can work with AOL's image and mail tools without logging onto AOL, perhaps saving some online fees. You'll need to connect to AOL to actually send the message, however.*

2. Double-click on the image and it will be loaded into a simple image editor. You can use this editor to fine-tune your image's appearance, such as changing the image's color, brightness, or size.

3. When you're ready, click on the Insert in Email button. The image appears in the mail window.

4. Address and send the mail message.

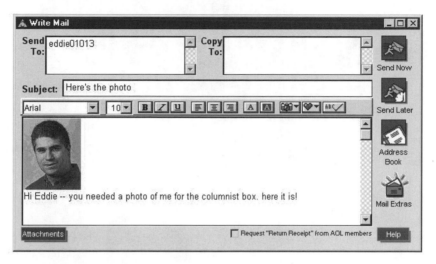

In older versions of AOL, you need to create a new mail message and add the image as an attachment. The new method is much better—if you haven't yet upgraded your copy of AOL to 4.0, you should do it now.

 Tip: *You can insert more than one image in a mail message if you have the new AOL 4.0.*

 ## How do I use AOL's "You've Got Pictures" feature?

"You've Got Pictures" is a new feature in AOL 4.0 developed in conjunction with Kodak. If you live near a participating photo developer, you can provide your AOL screen name and ask for electronic delivery of your images in addition to ordinary prints and negatives. When your pictures are ready, they are delivered to you via AOL, after which you can copy them to your hard disk or use them in e-mail.

Chapter 16

Digital Photography and Copyright Law

Answer Topics!

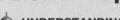

Digital Photography and Copyright Law @ a Glance

Copyright law is confusing and sometimes subject to broad interpretation, but it's there to protect you from the theft of your work, both intentionally and unintentionally. Read this chapter to understand what the law really says and what you need to do to be protected—and to keep yourself from accidentally infringing on the rights of others, too!

The copyright law has an effect on everyday life. You might want to use someone else's image as the basis for some artwork of your own—can you? What if you find that someone has used your image without asking your permission? It pays to know the extent of copyright law in everyday situations and also how fair use can affect your ability to use other people's images.

Getting published is the dream of many photographers, and thanks to new technology like the Internet, getting your images in front of an audience is easier than ever. But with publishing comes a slew of new terms and legal considerations. This chapter explains the most common kinds of publishing rights and the rules about getting permission from models that you want to photograph. Ever wonder if you were allowed to photograph a military tank in a local parade? Or take pictures of people in a crowd? The answers are here.

UNDERSTANDING COPYRIGHT

 ## What is a copyright?

A *copyright* is the name for the method used to protect the rights of an artist via the legal system, regardless of whether the work is text, music, painting, photography, sculpture, or software. Violation of copyright law—such as publishing a work without the artist's permission—is punishable by law. Since copyright violation is a *tort* (a wrongful act for which a civil suit can be brought), the artist can sue for punitive damages as well.

 ## What does a copyright not protect?

This is a good question, since it can help explain the extent of copyright law a bit better. While copyright covers images, both film and digital, it does not protect the ideas behind the photos.

In other words, a copyright doesn't protect facts, picture concepts, systems, or photographic methods. You may come up with a really clever special effect for your digital photography, but sorry—you can't copyright it to prohibit others from trying it on their own images.

 ## What rights do I have if I copyright a digital image?

In a nutshell, copyright law allows you to specify the way in which your image is used. You can sell, lease, give away, or just plain burn anything you copyright. You can also block others from using your image, since they need your explicit permission to use it.

Owning a copyright actually gives you a set of specific rights. These include:

- **The right to reproduction** You can reproduce your image as often as you like and prohibit others from doing the same.

- **The right to create derivative works** You can change your image in any way you see fit, such as cropping, changing the colors, or including the image

within another image. No one else has the right to modify a copy of your image without your permission, however.

- **The right to public display and performance** You can show your images off in any way you want, and others do not have the right to publish them without your permission.

How long will my copyright last?

A copyright lasts for the life of the artist plus another 50 years.

How do I copyright something?

There are really three answers to this question:

- Since 1988, any work you create is automatically copyrighted by virtue of having been made by your own hands. In other words, there is an implied copyright on all creative works, and you don't need to do anything at all to receive some protection under copyright law.

- On the other hand, there are copyrights and then there are copyrights. While no action is ever required on your part, simply putting a copyright notice on your work strengthens your copyright protection. To assert your claim on your image, just place a copyright notice somewhere on the picture. That's just a matter of inscribing the copyright symbol (©) followed by the year and your name.

- The most aggressive copyright action you can take is to actually register your image with the Registrar of Copyrights in Washington, D.C. There is a form to fill out and a small fee to pay (it's currently $20), but this provides you with the highest level of protection available under copyright law.

Why would I put the copyright notice on one of my images?

Having the copyright notice on an image gives you some leverage in a copyright dispute. While ignorance is no excuse

in a copyright case, infringers sometimes claim that they thought the image was in the public domain or that the owner wasn't enforcing their copyright. By placing the copyright notice on your image, you're announcing to the world that you're protecting your copyright. The infringer has less "wiggle room" in a dispute if your notice appears on your image.

Should I put my name or my business' name on the copyright notice?

Use your own name. That's because if you put the copyright in the name of your company and you later sell your business, then you've implicitly sold the copyright. If necessary, you can spell out ownership of copyright in the contract for the sale of your business, but I suggest you avoid confusion and keep it in your name to begin with.

I have a photograph that I took in 1980 and I recently scanned it for my Web page. Do I need to copyright the digital image separately from the film picture?

Surprisingly, this is two different questions. First, let's say you have made a digital image by scanning a 35mm photograph. You have only made a copy of the original image—which was already copyrighted and owned by you—and therefore the original copyright extends to any reproductions you make as well. So the short answer is no, you needn't copyright it again.

On the other hand, let's say the image is old and predates the 1988 change in copyright law that recognizes implicit copyright. If you've never taken any action to copyright the old image, you should do so now, since images made prior to 1988 must explicitly bear the copyright mark in order to be protected.

Should I officially register my images with the copyright office?

Generally, no, there's no compelling reason to do so, particularly if you're a casual digital photographer. Your image is protected from copyright infringement as soon as the work is created, and most people rarely need additional protection. But if you plan to use the work commercially— and you think your image has the potential to provide significant income—then formal registration is appropriate.

That's because you can't actually take anyone to court for copyright infringement unless the work is already registered. If you register your image before first publication, the court may award you more compensation than if you fail to register it until after the infringement occurs. Either way, your image needs to be registered before you ever step into court.

How do I register my pictures with the copyright office?

You need to supply the copyright office with a copy of their Form VA, a copy of the work being copyrighted, and the appropriate filing fee.

For more information, you can contact the copyright office at the following address:

Registrar of Copyrights
Library of Congress
101 Independence Avenue
Washington, D.C. 20559-6000

You can also contact the office by phone. To get information, call the Public Information Office telephone number at (202) 707-3000. Or, to actually order copyright forms, call (202) 707-9100.

Finally, you can get the forms directly from the Internet. The copyright office's Web site is http://lcweb.loc.gov/copyright/.

About six months after you submit your image for registration, you'll get a copy of your Certificate of Registration. This document certifies that your work is copyrighted, and you'll need that certificate to pursue a copyright infringement action.

Have Patience

The copyright office gets over half a million applications for copyright each year. As a consequence, registration is time-consuming. The copyright office does not notify you that your application has been received or that it is being processed. So sit back and wait—for six months or more—for your certificate. If you really want to know if the application was received, send it via registered mail. But remember, even that won't tell you if the application is lost within the copyright office.

How many copies do I send to the copyright office? Do I get them back?

You'll need to send one copy of your work unless it has been published—in that case, send two. The copies of your work are known as a *deposit,* and they are permanently stored in the Library of Congress. You don't get them back.

Can I send my deposit on floppy disk, Zip disk, or other electronic media?

No, the copyright office isn't generally equipped to receive works electronically, even those that are designed for the computer medium, as digital images are. The exception is CD-ROM; you can send images on CD-ROM as long as you also include the appropriate operating software and instructions. Alternately, you can print your work and send a hard-copy version of your image.

$20 is a lot of money for each image—can I copyright a bunch at once?

Yes, the copyright office allows you to perform something known as a *group registration* by submitting several images at once, under the same cover, and for the same $20 registration fee.

Unfortunately, group registration has some slightly confusing rules:

- If you've published a number of images in the same publication (such as a newspaper or magazine) then you can perform a group registration on them.
- If you've published a number of images in a book (such as this one) then group registration is not permitted. You need to register each image separately.
- If you have a number of unpublished images, you can group register them, though for added protection the copyright office recommends copyrighting them again after publication.

How long can I wait to register an image? After publication, is it too late?

No, you can register an image with the copyright office at any time, even years after publication. In general, the only reason you'd want to do that would be if you were preparing to take legal action against a copyright infringement. Also remember that the sooner you register, the more legal options you have available. If you register within three months of publication, for instance, you are eligible to receive statutory damages (see "What kinds of damages can be assessed for copyright infringement?" later in this chapter).

Are there any Internet-specific copyright laws?

At the time that I was writing this book, the United States Senate had just approved a controversial bill that would implement the first new copyright regulations since 1976. The bill essentially puts into law two UN treaties signed in late 1996 at the World Intellectual Property Organization. Among other things, it affirms that copyright law as applied to the Internet is essentially the same as copyright law as applied to traditional media.

The law also establishes a separate offense known as *circumvention*. While not directly related to digital imagery, the new copyright laws would make it a crime to defeat anti-copying technologies whether or not the source materials

are protected under copyright. This bill is obviously attracting a lot of attention from activists who suggest that this could mean trouble for those who perform research on the Internet. Only time will tell what the fate of this new law will eventually be.

If I've created a digital image under contract for someone, can I copyright it?

That depends upon the rights the contract or work agreement assigns to you and the employer. If you arc working in a "work-for-hire" arrangement, that usually means that all rights belong to the party that has hired you and they therefore own the copyright.

What does it mean for an image to be in the public domain?

Public domain describes any work that isn't protected by copyright. Your images are copyrighted unless you explicitly give up your copyright by failing to protect your image in the face of repeated infringement. Your images will also become a part of the public domain 50 years after your death. When images are in the public domain, anyone can use them for any reason without prior permission.

COPYRIGHT IN EVERYDAY LIFE

What if I take a picture that is very similar to one another photographer already published? Is that copyright infringement?

That depends. Copyright law does not protect ideas, such as the concept of photographing Niagara Falls with a long exposure. That means you can photograph—and even publish—an image that is for all intents and purposes identical to another, already copyrighted image.

On the other hand, you may be in violation of copyright law if you saw the published image and then decided to try to duplicate it. If you had *access* to the original and there is *substantial similarity,* then a court may find you guilty of infringement.

Remember that infringement is difficult to prove. Two people can independently develop substantially the same image and publish them separately—as long as they work in ignorance of each other, both images are fully protected under copyright law. No infringement has taken place. This means that a copyright dispute is held to a very different standard than applies in, say, patent law, in which the first person to patent a process has exclusive rights to the invention, regardless of how many other people come up with the same thing independently.

Is it possible to get permission to use someone else's image?

Of course it is—all you need to do is ask the owner. The worst they can do, of course, is say no, or ask for more money than you're willing to pay.

If you have no idea who owns the copyright to a particular published image, you can ask the copyright office to conduct a search. This is a last resort, since they charge $20/hour to look for this information for you. A better option is to contact the source where you saw the image, such as a magazine or Web site.

What is a digital watermark?

A *digital watermark* is an enhancement you can perform on your digital images that embeds information—like a copyright mark and your signature—into an image. Digital watermarks are generally invisible without special reader software, and they're fairly persistent, so even if the original image is altered, morphed, or otherwise edited, the watermark will survive. Some digital watermarks work in conjunction with tracking software that keeps tabs on where your images are posted on the Internet.

You should consider using digital watermark software if you intend to publish an image in a digital medium, such as on CD-ROM or on the Internet, where it can easily be copied and used without your permission.

Here are a couple of companies that offer water-marking software:

- **Alpha Tec Ltd.** Their EIKONAmark software is available at http://www.alphatecltd.com/.
- **Digimark** Find them at http://www.digimarc.com/dm_system.html.

How resilient are digital watermarks?

The ability of a digital watermark to survive when the image is changed in an image editor varies from one watermarking system to another. But though most watermark programs claim to be able to survive an almost infinite amount of digital editing, the reality is that there is a limit to how much you can mess with an image before the watermark becomes ineffective. Actions like resizing, cropping, compressing, and converting images among various file types can add noise to an image that renders the watermark unreadable. And tracking software can have trouble keeping tabs on marked images if those images get stored behind firewalls or on sites with password protection.

What is fair use?

Fair use is the term that refers to a part of the copyright law that allows others to use your images without your permission under a narrow set of conditions. Likewise, you can take advantage of fair use if you need to include someone else's image in a project you are involved with. Fair use is a poorly understood concept, however—people often believe that they're making fair use of a work when, in fact, they're really violating copyright. In its simplest form, fair use permits you to avoid copyright law as long as the copied material is used or redistributed for academic, journalistic, or satirical purposes.

What are the rules about making fair use of copyrighted images?

Unfortunately, there are no clear, well-defined rules about fair use. First and foremost, you need to be sure that you're using

the material for academic, journalistic, or satirical purposes. But that's not all. There are a number of tests that the fair use rule is held to. Here are some of the important ones:

● **Is the purpose and character of the use nonprofit in nature?**   While this is a consideration, keep in mind that being nonprofit or noncommercial is not a license to use copyrighted material with abandon. If you run a nonprofit organization's Web site and you egregiously violate a copyright, a court may very well find you guilty—even if you are noncommercial.

● **What is the amount of the work that you've copied or used?**   You are usually in violation of copyright if you use an entire work—or a substantial body of the work—without permission. Instead, you should use a subset of the work whenever possible. In photographic terms, this means that if someone extensively photographed an alien autopsy, you can't show all of the photos on your Web site without permission, even if you're reporting on the event. Instead, show just a few sample images.

● **Have you revealed the heart of the work?**   This is related to the amount of the work you've used, but is somewhat more subtle. Even if you use just a small sample of the work and claim fair use, you might be infringing if you choose the key element or the heart of the work. To extend the alien autopsy analogy, for instance, suppose you used the one key image that shows what the aliens have really been doing with all those cows over the years. The artist may claim you've revealed the heart of the work and therefore are in violation of the copyright.

● **What is the effect of your use on the marketplace?**   Since the goal of the copyright law is to allow artists to create and market their work in a free and unobstructed manner, then it stands to reason that the fair use clause shouldn't unduly limit the value of the original work in the marketplace. With that in mind, realize that any fair use of a work shouldn't adversely affect the value of the copyright.

 ## Is it OK if I infringe on a copyright accidentally or unintentionally?

If the damaged party is intent on suing, then the answer is probably no. Copyright law does not give much slack to the "innocent infringer," and consequently you can be held liable even if you didn't realize you were violating a copyright.

That means you can't use arguments like "I didn't see a copyright notice on the image." More surprising is that you're still accountable if you publish a work that you were "assured" was OK to publish but turns out not to be. Say, for instance, that you negotiate a one-time publishing right to an image for your Web-based newsletter and it turns out that the negotiating party didn't own the rights to the image. You didn't know that but guess what? You're guilty of copyright infringement.

In fact, there are three ways you can infringe on a copyrighted image:

● **Direct infringement**   In this case, you directly use someone else's work without permission.

● **Vicarious infringement**   Suppose you operate a Web site and publish pictures submitted by visitors to your site. If you edit the site for content, or you charge artists a fee to post images, then it can be argued that you had enough editorial control to be an infringer.

● **Contributory infringement**   In this instance, you operate a site that serves as a forum for posting images but you exercise limited control over the site's content. If someone posts something in violation of copyright, then you have contributed to the infringement and may be liable.

 ## What kinds of damages can be assessed for copyright infringement?

Damage awards for copyright infringement vary dramatically. Unintentional infringement can cost anywhere from $200 to $20,000. Willful infringement, on the other hand, can go as high as $100,000.

Also note that there is such a thing as *statutory damages*. If you filed a copyright registration with the copyright office within three months of the image's publication, then you are eligible to receive statutory damages regardless of how much you were paid for the image. If you only were paid $25, you can get $20,000 anyway.

What if I find someone is using my image without permission?

If you plan to challenge their use of the image in court, the first thing you need to do is register the image with the copyright office if you haven't done so already (see "How do I copyright something?" earlier in this chapter). You can then talk to an attorney and see if there's a case for suing the infringing party. Keep in mind, however, that copyright cases rarely pay enough to recover all the expenses. In order to recover damages, you'll need to demonstrate how you were, in fact, damaged by the infringement, and the burden of proof is on you.

Is there a statute of limitations on copyright infringement?

Yes, it's three years. After that, you have no legal recourse.

If I digitally edit someone else's image, can I use it without permission?

No. By establishing a copyright, the owner retains the exclusive right to modify an image and republish it. If you download, scan, or otherwise get a copy of someone's image, you are not allowed to edit it in any way. There have been some court arguments that severely modifying an image can constitute a whole new work, but the courts have generally dismissed that line of reasoning. In the music world, rap artists who "sample" songs must still get permission from the copyright holder to publish the new work.

Don't think that you may be able to change an image so much that it's unrecognizable. Digital watermarks can survive even severe tampering (see "What is a digital

watermark?" earlier in this chapter) and the image may even be tracked on the Internet.

 The right of reproduction is considered a specific right under copyright law. What does reproduction mean in the computer age?

Any copy of the original is a reproduction, and that's why computers make this so tricky. Some courts have ruled that the simple act of moving an image from the hard disk to memory is a "reproduction" in the legal sense. If you're offering to sell the rights to your work, then, be clear in your contract exactly what you mean. Contracts of this nature often give explicit examples to define what is meant, so a user can make copies of your image as necessary to use your work in the intended way.

PUBLISHING YOUR WORK

 If I sell my image to a Web site or magazine, do I lose my copyright?

No, not necessarily. You own the picture, and you own the copyright.

When you make a sale, you essentially bestow some rights on the publication. Which rights, and how comprehensive they are, is a matter to be decided between you and the publisher and is usually spelled out in a contract. See the following section.

If you do happen to sell all rights to an image, copyright law enables you to recover the rights to the image after 35 years.

What kind of rights am I selling when I sell my images?

That depends entirely upon the agreement you have with the publisher. In general, you should try to keep the rights as limited as possible—you want to make your images available to any given publisher for as little time as possible so you can resell your works over and over. That's increasingly difficult

in today's climate, unfortunately, but it's a goal. Here's a description of the major kinds of rights you'll encounter in a contract:

One-Time Rights

With one-time rights, the publisher has paid a fee to use your picture in print a single time.

First Rights

First rights are similar to one-time rights, except that you can generally get a higher fee since you're giving the publisher the opportunity to be the first to publish your work.

Exclusive Rights

This gives the publisher exclusive rights to publish your work in a particular market. That means you can sell the same image via exclusive rights to different publishers in different markets (such as a corporate Web site and also a calendar company). Exclusive rights typically expire after a certain time, and can be limited by corporate function (such as postcards, greeting cards, and calendars) or geographically (such as North America and Europe).

Serial Rights

Serial rights are similar to exclusive rights, though they are related to magazine publishing—they guarantee the publisher exclusive rights to publish your images in a magazine. Serial rights, in effect, block you from allowing competing magazines to publish the same images.

Electronic Rights

Electronic rights relate to permission to publish your images in a digital format, whether on the Web, CD-ROM, DVD, or in other formats. Electronic rights can be bought on their own or in conjunction with other rights.

All Rights

This is just what it sounds like: A publisher buys the rights to use your images exclusively. All rights can be permanent— essentially you sign the copyright over to the publisher—or you can negotiate a period of time after which the rights expire.

Work for Hire

Work for hire is the most restrictive category, since you do not actually own the copyright for the images you photograph. That means you receive a one-time fee for work and are not eligible for royalties or other payments, regardless of how valuable the image turns out to be.

In general, I highly recommend that you avoid work for hire, also known as WFH. While it'll get you some money in your pocket right away, you'll lose out on future earnings that could result from resale of your images or royalties on the initial sale. Work for hire is a very specific term and refers to work that meets one of these criteria:

● You are employed by the publisher and you took the image while in their employ. Unless you have a specific agreement with the employer to the contrary, anything you photograph belongs to them, along with the copyright.

● You sign a WFH contract with the publisher that specifically states that you relinquish ownership and copyright of the images.

● You sign an assignment letter that states that you assign the copyright to the publisher.

 When I sell rights for an image, are the specifics of the agreement negotiable?

Yes, they sometimes are. Increasingly, we're starting to see publishers who want to own all rights, such as when the phrase "all media now known or later developed" appears in a contract. Nonetheless, you can often negotiate rights that are different than those the publisher first offers. A work for hire contract, for instance, can often be changed into first rights.

Also be specific about electronic rights. While some contracts seem to be clear about what media they want permission to publish in, technology changes make this a difficult area to fully assess. If the publisher has asked for permission to publish on the Web, for instance, what about "push" technology that delivers information to the desktop automatically? As you can see, there are many kinds of permission you can negotiate, and there's no harm in asking.

If I get an image published in a magazine, does the magazine's "global" copyright notice apply to my image?

Yes, with a caveat—the publisher's copyright notice doesn't apply to advertising images, so advertisements aren't protected by the copyright notice in the masthead of the magazine. I recommend that you insert the copyright mark in your image if it's being used in this way.

What are moral rights?

You have a set of *moral rights* that accompany your copyright. These moral rights are designed to protect you and your work. Some of your moral rights include:

- The right to have your name associated with your work when it is published.
- The right of integrity; that is, your work cannot be substantially changed (recolored, for instance) without your permission, and your name may not be associated with the image if it is changed.

Moral rights are perpetual, which mean that even after the copyright expires, someone cannot modify your image in a way that isn't in the spirit of the original work and still connect your name to it.

If I allow other people to post images on my Web site, am I liable if they infringe on a copyright?

You might be (this would be a case of either vicarious or contributory infringement in the most strict interpretation of the law), but right now it seems that the answer is probably no. Copyright law on the Internet is still being refined, and copyright law to begin with is subject to differing opinions and interpretation.

The real test of copyright law on the Internet is to look at precedent—existing court cases that have involved copyrighted material. One of the most famous examples to date involves the Church of Scientology. The Church of Scientology sued an Internet service provider called Netcom in 1995 because a Netcom subscriber used the service to post copyrighted material—some secret Scientology materials.

Under traditional copyright law, the publisher is liable for violating copyright even if they don't know that an infringement took place. If the court had found Netcom to be a publisher, then they would have been liable for large punitive fines. In reality, the court found that Netcom didn't have intimate knowledge of what was being posted and was therefore innocent of copyright infringement. While that's counter to the kind of ruling that would probably occur with a print publication, it seems that the Internet is being treated slightly differently and has more latitude.

On the other hand, beware of applying the Scientology ruling to your own site without considering the differences. Netcom is a large ISP that can't possibly monitor everything that's posted to the Internet by its subscribers; if you're a small Web site that exerts some editorial control over content, things may be different. Specifically, editorial control implies that you are familiar with what gets published on your site, and therefore you may be held accountable for the copyright violations of those who use your site. I recommend that you consult a lawyer who is familiar with copyright law in order to strike a balance with your site, particularly if you want some control over what gets posted.

MODELING PERMISSION

 ### Can I photograph people in public places without their permission?

Absolutely. Depending upon the circumstances, it's often a common courtesy to get their verbal permission, but no one can bar you from photographing them in public. The First Amendment to the Constitution guarantees a free press, and that allows you to use your camera in public places.

Can the police require me to have a permit to photograph a public event or in a public place?

No. It's your First Amendment right to photograph in public. This is not an issue for negotiation or bargaining; public officials do not have a right to stop you. The only exception to this rule is if you are photographing the place or event expressly for commercial purposes, such as an advertisement.

If the military is participating in a local event, can I photograph their hardware?

Yes, you can. The military can only prohibit photography within the boundaries of their own installations. If they participate in a local event, they're displaying their hardware publicly, expecting photographs to be taken (don't expect to see anything top secret).

One exception: There are certain times when a deployed military force needs to set up a national security perimeter on public (or even private) land to protect certain kinds of hardware. This is rare but does happen—if you encounter such a thing and well-armed military guards warn you to put away your camera, do as they say.

What kinds of pictures aren't protected by the First Amendment?

Most of the kinds of pictures you're likely to want to take are within your First Amendment rights. However, in some situations you're simply not protected and you can be held liable for damages. These, as you can see, are fairly obvious, common-sense situations and easily avoided:

- **Photographing on private property**   You may not enter or photograph on private property without the owner's permission.

- **Libel or slander**   You may not misrepresent facts—implicitly or explicitly—through the use of a photograph and accompanying text.

- **Use of the photograph in a commercial application**   You need permission to photograph someone for an advertisement.

 ### Can I publish pictures of people I've photographed without their permission?

That depends upon the purpose of the picture. Here are the guidelines:

● If the purpose of the picture is *editorial in nature* or can be characterized as being to *inform* or *educate,* then you do not need the explicit permission of your subject. This is your First Amendment right.

● If the picture and any associated text may be libelous, be defamatory to the subject, or fall outside the "normal sensibilities" of the target audience, then you may need permission from the subject for your own protection.

● If the picture is used for commercial purposes, such as in an advertisement, then you need the permission of the subject.

 ### If I'm writing a book, do I need people's permission to place pictures of them in the book?

No. Unless the pictures are advertisements or product endorsements, you don't need explicit permission—though it's common sense that you'll secure their permission as a courtesy. You certainly don't need their permission in writing.

 ### Why is the subject's permission required for commercial photos?

You need to get the permission of the subject of your photos when you're creating images for commercial purposes because their role in an advertisement implies that they endorse the product. If you photograph a mother and baby in a local park, for instance, and the image ends up on a baby food Web site, then it appears that the mother uses the product, or at the very least endorses it. And that's the difference between commercial photography and publishing candid photos of strangers in a photo gallery, in a trade magazine, or on the Internet. There's no kind of product endorsement implied in the latter.

❓ How do I get the permission of my subject?

You'll do that with what is called a *model release form*. A model release is a document that the subject can sign, giving you permission to use the image in print. You generally only need permission from the subject of your picture if the image will be used for commercial (advertising) purposes.

If you have the flexibility to do so, you might want to get a model release for pictures even if you don't expect to use them for commercial purposes. That way if you later change your mind and have the opportunity to use the image in that way, you're all set.

If you never, ever take commercial photographs, then move along. But if you think you may have need of a release, feel free to work with this sample. There is no single legally binding format for a model release, but a typical model release looks something like this:

MODEL RELEASE

In consideration of receipt of ___($$)*___, I do hereby authorize _____ (the photographer) to use my likeness in any medium the photographer or the publisher sees fit for the purposes of advertising, editorial, or other use.

I affirm that I am more than 21 years of age.

Signature: ___(model)_____   Date: _____

Printed Name: _____

Signature: ____(photographer)_____   Date: _____

Printed Name: _____

*Indicate whatever compensation you and the subject have agreed upon, whether that is money, copies of the photo, or some other item of value.

Of course, if your model is still a minor, you'll have to use a slightly different kind of model release because you need the permission of a parent or guardian permission. This release looks like this:

MODEL RELEASE

I, _____, parent or legal guardian of
_____, a minor, in consideration of receipt of ____($$)*____,
do hereby authorize _____ (the photographer) to use the
likeness of said minor in any medium the photographer or the
publisher sees fit for the purposes of advertising, editorial, or other
use.

Signature: ___(parent or guardian)_____   Date: _____
Printed Name: _____

Signature: ___(photographer)_____   Date: _____
Printed Name: _____

*Indicate whatever compensation you and the subject have agreed
upon, whether that is money, copies of the photo, or some other item
of value.

Am I required to pay models in photographs that get published?

Certainly not. Any agreement that you have with someone who is in one of your images is a private transaction between the two of you. If you choose to pay, it probably shouldn't be more than 15% of what you're receiving as the fee for the publication of the image. Often, though, your model will be satisfied with a copy of the image or the publication that it eventually appears in.

Chapter 17

Printing

Answer Topics!

Printing @ a Glance

The proof, as they say, is in the printing. The essence of your camera is lost without the ability to print high-quality images, so look here for everything you need to know about printing pictures with a computer printer.

Are you shopping for a printer? Then you need to know the difference between laser, inkjet, and dye-sub printers. You also need to know what features and specifications are most important. Buying the right printer can make your digital camera a much more useful tool at home and in the office.

Printers can be a nightmare. So many things can go wrong—if it won't print properly, where do you start? Look here for a helpful guide to solving all your printer problems. That way you can get back to what you bought the printer for to begin with—printing!

PRINTING DIGITAL IMAGES

How do I actually print an image on my printer?

Of course, you'll encounter some variations in this process depending upon what program you print from, but here's the basic procedure:

1. Make sure your printer is turned on and the paper is loaded.

2. Open the image or file you want to print in the appropriate application.

3. Choose the Print command, usually found at File|Print. The Print dialog box appears.

4. Make sure all the print settings are correct. Choose the correct printer from the list, if you have more than one printer.

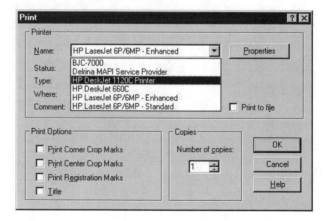

5. Set up the printer by clicking on the Properties button. Look for these settings:

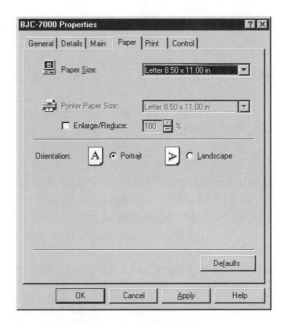

- **Correct paper type** Choose from plain paper, photo paper, and so on.

- **Correct paper size** If you're printing on paper that isn't 8.5×11 inches, you'll need to tell the printer software.

- **Correct orientation (landscape or portrait)** Landscape orientation turns the paper on its side.

- **Correct image quality** Choose from among the high-quality, normal, or economy printing modes supported by your printer.

6. Click on the Print button.

 ### How do I know what image resolution to use when printing to my inkjet printer?

For most inkjet printers, try to print at 150 or 200 dots per inch (dpi). You don't need to print at the printer's resolution

since, oddly enough, the printer's resolution and your image's resolution aren't directly related. Instead, you have to consider something called *line frequency* (a value you can probably get from the printer's manual). Line frequency has to do with the fact that a "dot" isn't exactly the same thing on a laser printer or magazine page as it is on an inkjet; it takes several dots to make a single dot of color in an inkjet.

So, to determine the file size of an image you want to print, simply multiply the output size by the dpi. A 4×6-inch print at 200 dpi works out to 800×1200 pixels—that's almost twice the default 640×480-pixel image most digital cameras take, so a megapixel camera is required to get the best quality at this size. In reality, you can still get pretty good results printing a 640×480-pixel image at 4×6 inches even though that's only 100 dpi. If you look carefully, though, you'll find that you can see jagged edges where there weren't enough pixels to fill in the image. For best results, pick a size where you can print at around 200 dpi, or whatever resolution best matches your particular printer.

In Figure 17-1, note at the top the entire image as it was printed on a Canon BJC-7000. Below, you can see a detail from the image first at 100 dpi, then at 150 dpi, and finally at 200 dpi. "Jaggies" in the picture are very obvious at 100 dpi, less obvious at 150, and nonexistent at 200 dpi.

The bottom line is that if you pack more pixels than you need into an image—and try to print the image above 200 dpi—odds are good that you won't improve image quality very much. Instead, you'll just make the file bigger, which takes more storage space on your hard disk and can slow down the printing process.

Tip: *Test your own printer by generating prints in high-quality mode at 100, 150, and 200 dpi. Use these to figure out what the resolution threshold of your printer is, and strive to use that setting as often as possible.*

Of course, the advice I just gave is specifically for someone who wants to know how much resolution an image needs to print well at a certain output size. If you just want to print an image and don't care how big it turns out, just print it. Most

Figure 17-1 An image printed at various resolutions on a Canon BJC-7000

image editors have an option to let you print the image at full-page size or at the image's normal size. If you choose normal size, the image will print smaller than full-page and probably look just fine. It's only when you force the image to

print at a certain size that the image's original resolution becomes important.

 ## How do I control how big my printer makes a picture?

You can print an image at any size you like, from postcard-size all the way up to 8×10 inches or larger if your printer supports those sizes. Some programs make the process of specifying print size easier than others, but here's the most general process used by many Windows programs including image editors like Paint Shop Pro:

1. Load the image you want to print into the desired program.

2. Choose File|Page Setup. The program's Setup dialog box will appear, allowing you to specify print settings.

3. Set the print mode to Fit to Page.

4. Choose your printer and select Properties.

5. Click on your printer's Paper tab and choose the appropriate paper type from the drop-down menu. If you're printing to a 4×6-inch paper stock or some other unusual size, choose Custom and enter the dimensions of the paper.

6. Click OK to exit the printer properties and print the image.

 ## Can a printer deliver output identical to 35mm prints from the corner store?

With the right printer and the right paper, you'd be amazed at the results you can get. Your printer should be a fairly recent model—one released in the last two years. Load photo-quality paper and be sure to use the photo-quality color cartridges recommended for your printer. There are even paper stocks designed for inkjets that come in the 4×6-inch format so your prints will be the same size as the ones from the photo store.

Technically, the resolution of a digital print won't match 35mm slides any time soon—film renders millions of pixels, while printers can only muster tens of thousands. In practical terms, though, the difference between an 8×10-inch enlargement and a good inkjet print can be beyond the limits of visual acuity, so you won't be able to tell the difference.

One caveat: the texture of your images will never be exactly the same as you'd get from a photo-finisher. The surface of prints made with photo-quality paper is rough and easily damaged, so you need to handle these pictures even more carefully than you might handle ordinary prints.

How large can I make prints with a printer? How small?

With the right printer and paper, you can print images as small as ordinary photos or as large as posters (11×17 inches being the standard). For small prints, I've had excellent results with Hammermill Jet Print Photo paper, which is a 4×6-inch photo stock that sells in packs of 24. For large prints, Hewlett-Packard sells 11×17-inch photo paper that yields incredible results on wide-format printers like the HP DeskJet 1120C (see Figure 17-2).

There are many kinds of paper stock to choose from. Which should I buy?

That's a good question, because there are so many kinds of paper floating around, particularly for inkjet printers. If you're printing on a laser printer, I suggest that you use ordinary 20-pound laser or copier paper that is at least 80 bright. Decent paper shouldn't cost more than about $7 per 500-sheet ream. I'd be reluctant to buy really inexpensive paper ($3/ream or less) since loose paper fibers can slowly affect the performance of your printer.

When it comes to inkjets, there are more decisions to make, since the quality of the colors is directly related to the paper you use. Use quality paper, since cheap stock can plug the nozzles and decrease the effective resolution of the printer. For general-purpose printing, you can use the same stock that I recommend for laser printers. Of course, I'm assuming that the majority of what you print isn't going to be mounted at the Louvre.

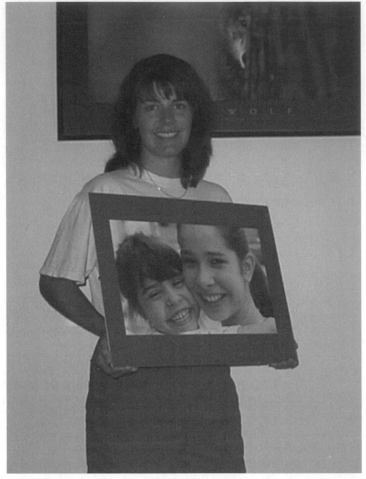

Figure 17-2 People can't tell that my 11x17-inch prints come from a digital camera and are printed on an inkjet—that's how good technology has gotten

But not every print job is appropriate for ordinary, plain paper, and there are several grades of paper in the stores:

- **Plain paper**   This is good for general text and ordinary graphics printing. The paper is inexpensive, but the ink tends to absorb quickly into the paper and blur the image.

- **High-quality or coated paper**   This is one step up, with some sort of clay embedded into the paper to stop the inks from spreading before they dry. For most printing you won't notice a big difference, but this paper improves photographic prints.

- **Photo paper**   The best stuff around, this paper is expensive, costing as much as a dollar a sheet. Certainly you won't use it all the time, but if you plan to frame a picture or give your digital prints away to family or friends, definitely use the special photo paper. Note that you can only print on one side of photo paper; I don't even recommend running this stuff through a laser printer on the flip side.

In Figure 17-3, you can see the differences among the three major kinds of inkjet paper. Photo paper (top left) offers the truest reproduction, while both coated (top right) and plain (bottom) paper suffer from color matching and bleeding problems. The plain paper also curled and wrinkled.

Tip: *No other factor has as great an effect on your final image quality as the kind of paper you use. If your prints don't look good, try better paper.*

If I have a Canon printer, should I use Canon paper?

This is a good question, and obviously applies to other printers as well. Hewlett-Packard wants you to use HP paper with their printers—does that mean you should, or is it just a case of the company wanting you to use their brand exclusively for no good reason?

In reality, vendors like Canon and HP can fine-tune their paper to match their inks so colors won't bleed and they'll be as vivid as possible. So it's not a bad idea to at least start with the same brand paper as your printer. On the other hand, many companies make excellent paper for inkjets—some more expensive, some less expensive than the same-brand paper. I suggest you experiment. Print the same image on different kinds of paper and compare them side by side. Then use the one you like the best. Certainly, you won't

Figure 17-3 The difference in image quality is obvious on photo, coated, and plain paper

hurt the printer by using different kinds of high-quality paper.

Personally, I've found that photo paper is uniformly excellent regardless of who makes it—so in my experience, at least, I don't feel compelled to match brands.

 ## Does it matter which side of the paper I print on?

Often, yes. Plain old laser paper is the same on both sides, so if you print on a laser printer or you use plain paper in an inkjet, it doesn't matter. But if you print specialty paper in an inkjet printer, make sure you load the paper the right way. Keep these tips in mind:

- Usually, the brighter or shinier side of the paper is the printing side. Sometimes it's also rough, like sandpaper.

- If you're printing on photo paper, the back will probably have writing (like "Kodak") on it.

- Many papers are labeled with small marks to indicate the proper print side.

Be sure you look carefully at the printing directions the first time you try a new paper. Ink won't adhere well—or at all—to the wrong side of specialty papers, and you could end up with a real mess when the ink runs everywhere.

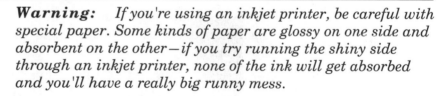 ## Can I print on both sides of plain paper?

Warning: *If you're using an inkjet printer, be careful with special paper. Some kinds of paper are glossy on one side and absorbent on the other—if you try running the shiny side through an inkjet printer, none of the ink will get absorbed and you'll have a really big runny mess.*

If you create newsletters, brochures, or other documents in bulk that might benefit from a splash of color, you can print in color on one side with an inkjet printer and in black and white—with a less costly laser printer—on the other side. Here's how I suggest you do this:

1. Start with the laser-printed side. If you started printing with the inkjet, the ink might melt in the laser printer due to the laser's extreme heat. If you are using special paper, print on the side that you can't print with an inkjet printer. If you're using plain paper, print on either side.

2. Take a stack of documents that have been laser-printed and load them in the inkjet printer. Usually, you'll need to load the paper printed side up, with the head of the page toward the printer. It's a good idea to print a test page in "economy ink mode" to be sure.

? **After I print a picture, the ink seems a bit tacky. Is this normal?**

Yes, if you're printing on photo paper, the ink may seem very rough and just slightly tacky long after the print is made. The ink will also be very sensitive to fingerprints, dust, and other contaminants, so handle the paper very carefully.

? **My inkjet printer is a year old and doesn't seem to print as well as it used to. Do I need to replace it?**

No, you probably don't need to replace the printer. However, you may need to clean the nozzles (see Figure 17-4). First try to run the nozzle cleaning software that came with your printer. Look for it in the printer properties. If you can't find such a utility—or it doesn't work that well—then try this method:

1. Remove the cartridges one at a time, being careful not to touch any part of the cartridge near the nozzles with your fingers.
2. Gently clean them with Q-tips dipped in alcohol.
3. Dab the nozzles with a tissue. Be gentle!
4. When you're done, simply replace the cartridges. Your printing should be significantly improved.

? **Why don't the colors in the printout match the colors onscreen?**

They never will match exactly, particularly your most vibrant, saturated hues.

All printers use the CMYK (cyan, magenta, yellow, and black) color model. But CMYK color cannot reproduce the full range of colors displayed onscreen in RGB (red, green, and blue). That's because RGB colors are just made of light, while your printer needs to be able to actually mix those colors using real ink. No printer can get the really saturated reds, for instance, that a computer can display.

Figure 17-4   Periodically cleaning the inkjet nozzles can improve
image quality

 Will my prints fade?

All picture colors tend to fade over time, but inkjet photos
do tend to fade somewhat faster. In fact, inkjet inks are
sensitive to ultraviolet light, and your images will fade
faster if exposed to direct sunlight for extended periods. If
you plan to frame pictures and leave them exposed to
sunlight, consider using UV-shielded glass, available at
some framing shops.

Tip: *Keep the original file on your hard disk so you can
reprint it when it starts to noticeably fade.*

 I want to make a high-quality print of a particular picture. Can I have it done professionally?

> You can always enlist the aid of a print shop or service bureau. While such businesses are not cheap, they may be able to take your image on disk and provide you with a very high-quality image. And modern print shops aren't nearly as intimidating as they used to be, since local copy centers have started offering similar services.

 What do I need to know if I want to get images printed by a print shop or service bureau?

> If you want a print shop to make prints for you, you should shop around and find out a few important things before you decide which one you want to use:
>
> - What are their rates?
> - How does the volume affect the cost? (If you want 50 copies, it may begin to get a lot cheaper on a per-image basis.)
> - What format do they require the image in?
> - How can you submit files—on floppy or Zip, or by e-mail?
> - What kind of paper do they use?

 How many pages should I expect to print with my printer toner or ink?

> You should look at the manual that came with your printer for this information. In general, you'll get a few hundred pages out of a set of color cartridges and a few thousand pages from a toner cartridge. In fact, that makes a laser printer very cost-effective—the toner lasts quite a long time, dropping the cost per page significantly.

> ***Tip:*** *I suggest you avoid using services that refill your ink cartridges. Their quality is unpredictable, and I don't think it's worth saving a few bucks.*

CHOOSING A PRINTER

 ## What are the different kinds of printers I can choose from?

Buying a printer isn't an easy decision because not only are there many different brands of printers competing for your attention—and lots of different models from each manufacturer—but you have to figure out what kind of printer you want. Here's a short guide to the type of printers you might want to install in your home or office.

Inkjet printer

Inkjet printers, which work by spraying microscopic drops of ink onto the paper, are the best all-around printing solution for many people. They produce good color and yet aren't too slow at printing plain text. Inkjet printers are also pretty affordable, costing as little as $150 and usually no more than about $500.

Many people are concerned about the quality of inkjet printers based on experiences they had with older printers several years ago. Since then, the technology has improved so dramatically that there's almost no comparison between those old printers and the ones being made now. I have digital images framed, matted, and hung on my wall that are pretty much indistinguishable from professionally printed 35mm pictures.

Laser printer

Laser printers are better at text printing than graphic printing, largely because most lasers are black-and-white devices. Yes, you can get color laser printers, but they cost $2,500 at the very least and can be significantly more. An ordinary laser printer, on the other hand, can be had for between $250 and $1,000.

Laser printers can certainly be used to print images, and they can do it well—as long as your needs don't include color. You can print a large quantity of family newsletters with a laser faster than with an inkjet, for instance.

Dye-sublimation printer

The smallest segment of the printer market is occupied by dye-sublimation printers (also called dye-sub for short). Dye-subs work by spreading ink onto the paper from long rolls of heated, colored, plastic ribbons. The results from dye-sub printers are nothing short of stunning—they typically look just as good as 35mm prints and even magazine photos.

The downside is that they're not much good for printing text, so your dye-sub printer will almost by definition have to be a second printer that you only use when you're expressly printing photos. Also, the selection is much more limited. There are just a few dye sublimation printers on the market. A company called Fargo is a popular dye-sub manufacturer, and they sell small printers designed just for creating photo prints in the $500 price range. To print a full 8.5×11-inch page, however, you'll need to step up to the $1,500 price range. Many print shops have dye-sub printers, so you can use their services if you only want to print an occasional image at this quality. See "I want to make a high-quality print of a particular picture. Can I have it done professionally?" earlier.

 ## What's a "bubble jet" printer?

"Bubble jet" is the name that Canon uses to describe its inkjet printers. They're really inkjets at heart, but the name distinguishes them somewhat from other, similar printers on the market.

 ## Which kind of printer should I get?

That depends, of course. Nonetheless, I think you should probably get an inkjet. In comparison to a dye-sub printer, inkjets are more versatile, since you can use them to routinely print text as well as graphics. They're also a bit cheaper.

On the other hand, I really like laser printers as well, and many people choose to buy one of each since they're reasonably affordable (you can get a laser and an inkjet today for what just one of them would have cost five years ago).

Lasers typically can print sharper text than inkjets, too, so you might not want to routinely print Word documents and spreadsheets on an inkjet. And lastly, lasers are cheaper in the long term—a $75 toner cartridge in a laser printer may last for 4,000 pages, while a $50 ink cartridge in an inkjet will only last for a few hundred pages.

How should I shop for a printer?

Start with the printer's specifications. You should look for the printer's speed (measured in pages per minute, or ppm) and resolution. Slow laser printers run at 4 ppm; the fastest are around 16 ppm. Remember that inkjets print much more slowly; color is their selling point, not speed.

Resolution is measured in dots per inch (dpi), and most printers are 300 dpi. Some printers offer four times higher resolution with 600 dpi; anything higher than that approaches publication quality, and you're unlikely to need that level of quality (especially considering the price of those printers). Price/performance-wise, the sweet spot for laser printers right now is 600 dpi, so I suggest you look for a printer with that resolution. Inkjets typically print at 300 dpi, but the presence of color can make the images appear to have a higher resolution.

After specifications, I suggest that you consider ease of use. Many printers use the capabilities of the bidirectional parallel port to tell you about the printer's status. These status monitors are handy. If you have a notebook PC, you might want to print directly to the new printer via the wireless IrDA port found on most portables. Few printers have IrDA support, however, so you'll have to shop around. The Hewlett-Packard LaserJet 6P, for instance, is a 600 dpi, 8 ppm printer with an IrDA port for wireless printing. Another one of my favorites is the NEC SuperScript 860, a printer with the 6P's specifications minus the IrDA port.

Few inkjets offer much in the way of advanced features, so the key for them is simply to look for the one with the best output at a price you want to pay. See the following section for more information.

You should also make sure the printer is designed to accommodate any media you often print, such as envelopes,

transparencies, and heavy cardstock. Can you load a stack of envelopes at once, or do you need to buy an optional envelope feeder? To cut down on jams, look for a printer with a fairly straight paper path, meaning the paper is pulled straight through the printer's internals, not curled up and around.

Finally, trust your own eyes. Try to test a few competing printers in a PC store before making your decision. Test both text and graphics. Avoid graphics that are too dark or lack contrast or definition, and in the case of inkjets, try to determine which printers do well on plain paper as well as on special photo paper. People are often disappointed when they discover that their new printer does poorly on plain paper despite impressive results on expensive premium stock.

 ## Which inkjet should I buy?

There are a lot of variations among inkjet (and bubble jet) printers. When it comes to image quality, one of the most important issues is the number of colors the printer can produce. In the old days, inkjets had just three color tanks. Combining all three colors should have made black, but it was more like a dirty brown. That's why inkjet images weren't very satisfying and no one took them seriously for creating photograph-quality output. A few years ago, though, we started seeing four colors (cyan, yellow, magenta, and black) in printers. Since then, the newest printers on the market have featured even as many as six or seven colors. Manufacturers found that by adding extra colors, they could achieve more photorealistic prints.

Today, many inkjet printers allow you to insert a "photo cartridge" that has extra colors when you're ready to print photos (see Figure 17-5). When you're printing ordinary, non-photographic graphics or just plain text, you don't need the photo cartridge and can swap it out for the normal array of four colors. The results from these printers are outstanding and come close to the results you can get with a dye-sub printer. Personally, I use a Canon BJC-7000, and I'm extremely pleased with the output.

Most inkjets can only print on an 8.5×11-inch sheet of paper. What if you want to create larger works? There are a few wide-format printers around that let you print up to 11×17 inches. The Hewlett-Packard DeskJet 1120C, for

Figure 17-5 Many inkjet printers let you swap out the normal color cartridge for an enhanced photo-color unit when printing photographs

instance, is an affordable wide-format inkjet printer that I've used to create stunning poster-sized pictures. Though the 1120C only uses four ink cartridges, not the six or seven that are becoming more common, that doesn't seem to affect the image quality. To my eye, its output is stunning. As a testament, the output from this printer hangs on walls throughout my home.

 I keep seeing that some laser printers use image enhancement technology. How does that work?

Many laser printers offer higher apparent resolutions than the print engine is actually capable of delivering through some sort of image enhancement technology. By varying the size of the dots in graphics and text, these printers can make the output smoother than the rated resolution would ordinarily allow (see Figure 17-6). Each manufacturer has its own name for it, but the basic idea is the same in every case.

How a Laser Printer Works

A laser printer is an interesting device. It works in a manner similar to a photocopier, but curiously enough, it actually needs more reliability than a photocopier, which is visited frequently by a technician on a service contract.

A laser printer has at its heart a photo-conductive drum. A charging roller imposes an electrical charge on the roller that causes it to repel toner. Without any more components, this printer would produce elegantly white sheets of paper. A laser, however, scans quickly across the drum to draw an image of the page that is being printed. In the process, it dissipates the charge wherever it strikes. When the toner comes in contact with the drum via a toner roller, toner sticks to the drum wherever the laser made contact. Paper is rolled across the treated drum, and a fuser roller melts the toner in place.

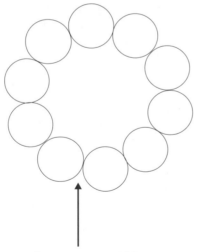

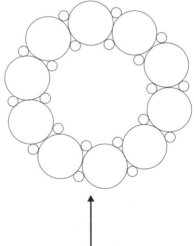

A normal image is jagged because the uniform-sized dots can't form smooth curves or diagonal lines

Enhancement technology smooths curves by using variable-sized dots

Figure 17-6   Many laser printers vary the size of dots to reduce "jaggies" and pixelation when printing irregular shapes

Do I need a PostScript printer?

Nope. PostScript is a page definition language that is popular with the Macintosh and some high-end page layout and graphics programs. If you're a graphics professional, or if you want to work in Mac/PC hybrid workgroups over a network, then you should definitely consider PostScript. In general, however, you won't need PostScript and can save a few dollars by buying a "Windows" printer that doesn't include it.

Do I need to buy a printer with lots of fonts? How about font cartridges?

No, rank this pretty low on your priority list. Printers with lots of fonts were all the rage a few years ago when lots of people printed from DOS and used the fonts built into the printer. Windows, however, uses TrueType fonts— standardized, scalable fonts that are stored on your hard disk and sent to your printer as high-resolution graphics. When you're shopping for a printer, you can disregard whatever marketing blurb they put on the box about how many fonts are included.

USING YOUR PRINTER

How do I install a printer?

Installing a printer is a simple task because it docsn't involve removing the cover from your PC. Here's what you need to do:

1. Turn off your PC.

Not as Many Fonts as You Think

Many printers advertise that they have 20, 30, or even 50 fonts preinstalled. Often, that's not 50 distinct typefaces (like Times, Arial, and Courier), but just a few typefaces in many, many different sizes.

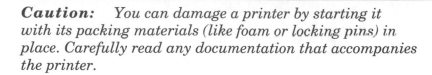

2. Locate the printer and a parallel cable. If a parallel cable didn't come in the box, you'll need to purchase one separately.

3. Remove all the packing tape, "before flight" stickers, and other artifacts of the shipping process from your new printer. Often you'll need to open the printer up and take bits of foam or locking pins out of the printer's insides.

! ***Caution:*** *You can damage a printer by starting it with its packing materials (like foam or locking pins) in place. Carefully read any documentation that accompanies the printer.*

4. Install the toner cartridge (if it's a laser printer) or ink cartridges (if it's an inkjet). Follow the manufacturer's warnings about not touching delicate parts and not shaking and turning anything in such a way that you spill ink or toner all over the place. Laser printer toner in particular is virtually impossible to clean up.

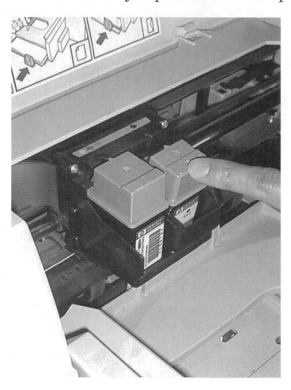

5. Load some paper in the paper tray.

6. Plug the parallel cable into the printer and then into the parallel port on the back of your PC. Use the tensioners to lock the cable on the printer; screw the cable securely into the computer.

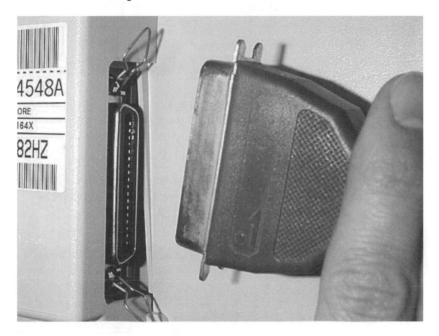

7. Plug the printer's power cable in.

8. Start your PC and power-on the printer. When Windows starts, it will probably recognize the printer and prompt you to install the drivers. If not, wait until the PC is fully booted and then choose Start | Settings | Printers and add the printer manually.

How do I know if the printer is working right?

There are two different kinds of self-tests you can run: the one within the printer itself and the one from Windows. If you're having trouble getting your new printer to work, try both to figure out where the trouble lies.

Does the printer work at all?

If you're having a problem, you should first make sure that the printer works all by itself, without involving Windows. Every printer is a bit different—you'll need to take the printer "off-line" and press the one-, two-, or three-button combination identified in your printer manual. If you're not sure if the printer is functioning properly, that's the way you need to test it.

Is the printer communicating with Windows?

If the printer works but you can't print anyway, then it might be a problem within Windows or with the connection to the printer. Try this:

1. Choose Start | Settings | Printers.

2. Find your printer icon in the Printers folder and right-click on it. Choose Properties.

3. Click on the General tab and choose Print Test Page.

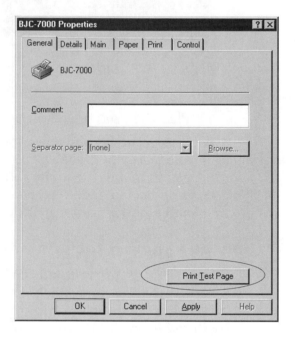

If all is well, a page of text and graphics with the Windows logo should come out of your printer.

I want to install a printer but there's no Windows driver for it. Can I use the printer?

Sure. Most printers are designed to emulate other printers. That way you can easily connect a printer and, even if it doesn't have its own set of drivers for your application or operating system, it'll understand a fairly universal set of commands used by a more popular printer. Windows has eliminated the need to install printer drivers for every application on your hard disk (if you aren't old enough to remember that, it's true—in the old days, you had to install your printer separately for every program you owned!). Thus, all you have to do is let Windows know what kind of printer you have. If you don't have a driver disk for your printer, try installing it with alternate drivers in this order:

- First see if Windows has your printer listed by name in the Settings | Printers dialog box (double-click on Add Printer). If so, select it.

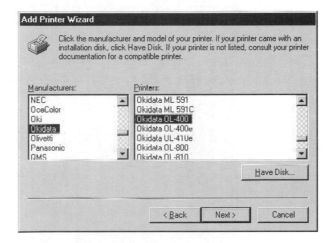

- If not, next try a similar printer from the same manufacturer. If you have an HP Deskjet 660C, for instance, the 550 driver works just fine.

- Last, but not least, see if the printer will emulate a more common printer from another vendor. If you're installing a laser printer, try Hewlett-Packard.

 Always see if your printer's manufacturer has a Web page where you can download a new printer driver. Here is a short list of common printer manufacturers and their Web addresses:

Manufacturer	Web Site
Brother	www.brother.com
Canon	www.ccsi.canon.com
Epson	www.epson.com
Hewlett-Packard	www.hp.com
Lexmark	www.lexmark.com
NEC	www.nec.com
Okidata	www.okidata.com
Panasonic	www.panasonic.com

Can I connect more than one printer to a computer?

Yes, you can use a simple A-B switch box to connect two printers to a single parallel port.

Switch boxes are inexpensive and available at most PC stores. Keep in mind, however, that some printers that rely on the bidirectional parallel port may not work properly with a switch box between them and the PC. Hewlett-Packard laser printers are notorious for not supporting switch boxes. If your printer is so affected, return the switch box to the store and try one of these three alternatives:

- Install an I/O card to get a second parallel port.

- Purchase an active, powered switch box. These cost over $100, so they're not an inexpensive solution.

- If you have two PCs, install a simple network and attach a printer to each PC. If you "share" the printers in the network, you can print to either printer from either computer. See "How do I install a printer on a network?" later in this chapter for more information.

Warning: *Always power down your PC and printer before moving cables around—even to connect a switch box.*

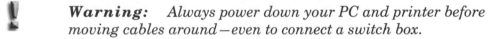

Can I let two computers share one printer?

This is the opposite of the previous question. You can either connect one printer to two computers with a custom switch box or network the computers together and share the printer so either computer can print to it. See "How do I install a printer on a network?" for more information. You can also learn all about this topic in another book of mine, *Upgrading & Repairing Your PC Answers!* (Osborne/McGraw-Hill, 1998). Sorry about the shameless plug.

Can I add memory to my printer?

You'll need to check your printer's manual to be sure, but inkjets and dye-sublimation printers don't generally accept memory upgrades. The main reason for this is that data is sent from your PC to the printer a little at a time, so having more memory on the printer isn't much of an advantage.

Laser printers, on the other hand, are called *page printers* because an entire page of data must be sent to the printer before it can print. So if you're printing a page with lots of graphics at a high resolution, you may need more memory to

print. Most laser printers accept memory modules that you can install yourself. If you experience data overflow errors (see "Why doesn't my laser printer always print the entire page?" later in this chapter), then you might want to look into a memory upgrade.

How do I install a printer on a network?

If you've installed a Local Area Network in your home or office, you can configure the printer so all the PCs on the network can print to it. There are two steps to enabling the printer. First, you need to make sure that Windows will share your printer with the rest of the network. Then you need to visit each computer on the network and show it where the printer actually is. Here's how you do it:

1. Choose Start | Settings | Control Panel and open the Network applet.

2. On the Configuration tab, click the File and Print Sharing button.

3. Make sure that there's a check mark in the box for "I want to be able to allow others to print to my printer(s)."

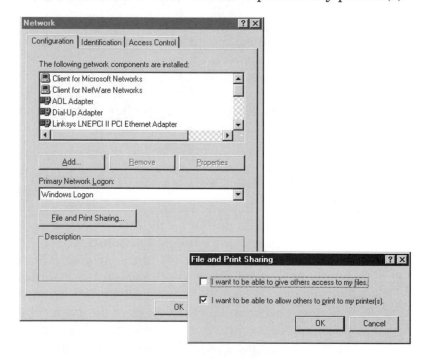

4. Click OK twice to close the Network applet.

Next, go to each computer that isn't directly connected to the printer via a parallel or serial cable and do the following:

1. Choose Start | Settings | Printers.

2. Select Add Printer and click Next.

3. Choose Network Printer and click next.

4. Click the Browse button and look for the computer with the printer attached. Click on the plus sign to its left and choose the printer when it appears. Click OK.

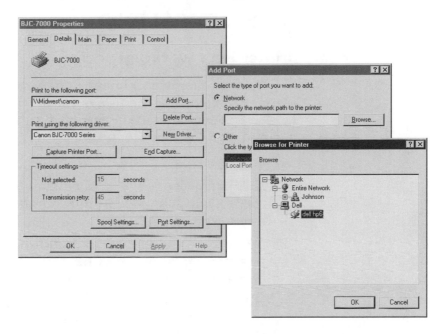

5. Name the printer and click Next.

6. Click Finish to complete the printer's installation.

Now your printer can serve not just the PC it's attached to, but also the other PCs on the network.

 ### What should I do if I need to ship the printer off for repairs?

Make sure you remove the toner cartridge before shipping it anywhere. I've actually made the mistake myself of mailing not just one, but two, printers to a photo studio during a magazine review, with the toner cartridges still installed. When they arrived, the printers were "toner bombed"—irreparably drenched, inside and out, with ink. Don't make the same mistake yourself.

If you need to ship the printer, you should also apply tape to any doors or moving parts that could come loose and get broken during shipping. Your best bet is to save the packing materials and shipping box that came with the printer in the first place.

PRINTING PROBLEMS

 My printer isn't working!

Any number of problems might contribute to this general alarm, so let's review the things you should check. Follow these steps in order, since I designed it to progressively narrow down the source of trouble.

1. **Try the obvious.**   Make sure the printer has paper, it isn't jammed, and it's plugged in and turned on. Check the LCD display (or LED indicators) on your printer for a trouble message.

2. **Make sure the printer is "on line."**   If you had a problem, the printer may have taken itself off-line and be waiting for you to press a button on its front panel.

3. **Recycle the printer.**   Turn it off, wait a minute, then turn it back on again. Try printing. If that doesn't work, then keep going.

4. **Run the printer's self-test.**   You may need to check the user's manual for the correct keypresses, but this will determine if the printer works. If it does, the problem is elsewhere.

5. **Is it Windows?**   Run the Print test in Windows. See "How do I know if the printer is working right?" earlier in this chapter.

6. **Does it work in DOS?** From a DOS prompt, try sending something to the printer. Type, for instance, **type config.sys > lpt1:**. If your CONFIG.SYS file spits out of the printer, the printer works and the connection to your PC is fine—so it's a Windows problem after all. If not, the problem is with the printer or cable.

7. **Do you use a status monitor program in Windows?** If so, this may be the culprit. It can get corrupted and interfere with printing from Windows. Change printer drivers to bypass this status monitor—choose an older version of your printer from Start | Settings | Printers or use an alternate driver provided by the manufacturer. Then remove the status monitor from your Startup folder and reboot the PC. Can you print now? If so, uninstall and reinstall the status monitor.

8. **Replace the cable.** If you've isolated the cable as your source of trouble, replace it.

9. **Check the parallel port.** It's very unlikely that the parallel port has blown, but it does happen; if you suspect that the port is your problem, try the printer on another computer.

Once you narrow down the problem, you can take some action. Some solutions are self-evident. If the printer fails its own self-test, for instance, it needs to be repaired or replaced. If you narrow the problem down to Windows, however, you may need to remove and reinstall the printer driver.

What's the difference between the printer's print test and Windows' print test?

The print test built into your printer is the best way to determine if your printer works properly—the test will work even if the printer isn't connected to a computer at all. Windows' print test, on the other hand, sends data from your PC to the printer; so if the printer's print test works but the Windows test doesn't, you know the problem is with either the connection or Windows itself. If you can print from DOS, you can eliminate the connection as a possibility and you know the problem is with Windows.

 Why doesn't my 8 ppm printer print at 8 ppm?

First, remember that your printer is rated by its ability to print text; if you throw a page of graphics at it, don't expect to get the speed marked on the box. If you're printing plain text and the printer is noticeably slower than the rated speed, however, here are a few things you can try:

● Turn off any image enhancement technology in the printer's software control panel. That can affect print speed significantly.

● Drop down to the printer's base resolution (probably 300 dpi).

● Disable the printer's power management tools.

● Check that you're using the correct printer driver for the printer.

One or more of those changes should get your printer printing at top speed, but realize that the cure may be worse than the symptoms. I'd rather enable image enhancement, for instance, and sacrifice some print speed.

 Why doesn't my laser printer always print the entire page?

The most likely problem is a "data overflow" caused by a lack of memory in your laser printer. Other printers—like inkjets and dot-matrix printers—don't need to worry about this, because they get data in small chunks from the computer. They print as they receive data, and hence stay ahead of their small printer buffer.

A laser, as I've said, is a page printer. Page printers need to build an image of the entire page in memory at once before they start printing, because the print mechanism—in this case, a laser heating toner on a rolling drum—doesn't allow for pauses in the print process while more data arrives.

So much for theory. The bottom line is that you need to have enough memory in your laser printer to handle all of the text and graphics. Usually the amount of RAM that comes with a printer is sufficient, but you can easily send print jobs to a laser printer that overtax its capabilities. That commonly

happens when you send a file with lots of graphics, like a PowerPoint presentation, to a printer that doesn't have enough RAM.

The problem is exacerbated by the fact that it's hard to tell exactly how much memory you need. Modern printers use sophisticated compression to do more in a limited amount of RAM. But when a particular page can't be compressed as much as the software expected, you get a data overflow and the page doesn't print.

You have two ways to solve this problem:

- Drop down to a lower print resolution. If you're usually printing at 600 dpi, set your printer to 300 dpi using the Start | Settings | Printers dialog box. That gets you about four times as much memory for printing.

- Add memory to your printer. Contact your vendor and find out what your memory upgrade options are. You can probably add 2 or 4MB of RAM to the printer and avoid those overflow errors forevermore.

How do I replace the toner cartridge in my laser printer?

After a few thousand pages, your toner cartridge will wear out and you'll have very light output or streaks of white through your documents. The cartridge is easy to replace yourself:

1. Shut off your printer and open the access cover.

2. Remove the old cartridge. Pull it straight out and slip it immediately into a plastic bag to prevent residual toner from messing up your office.

3. Take the new cartridge out of the sealed bag and shake it gently or rock it from side to side to distribute toner evenly inside it.

4. Find the plastic strip that seals the toner cartridge and pull it evenly, firmly, and continuously out of the unit. Don't jerk it or it might break—if it does, the toner cartridge is ruined.

5. Slip the cartridge into the void left by the old cartridge and make sure it is seated firmly in the printer. Close the cover and turn the printer back on.

6. Run the printer self-test to be sure the toner is flowing evenly out of the cartridge.

Tip: *Keep the bag from the new toner cartridge handy in case you need to remove it or ship the printer.*

How do I prevent paper jams?

Paper jams eventually happen, but you can take some steps to minimize them:

● Don't overfill your paper tray or paper cassette.

● Fan stacks of paper before loading them.

● Keep paper in a cool, dry place. Damp paper is more likely to jam.

● Don't print on scrap paper that has already been printed on the other side. (Although you might want to do this anyway to conserve paper and just deal with occasional jamming.)

● Use quality paper. Cheap paper is more likely to jam.

● Be sure the stock you're printing on—especially if it's something special like labels—is approved for laser printers.

● When printing labels or stock heavier than 20 pound, use the straightest paper path available. Often, that's the single-sheet accessory tray.

How do I fix a paper jam?

When clearing paper jams, be aware that the inside of a laser printer or a dye-sub printer is very hot. Turn the printer off and wait a few minutes for the inside of the machine to cool. In an inkjet, heat isn't a concern.

Locate the jammed paper. It might be jammed at the entryway from the paper cassette, at the rollers, or in the rear of the printer. Wherever it is, pull the paper straight out—not by a corner—and pull it slowly. These precautions should prevent the paper from tearing. If it does tear, make sure you remove all the shards of paper to prevent future jams.

When the paper jam is cleared, be sure to return the printer to its on-line state before trying to print.

! ***Caution:*** *If you have a jam with an inkjet printer, make sure you allow the printer to attempt to cycle the page through first. If you must physically remove the paper, pull it slowly in the direction of the paper path. Inkjets tend to jam less often, but yanking paper out of their mechanisms can be more damaging.*

? Why does my paper crease when it prints?

Damp paper can do that. Try to store your paper in a cool, dry pace, particularly if you live in a high-humidity part of the country.

Extending the Life of Your Laser Toner Cartridge

If you notice that your laser toner is running low—i.e., your output is very light or streaked with white—you can get another 50, 100, or more copies out of your cartridge before discarding it. Open your printer and locate the toner cartridge. It usually looks like a long, black tube that runs across the width of the printer. Pull it out and give it a few good shakes to distribute the toner across the drum. Replace the cartridge and you should be able to print normally again for a while. This trick may even work a second time, but probably not very well after that.

Warning: *Don't go nuts when you shake the cartridge. If you flip it over or shake it up and down too vigorously, you'll spray impossible-to-clean toner all over your rug. Try to shake it gently from side to side.*

Why does my inkjet's output have big splotches of ink on it?

The nozzles of your cartridges might be gunked with ink. You can solve this by cleaning them—see "My inkjet printer is a year old and doesn't seem to print as well as it used to. Do I need to replace it?" earlier in this chapter. When you're done, your printing should be significantly improved.

Why has my laser printer's output suddenly turned all white?

If your laser printer suddenly starts producing completely white output, the charging roller (often not really a roller but actually a wire) has broken. If the charging roller is contained in the toner cartridge, replace the cartridge. If it's an integral part of the printer instead, you'll need to get the printer serviced. Check your printer manual to see which kind of printer you have.

Do I ever need to use "cleaning paper"?

Usually the manufacturer recommends that you pass a page or two of cleaning paper through your printer whenever you replace the toner or color cartridges. Don't be thrown by the term "cleaning paper"—it's usually just ordinary paper that you run through the printer when you select the printer's cleaning or self-test mode. The cleaning paper helps ensure a uniform distribution of toner or ink when you start printing for real. Check the printer manual for details.

Someone sent me a file but it prints differently on my printer than theirs. Why?

It's not a problem with your printer—it's the software. Often, word processing and graphics files were created with fonts that you don't have installed on your PC. If you try to open or print the file, the software substitutes "similar" fonts, and the end result looks quite different than the original file on the other PC. Ask your friend to e-mail you the fonts used in the document and drag them into your Fonts folder.

> ✻ **Note:** *In some cases, it may be a violation of the font software company's copyright for you to install fonts from your friend's computer. In this case, you can buy and install the fonts yourself or ask your friend to reformat the document using more typical Windows fonts.*

Can I safely remove and store a partially used cartridge?

There are many reasons why you might need to do this. You might have an inkjet printer that enables you to swap in cartridges containing unusual colors, like fluorescent and glitter inks. Or you might need to remove a toner cartridge from a laser printer if the printer is going in for repairs.

The bottom line for storing laser printer toner is this: Never turn it upside down and never store it where it is exposed to light, even fluorescent office light. You should keep the opaque plastic bag that the toner comes in for storage situations like this. Tape the end of the bag shut and lock it in a drawer where you won't accidentally tip it over.

For inkjet cartridges, you don't have to worry quite so much about exposure to light or spilling ink. You should be careful to store them upright, however, and never, ever touch the bare metal plate with electrical contacts. Many vendors provide (or sell as an accessory) special containers that hold ink cartridges when they're removed from the printer. I recommend that you use them.

How far from my computer can I place my printer?

If you have a parallel-port printer (and virtually all PC printers are of the parallel variety), then your standard parallel cable can be no longer than 6 feet. If you spend a bundle on a specially shielded parallel cable, you can get perhaps 9 or 12 feet, but signal degradation prevents anything longer. If your printer has a serial connection, about 200 feet is the limit.

Chapter 18

Digital Video

Answer Topics!

Digital Video @ a Glance

Many digital cameras come with a video-out jack that lets you display images on video. Sounds great, but almost no one really uses this feature. Look in this chapter for tips and advice on how to get the most mileage out of the video-out feature of your digital camera.

How do you get video from your camcorder into your PC? Look in this chapter for the skinny on topics like video capture cards, FireWire, system requirements, and Audio Video (AV) hard disks.

A close cousin of the digital camera is Digital Video. By capturing video from a camcorder or a DV camcorder, you can turn your PC into a desktop video studio. If you want to make videos for your family or a small office, video editing on the PC has come of age. Read about it here.

Use your camera to reach out and touch someone who lives 2,000 miles away. Digital cameras can be used to video conference with people over vast distances without spending a penny on long-distance phone charges. Or use a digital camera to broadcast images of your office, your backyard, or your pet hedgehog to the world via your Web page. You can even monitor your kids while you're at work via a Web page and a Web cam.

TRANSFERRING TO VIDEO

 Can I transfer digital images to video?

That depends upon your camera. Many digital cameras come with a video-out jack that allows you to show the images stored in your camera on a television or other video unit (see Figure 18-1). If your camera is one of these, you can easily connect your camera to a VCR. You can create a slideshow on videotape by using the camera's preview control buttons to advance through the images while recording the results to videotape.

Figure 18-1   The Canon PowerShot 350 has a video-out jack for displaying images on television

Why do some of my pictures look really bad on videotape?

Some images you take with your digital camera might look particularly bad on video. This is a result of the fact that very saturated colors—red in particular—are beyond the ability of video to properly process and display. As a result, oversaturated colors tend to bleed onscreen.

If your camera has a feature that lets you transfer images from the PC back to the camera again, then you can fix this. Find images that will bleed on the video screen and use an image editor to reduce the color saturation slightly. Then load the images back into the camera and transfer them to video.

 What are some ways I can take advantage of the video-out port on my camera?

The video-out port on your camera is an oft-neglected tool. If you think about it, though, I'm sure you can come up with a bunch of innovative ways to utilize that port. Here are some suggestions:

- Create a video slideshow of digital images and send it to friends or family.

- Transfer old, aging photographs to video. To do that, you'll need to first scan them into your PC, then upload them to your digital camera, where you can easily transfer them to VHS.

- Use your digital camera as the world's smallest, lightest video projector while you're on the road. Transfer images or PowerPoint presentations to your camera an image at a time and then use the forward and back keys to display them on a video system when you're away from the home office.

- Use a digital camera as a real-time surveillance system that displays the current scene in front of the lens on a video monitor. For instance, you can use a Web cam to show what's going on in your home on a Web page. Even when you're away at work, you can have peace of mind by checking in on your kids and your day care provider.

 ## How do I synchronize music to a video slideshow?

If you'd like to make a video slideshow, you can easily play music at the same time for a more immersive experience. Just follow these steps:

1. Determine how many images you need to play and multiply that number by about six. The result is the approximate run time of your show in seconds.

2. Practice cycling through the slides a few times to fine-tune the actual run time. The number you end up with should be the length of the music you select for the show.

3. Configure your VCR to accept audio from one source (your CD player, probably) and video from another. You may need to set a multi-source option, or physically move cables so the two desired sources are feeding into the VCR. The easiest—but least elegant—way is to simply plug the audio out of your CD player into the audio in of the VCR, while the video in of the VCR is connected to the camera.

4. Start the VCR and CD player with the first image already displayed. Then cycle through the images just the way you practiced.

VIDEO CAPTURE

 ## Can I capture video with my digital camera?

The easy answer is no, a digital camera is a very different beast than a camcorder. Its memory system is designed to store one image at a time, and the capture and storage process is far too slow to capture any useful series of video frames.

But what if you captured the image data not in the camera, but on your computer instead? That's the premise behind a product called ZipShot from ArcSoft. The ZipShot is a small peripheral for your PC that plugs into your parallel port and

NTSC, PAL, and Image Resolution

Depending upon where in the world you live, you will have a particular video standard. The most common ones are PAL and NTSC. PAL (which stands for Phase Alternating Lines) is used throughout most of Europe and is incompatible with the American NTSC (National TV Standards Committee) broadcast scheme. NTSC is transmitted at 525 of lines of resolution, 60 times each second. PAL, on the other hand, uses 625 lines at 50 times per second, providing somewhat better resolution.

Your digital camera is designed to use one or the other (if you're in the United States, it uses NTSC). If you take your digital camera overseas, it won't work on a television in another country.

And while we're on the subject, let's put the whole VHS/Beta argument to rest once and for all. A VHS VCR is a fairly low-resolution device, providing only about 240 lines of resolution (compared to the 525 lines that a television is designed to display). Beta was never all that much better, though—it only offered about 10% better resolution, which was so slight that most people couldn't even tell the difference. The Beta/VHS marketing war is now almost legendary since it is the story of how marketing squashed the little guy, but remember that much better video devices still abound. You can buy S-VHS, laserdisc, or DVD and get significantly better resolution than Beta ever had.

captures any incoming image data as a continuous video stream. Hook up your digital camera, point it at the action, and the data streams into your PC where it is saved as a Video for Windows file (see Figure 18-2). It's a clever product that might be exactly what you need for making short videos without a camcorder or other video capture device.

There is also a new crop of digital cameras that have limited video capture capabilities built in. Casio, in particular, sells digital cameras that in addition to still images can store several seconds of video, which you can download to your PC.

Figure 18-2 The ZipShot is an easy way to capture live video with your digital camera

? Can I capture video into my computer with just an ordinary camcorder?

Absolutely, but you'll need extra hardware. To capture video from a camcorder, you'll need a video capture card that has inputs for video from your VCR or camcorder. There are a number on the market, so you have a lot of choices. If you want to replace your existing video card, look for a system like Matrox's Rainbow Runner. Otherwise, you can get a stand-alone video capture card that works in addition to your existing video display card, like Miro's DC10 or DC20.

In addition, many new multimedia PCs ship with video cards that already include video-in ports. To see if your computer already has what you need, look on the back of the

PC at the video card (where the monitor is plugged into the computer). If you see video-in RCA or S-Video jacks like the ones in Figure 18-3, you've already got the hardware. Just plug in the camcorder.

Is the video on my camcorder digital?

No, it's not. A camcorder doesn't record scenes digitally (that is, as a set of ones and zeros). A new kind of device does record video digitally, and it's called a DV camcorder (the DV stands for Digital Video). For more information on DV devices, read "What is the difference between Digital Video and a regular camcorder?" and subsequent questions later in this chapter.

What kind of system do I need to capture video?

Capturing video is one of the most demanding, processor-intensive tasks you can ask of your PC. The problem is that analog video—like the kind you record with your camcorder—is extremely densely packed with information. Since NTSC video is roughly equivalent to a 24-bit, 640×480-pixel display, you can see that just one frame is almost a megabyte all by itself. If you then try to capture 30 frames of it per second, you're asking the processor to encode and store on a hard disk about 240MB of uncompressed video per second.

Of course, no PC hard disk in the world can hope to record that much data that quickly, so the processor also has to contend with compressing the video as it is read from the video input port. That's a tall order, but modern PCs with good video cards can not only do it, but create video that looks nearly broadcast-quality when you send it back out to tape.

Figure 18-3   Many PCs come with video-in and video-out jacks as standard equipment

If you want to digitize full-motion video, here's the kind of system you should have:

● At minimum, a 100 MHz Pentium processor. I'd recommend having a 166 MHz Pentium or better.

● 32MB of RAM. More RAM helps, and 64MB is really almost essential for efficient video editing.

● A fast AV SCSI hard disk. An AV drive is important, because it'll spin at 7200 RPM (faster than most ordinary hard disks) and only write data sequentially to the drive—that prevents the playback hiccups that can result from disk fragmentation. You can use an IDE drive, but SCSI offers better performance.

● In addition, look for a PCI-based video capture card that offers Motion-JPG hardware compression and broadcast video output.

 How do I install a video capture card?

If you want to download video from a camcorder to your PC, you'll need a video capture card to act as the interface between the two. Your PC may have come with a video capture card, particularly if it's a fairly new multimedia PC, but if not, follow these steps to install your capture card:

1. Shut down your PC and remove the cover.

2. Ground yourself by touching something metallic, like the power supply chassis.

3. Remove the backplate from an empty PCI slot and set it aside.

4. Take the capture card out of the anti-static bag and slip it into the empty PCI slot.

5. Screw the video card in place securely.

6. Attach video and sound cables to the back of the capture card. Don't be confused by the nomenclature. If it says "video in," that means you should run a cable from the video out of your camcorder or VCR to that port.

7. Replace the cover on your PC.

8. Start your PC. Follow the Plug and Play instructions to add the new drivers for your capture card. If Windows starts but doesn't detect the new card, open the Display Properties and add the card manually.

9. Your card probably came with a nonlinear video editor like Adobe Premiere or Corel Lumiere. Start the program and test your card according to the instructions that came with the video card.

If your capture card doesn't seem to work, check for these possible problems:

● Some cards require you to start a program that initializes the capture card before it'll work with capture and display software. Check to see if it's running.

● Make sure the video card is securely seated, and not sticking up at either end of the slot. If all the PCI slot's pins aren't making good contact, the card won't work.

● Some video devices need to be in a "bus master" slot. Most PCI slots are bus masters, but that's not always the case. Try putting the video capture card in a different slot, and see if it works in the new location.

What is the difference between Digital Video and a regular camcorder?

One of the newest innovations in digital imaging technology is the Digital Video (DV) camcorder. Several companies now make cameras that meet the DV specification, though the most popular is Canon's Optura (see Figure 18-4).

DV systems record their video digitally onto a tiny magnetic tape. Since the data is recorded digitally, there's no "generation loss" when you make copies. Just as important, these cameras usually record 30 or even 60 blur-free frames each second—that means perfect freeze frames all the time.

Not particularly cheap, these cameras will set you back around $2500 right now. On the other hand, prices should start to fall soon. In time, Digital Video camcorders may replace ordinary analog camcorders, both because they capture higher-quality video and because they make it easier

Figure 18-4 The Optura is a Digital Video camcorder that captures 60 frames of 640×480-pixel images each second

to connect with a PC and work with video editing software. At the moment, however, DV is an expensive alternative.

Can I play a Digital Video tape in my VCR?

No, it's a completely different format. Video from your camcorder or VCR is stored in an analog format, while DV camcorders write the data to their tapes in ones and zeros. Aside from the fact that both formats use a magnetic tape, they share nothing else in common (see Figure 18-5).

How do I connect a Digital Video camera to my PC?

You'll need a compatible interface card. In most cases these cards do not come with the camera, but cost extra. These

Figure 18-5   The DV cassette format is much smaller than a VHS tape

days, most DV cameras use FireWire cards to transfer data, though it's possible that future cameras might use USB as well. Several manufacturers make FireWire cards that work with DV camcorders, including Adaptec and Radius.

Can I use a Digital Video camera to take still images?

Yes, you can. Many photojournalists, in fact, are forgoing the traditional 35mm camera in favor of just carrying a DV camcorder. Since these cameras take 30 or even 60 pristine frames of video each second, you can transfer specific frames to your PC and get great still images. One product that makes this easy is Radius's PhotoDV, a software package that lets you choose specific frames from a DV video and store them on your PC's hard disk.

 Are there special hard disks for capturing video?

While you can use an ordinary hard disk for capturing video, I recommend an AV drive. The AV stands for Audio Video, and they're specially designed to spin faster and record data in a special way to let video play back smoothly. Some of the companies that make AV drives are Micropolis, Quantum, and Seagate.

Whatever you choose, you should be sure to only put video on the drive—don't mix it up with applications, word processing files, or other data—and defragment the drive before you work with it.

VIDEO EDITING

 Why would I want to edit video on my PC instead of a VCR?

Aside from the greater control you have over the video in your PC, a great reason to edit video on your computer is that it's a lossless environment. Every time you make a copy of a video in the "real" world, like on a VCR, you lose some quality, introduce noise and hiss, and reduce the resolution of the image. Each copy is called a *generation*, meaning that each subsequent version is an imperfect copy of the previous one. A typical editing session could mean aging the video through as many as three generations.

On your PC, however, there's no generational loss. From the moment video gets copied from your tape to the computer, it remains in lossless digital format. Copy and paste it as much as you like and there's no loss. Finally, when you're done just copy it back out to tape again and you're still working with a first-generation video source.

 What are some applications of video editing on my PC?

There are a lot of ways to take advantage of video editing on your PC. Here are some applications you might want to try:

- **Family videos**   You can create home movies that have professional-looking titling and transitions, plus you get to cut out bad video segments that would otherwise stay in the finished product.

- **Company videos**   Now even a staff of one can create training videos and messages from the boss on videotape.

- **Spruce up PowerPoint**   Create short video segments and insert them in PowerPoint presentations.

How much compression should I use when capturing video?

One of the advantages of Motion-JPG is that you can adjust the compression for better video quality or more efficient hard disk storage. Table 18-1 is a guide to how much to compress the video you capture.

What is a nonlinear editor?

A *nonlinear editor*, or NLE, is a software program that allows you to edit video in the same way that you might edit text in a word processor. Your video clips can be rearranged, clipped, cut, and pasted in order to create a finished video. NLE software usually lets you attach audio, music, wipes, fades, and transitions as well.

The most popular NLE software for Windows is Adobe Premiere (see Figure 18-6), though there are less expensive alternatives, like Corel Lumiere, as well. If you want to edit video and create home movies, training films, or similar projects, you'll need NLE software to accompany your analog camcorder or DV camcorder.

Compression Ratio	File Size for One Minute of Video	Quality
4:1	300MB	Broadcast
8:1	150MB	Professional
16:1	75MB	Consumer
25:1	48MB	Multimedia

Table 18-1   Compression Rates for Full-Motion Video

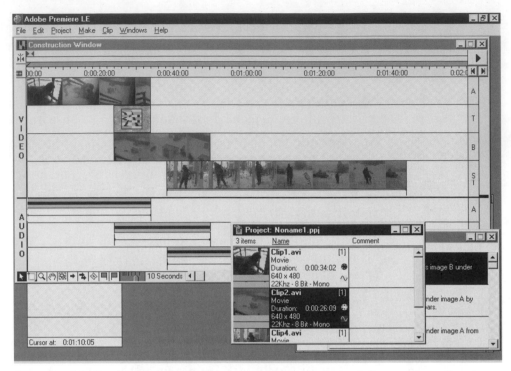

Figure 18-6   Using NLE software, you can drag and drop video clips to make a professional-looking video and copy the finished product onto VHS

 I've heard of products like Trinity and the Video Toaster. What are they?

Play's Trinity and NewTek's Toaster are combination hardware/software products that are essentially video editing and production studios crammed in a single box. A few years ago all the stuff you'd find in one of these products might have cost $100,000, but now these boxes make it possible to essentially create a complete broadcast-quality video studio for $10,000 or less. They perform special effects and have integrated paint, titling, multi-source video switching, and more. They're great for the professional (or even the amateur with money to burn) who wants to produce complete videos like promotions, commercials, corporate training videos, and so on.

VIDEO CONFERENCING AND WEB CAMS

What is so great about video conferencing?

It's free. Video conferencing allows you to talk face to face with someone in real time, no matter how far away they are, for the price of the Internet connection. Even if you're separated by a thousand miles or an ocean, there are no long-distance telephone charges because your ISP connection is a local call. For that reason, video conferencing will only get bigger as time goes on and the technology improves.

What kind of camera do I need if I want to video conference?

You certainly don't need a video capture card designed for broadcast video—but if you already have one, it'll work. In fact, you can connect a camcorder to the video card and video conference with that. A cheaper solution, however, is one of the many "tethered cameras" now for sale for the PC. These cameras typically connect to the always-in-demand parallel port and capture low-resolution images that are fine for the current state of Internet video broadcasting. Alternately, you can use a digital camera connected to your PC via a device like ArcSoft's ZipShot, which captures video from your camera and sends it to the computer in real time (see "Can I capture video with my digital camera?" earlier in this chapter).

Why is video conferencing so prone to problems?

Making voice and video calls on the Net hasn't become widely accepted yet, thanks in large part to technical obstacles laid down by the Internet itself. Information is transmitted over the Internet in small packets, designed to keep everyone on the Net moving regardless of how much traffic there actually is. Someone sending a large multimedia file, for instance, doesn't unduly bog down an e-mail sender because the large file is sent in small packets, interspersed with smaller e-mail messages. That way everyone stays, if not happy, at least satisfied.

The packet convention wreaks havoc with streaming data, however. Video conferencing is considered streaming data because it sends real-time audio and video data using the

Internet's TCP/IP protocols. But the Net might delay certain packets due to network congestion, meaning that the message plays back choppily, distorted, or long after it was supposed to arrive.

Do I need a special kind of modem to video conference?

You'll need at least a 28.8 Kbps modem—preferably faster. The key part of the equation, though, is the modem's duplex: For best results, you'll need a full-duplex model. Full-duplex modems let both parties talk at the same time. With an older half-duplex modem, each person has to take turns talking, much as if you were using a walkie-talkie. Don't upgrade your old half-duplex just for this, though. Chances are you can tolerate half-duplex operation, particularly if it's not mission-critical communication.

What kind of video conferencing software should I use?

Don't forget that you'll probably need to use the same telephony software as anyone you plan to talk to. Unlike Web browsers and ordinary telephones, there's no universal standard for video conferencing. It's as if people with Sprint could only talk to other Sprint users, and AT&T customers were on their own. So while ideally your decision would be based on which product is the best, in fact you may need to adopt what the other people in your communication group already have. Thankfully, you can install more than one communication program on your PC, so you can use, for

Telephony and Your PC

Telephony is a term that refers to telephone and communication technology—video conferencing and Internet voice call software are examples of common telephony applications. This is an increasingly important use of many people's computers.

instance, NetMeeting for business, NetPhone for family, and WebPhone for a few other friends.

On the other hand, the future looks bright for cutting through all this incompatibility muck. A new standard, called H.323, defines the way telephony software can make and break connections, and what CODEC (compression and decompression codes) the software will use. Right now only a few programs, like Microsoft NetMeeting and NetSpeak WebPhone, use H.323, but expect that to change as users see the convenience of connecting to anyone's PC regardless of what software is in use.

It's easy to experiment with voice over the Internet—some telephony software is even free. Intel offers their Intel Internet Video Phone free from its Web site at http://www.intel. com/cpc/index2.htm. Once you download this application, you can make voice and video calls. Intel includes a "People Finder" directory to track down other phone users. The phone isn't as full-featured as other products on the market, but the price is certainly right.

Other free Internet telephony products include Microsoft's NetMeeting. NetMeeting is a voice and video conferencing system that comes with Internet Explorer 4.0; you can download it from Microsoft's Web site or order a CD-ROM. NetMeeting is packed with features, like a whiteboard you can use to draw and share images while talking to others and a text-based chat window. Perhaps the most impressive feature in NetMeeting is the capability to share applications. While talking to another conference member via the Net, you can surrender control of an open program, like Word, and let the other participant actually work with your document remotely. NetMeeting is a great way to experiment, though its directory system for locating other users is difficult to manage, and it doesn't seem to handle voice communication as well as some other programs.

If you're looking for a telephony program with a tremendous array of features, check out NetSpeak WebPhone 4, seen in Figure 18-7. This "Internet telephone" broadcasts both voice and video (if you have a camera) and manages the available bandwidth to give priority to audio data. That means that if the Net is congested, WebPhone smartly steps down the video frame rate so your voice stays intact. The

Figure 18-7   WebPhone is one of many products that let you use your
camera and PC like a videophone

audio part of WebPhone behaves like a business phone with
four separate lines, hold and mute controls, and the option to
create multiple outgoing messages. In fact, you can target a
specific message—like "be right back"—to particular people,
so only they will hear it when they call you.

Another popular program that has been periodically
updated since the dawn of Internet telephony, VocalTec's $49
Internet Phone, supports both audio and video communication over the Internet. A straightforward interface eschews
the telephone handset graphics for a simple call box, a video
window, and a logical set of buttons and menus.

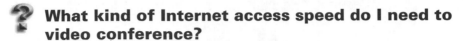

What kind of Internet access speed do I need to video conference?

Video conferencing takes up a lot of communications bandwidth. The easy answer is that the faster your connection speed is, the better off you are.

Don't even try to video conference with only a 14.4 Kbps modem. 28.8 Kbps is better, but only marginally acceptable. Many people who have ISDN service get great results, though, as do 56 Kbps modem users. Another solution: You can get about 100 Kbps by "bonding" two 56 Kbps modems with two phone lines working together.

What is a Web cam?

A Web cam site is one that has a live camera attached. Every time you visit you can see what's going on at the remote location in real time. Sometimes the subjects are interesting, like the view of a crowded tech support facility. Sometimes it's a bit boring but interesting just for the cheesiness—like a Web cam pointed at a vending machine or a fish tank.

Figure 18-8 shows the Pikes Peak Cam, which is always pointed at Colorado Springs' most famous mountain. It has a practical benefit, believe it or not—the weather over the mountain is Colorado Springs' weather an hour or two later, so you can use the Web cam as a weather predictor.

Whatever the subject, there's a certain thrill in simply being able to see what's going on a few thousand miles away at the click of a button. Some of the most popular sites are those that display what's happening in someone's home. The most famous of these is the JenniCam. Jenni's Web site is at http://www.jennicam.org.

If I wanted my own Web cam, would I need a dedicated Internet connection or my own server?

No, you can use an Internet service provider and keep the Web page the way it already is. You'll simply need special software that can take a picture, dial up your ISP, and

Figure 18-8   Web cams are usually updated every few minutes so you can see what's going on around the world almost as it happens

upload the image on a regular schedule (see the following section).

 ## How do I create a Web cam?

You can create your own Web cam if you're so inclined. Remember that a Web cam must periodically capture an image, convert it into a JPEG or GIF file, and then transmit it to your Web hosting server.

You need both a camera and Web cam software that can take care of automating those steps for you. Many are shareware and easily found in file libraries on the Web (see "What are some common Web cam programs?" later in this chapter). You also have to set up your computer to dial your

ISP on request (unless you leave your system connected to the Internet all the time).

The way most of these programs work is they upload a file to your Web server at an interval you specify (such as every 10 minutes) using the same filename each time. That way the Web page never needs to change—it can simply display a file called myroom.gif, for instance, and every request to see that image will retrieve whatever file is newest (see Figure 18-9).

What on earth is a Web cam good for?

A good question indeed. Here are a few suggestions that may spark your interest:

- Liven up your Web site. People seem to love to look at other people and their domiciles via the Web.

- See your kids while they're in day care.

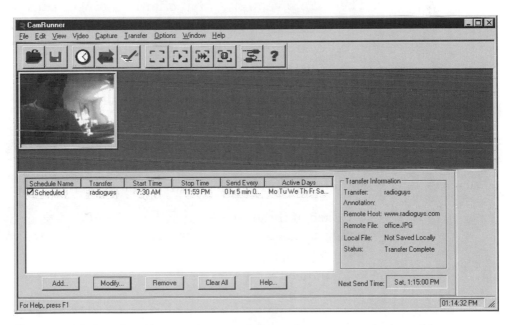

Figure 18-9   CamRunner is one of several programs designed to manage a Web cam for you

- Keep tabs on your home while you're away at work.
- Watch your pets while you're at work.
- Monitor a branch office while you're at the main office.

What are some common Web cam programs?

Web cam drivers are easy to find on the Web. Here are a few of the most common ones to get you started:

- **CamRunner** Find it at http://www.dcn.com/cr/.
- **Ispy Webcam** This program can be found at http://www.ispy.nl/.
- **NetSnap** Download this program from http://www.netsnap.com/.

Is there a place on the Web where I can look for a complete list of Web cams?

There are several sites that offer lists of Web cams you can visit. Here are some starting places:

- http://www.dcn.com/us/index.html
- http://www.dcn.com/world/index.html
- http://www.geocities.com/TheTropics/Shores/3245/camcoll2.htm
- http://www.dreamscape.com/frankvad/cams-links.html
- http://www.iwaynet.net/~kwroejr/livecams.html
- http://www.crk.umn.edu/technology/webtech/cameras.htm

Each of these sites maintains a list of dozens or even hundreds of other sites that have active Web cams you can visit.

How do you set up a robotic camera that people can control over the Internet?

Right now, there's one major company that sells this kind of capability: Perceptual Robotics. If you visit http://www.perceptualrobotics.com/, you can try out this technology and learn more about implementing it yourself.

Index

IF YOU THOUGHT YOU'D CONSIDER

A DIGITAL CAMERA WHEN HELL FREEZES OVER,

OBSERVE THIS RECENT SHOT OF HELL.

Take heart, photographers, for there is finally a digital camera designed just for you. The Coolpix 900 features a 3X Zoom Nikkor lens, 3-mode TTL Metering, and 1280 x 960 resolution. There's precise 945-step autofocus, a 5-mode speedlight, plus optional wide-angle and fish-eye lenses. All of which helps produce an 8 x 10 print serious photographers will be proud to call their own. The Coolpix 900. Thank heaven you held out for a Nikon. To learn more, call 1-800-52-NIKON, or visit www.nikonusa.com.

Photo shown is unretouched and was taken by B. Moose Peterson with a Coolpix 900. © 1998 Nikon Inc.

The Nikon Coolpix™ 900

At home or the office, you'll spend less time looking for images and more time communicating with them!

Clutter. Everyone tries to avoid it. But if you're an imaging enthusiast or professional, you know that clutter is a way of life. You have hundreds of images scattered across your hard drives. Thousands of photos and clipart on CD. Millions of pictures available for free on the 'Net. And if you own a digital camera or scanner, those numbers are probably increasing daily.

So how do you bring order to the chaos? Simple. Award-winning PhotoRecall Deluxe, from the experts in image management technology.

PhotoRecall Deluxe rapidly locates and organizes digital images and clipart, no matter where they're stored. And PhotoRecall Deluxe does it all automatically. Spend more time on reports, presentations, web pages, and other documents, and less time hunting for graphics. Distribute image archives to friends and colleagues. E-mail sound-enabled, self-running photo albums or publish your albums on the Web.

No matter what your level of expertise, PhotoRecall Deluxe offers a better, easier way to banish clutter and communicate more effectively.

LOAD YOUR IMAGES FROM...

 or  **or**

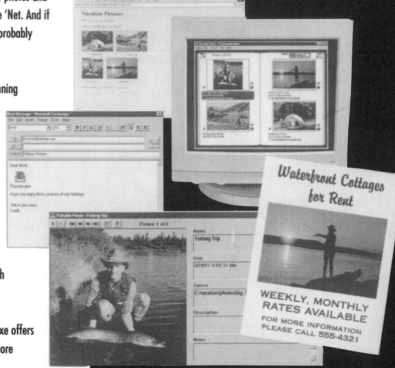

PhotoRecall 2.0 DELUXE

Photo Management Made Easy And Fun!

PC MAGAZINE Named One of 125 Best Software Titles
(PC Magazine, Your New PC, Winter 1998)

FamilyPC
"The best program we've found for maintaining a useful photo catalog is PhotoRecall"
(Family PC, July/August 1997 Copyright© Family PC 1997)

Visit our website at
w w w . p h o t o r e c a l l . c o m

G&A Imaging

DISCOUNTS ON TOP PANORAMA SOFTWARE!

$5 off on QuickStitch!

QuickStitch is an easy-to-use application that turns overlapping photos into wide angle, high resolution shots in seconds.

$10 off on QuickStitch 360!

QuickStitch 360 combines photos into high quality panoramas and QuickTime VR up to 360 degrees.

To Order
Download QuickStitch and QuickStitch 360 and purchase CD-ROM versions from Enroute at http://www.enroute.com. Or, call 1-800-946-0135 or fax to (650) 813-9089. Please have the following order code ready when placing your order. OSB-D9810A

QTY	Description

Billing Information

Payment Type:

Cardholder Name:

Card Number: Expiration Date:

Shipping Address

Last Name: First Name:

Company:

Street Address (no PO boxes please):

Address (cont.)   City:

State/Province: ZIP/Postal code:

Day Phone: E-mail:

Shipping Method (US and Canada only):   US Mail $3.75 (US only)   Priority Mail $5.75   Fedex 2nd Day $8.75   Fedex Overnight $13.75

Where did you hear about the product(s) you ordered?

8.25% tax will be added to all California orders.

ENROUTE

For mail orders, mail this form with a check made out to Enroute Imaging to:
Enroute Imaging
Sales Department
530 Showers Drive, Suite 200
Mountain View, CA 94040